After the Collapse of Communism
Comparative Lessons of Transition

This collection of essays is the result of a conference convened at Princeton University marking the ten-year anniversary of the collapse of the Soviet Union. Some of the best minds in post-Soviet studies focused on the task of identifying in what ways the postcommunist experience with transition has confirmed or confounded conventional theories of political and economic development. The result is a rich array of essays examining vital aspects of the transitional decade following the Soviet collapse and the comparative lessons learned. This collection of essays explicitly tallies the gains and losses to post-Soviet countries of the last ten years as well as comparing the post-Soviet experience implicitly and explicitly with that of other developing countries. Each essay blends political science theory with fresh empirical analysis.

Michael McFaul is the Peter and Helen Bing Senior Fellow at the Hoover Institution. He is also an associate professor of political science at Stanford University and a nonresident associate at the Carnegie Endowment for International Peace. Before joining the Stanford faculty in 1995, he worked for two years as a senior associate for the Carnegie Endowment for International Peace in residence at the Moscow Carnegie Center. McFaul is the author and editor of several monographs including *Russia's Unfinished Revolution: Political Change from Gorbachev to Putin*, *Russia's 1996 Presidential Election: The End of Bi-Polar Politics* with Tova Perlmutter, and *Privatization, Conversion and Enterprise Reform in Russia*. His articles have appeared in *Constitutional Political Economy*, *Foreign Affairs*, *Foreign Policy*, *International Organization*, *International Security*, *Journal of Democracy*, *Political Science Quarterly*, *Post-Soviet Affairs*, and *World Politics*.

Kathryn Stoner-Weiss taught in the Politics Department and at the Woodrow Wilson School at Princeton University before becoming the Associate Director of Research and Senior Research Associate, Center on Democracy, Development and the Rule of Law at Stanford University. Her work has been funded by the Smith Richardson Foundation, the Carnegie Corporation of New York, and Princeton University's Center of International Studies. She is a frequent traveler to Russia and the former Soviet Union. Her other books include *Local Heroes: The Political Economy of Russian Regional Governance* (1997) and *Resisting the State: Reform and Retrenchment in Post-Soviet Russia* (Cambridge University Press, forthcoming).

After the Collapse of Communism

Comparative Lessons of Transition

Edited by

MICHAEL McFAUL
Stanford University

KATHRYN STONER-WEISS
Stanford University

CAMBRIDGE
UNIVERSITY PRESS

32 Avenue of the Americas, New York NY 10013-2473, USA

Cambridge University Press is part of the University of Cambridge.

It furthers the University's mission by disseminating knowledge in the pursuit of
education, learning and research at the highest international levels of excellence.

www.cambridge.org
Information on this title: www.cambridge.org/9780521834841

© Michael McFaul and Kathryn Stroner-Weiss 2004

This publication is in copyright. Subject to statutory exception
and to the provisions of relevant collective licensing agreements,
no reproduction of any part may take place without the written
permission of Cambridge University Press.

First published 2004
Reprinted 2007
First paperback edition 2010

A catalogue record for this publication is available from the British Library

Library of Congress Cataloguing in Publication data

After the collapse of communism : comparative lessons of post communist transition /
edited by Michael McFaul and Kathryn Stoner-Weiss.
   p. cm.
"This collection of essays is the result of a conference convened at Princeton University
marking the ten year anniversary of the collapse of the Soviet Union."
Includes bibliographical references and index.
ISBN 0-521-83484-8 (cloth)
1. Europe, Eastern – Politics and government – 1989 – Congresses.   2. Former Soviet
republics – Politics and government – Congresses.   3. Russia (Federation) – Politics and
government – 1991 – Congresses.   4. Post communism – Europe, Eastern –
Congresses.   5. Post communism – Former Soviet republics – Congresses.   6. Post
communism – Russia. (Federation) – Congresses.   7. Democracy – Europe, Eastern –
Congresses.   8. Democracy – Former Soviet republics – Congresses.   9. Democracy –
Russia (Federation) – Congresses.   I. McFaul, Michael, 1963–   II. Stoner-Weiss,
Kathryn, 1965–
JN96.A58A34   2005
320.947′09′049 – dc22   2004040737

ISBN 978-0-521-83484-1 Hardback
ISBN 978-0-521-15355-3 Paperback

Cambridge University Press has no responsibility for the persistence or accuracy
of URLs for external or third-party internet websites referred to in this publication,
and does not guarantee that any content on such websites is, or will remain,
accurate or appropriate.

Contents

Contributors		*page* vii
	Introduction: The Evolving Social Science of Postcommunism *Michael McFaul and Kathryn Stoner-Weiss*	1
1	The Triumph of Nation-States: Lessons from the Collapse of the Soviet Union, Yugoslavia, and Czechoslovakia *Philip G. Roeder*	21
2	The Fourth Wave of Democracy and Dictatorship: Noncooperative Transitions in the Postcommunist World *Michael McFaul*	58
3	Circumstances versus Policy Choices: Why Has the Economic Performance of the Soviet Successor States Been So Poor? *Vladimir Popov*	96
4	Whither the Central State? The Regional Sources of Russia's Stalled Reforms *Kathryn Stoner-Weiss*	130
5	Parties, Citizens, and the Prospects for Democratic Consolidation in Russia *Timothy J. Colton*	173
6	Comparative Democratization: Lessons from Russia and the Postcommunist World *Valerie Bunce*	207

7 Russians as Joiners: Realist and Liberal Conceptions of
   Postcommunist Europe   232
   James M. Goldgeier and Michael McFaul

Index   257

Contributors

Valerie Bunce, Cornell University

Timothy J. Colton, Harvard University

James M. Goldgeier, George Washington University

Michael McFaul, Stanford University

Vladimir Popov, Carleton University, Canada, and the New Economic School, Moscow, Russia

Philip G. Roeder, University of California, San Diego

Kathryn Stoner-Weiss, Stanford University

Introduction

The Evolving Social Science of Postcommunism

Michael McFaul and Kathryn Stoner-Weiss

This volume is the product of a conference, entitled *Ten Years since the Collapse of the Soviet Union: Comparative Lessons and Perspectives*, held at Princeton University in the autumn of 2000. The genesis of the conference lay in our shared belief that the study of the formerly communist world had much to offer comparative politics, but that few if any volumes actually had yet attempted to explore what these contributions might be. We wanted to move away from the often shrill debate between area specialists and general comparativists toward a more constructive blending of comparative political science and the best of area specialization. As a result, we gathered together a distinguished group of scholars pursuing research in Eastern Europe and the former Soviet Union within a distinctly comparative framework.

In producing this volume, we set out to answer three questions: First, more than ten years after the collapse of the Soviet Union and the initiation of sweeping economic, social, and political change in the post-Soviet states, what have we learned? Second, how are we to understand theoretically the complicated and multidimensional components of triple transitions? Finally, what new theoretical insights into democratization, political economy, and state formation does the post-Soviet transition experience offer the study of comparative politics and international relations more generally?

We began our project with the assumption that "change" was the generic dependent variable in need of explanation. The collapse of the Soviet Union and the emergence of new polities and economies in the former Soviet space constitute a rare turning point in world history. Revolutions in Eastern Europe and the Soviet Union fundamentally altered the borders of the states in the region, the internal organization of the economies of these states, and political and social institutions of the communist world. After nearly a century during which competition between authoritarian communism and democratic capitalism divided and polarized the international system, internal changes within the Soviet Union have transformed international relations in Europe and Asia as well as relations between East and West.

Or did they? Since the collapse of the Soviet Union, action verbs and motion adjectives have dominated descriptions of events in the postcommunist world. Yet, more than ten years later, what is most striking about the region as a whole is the resultant mix of change *and* continuity and the variation that this mix gives to different kinds of outcomes. Some states have disappeared entirely (the Soviet Union, East Germany), others have divided (Czechoslovakia, Yugoslavia), and others remain intact but marked by deep internal changes and conflicts (Russia, Kazakhstan, Georgia). The economies of some postcommunist states have moved far from their formerly planned systems, while others have moved scarcely at all, and still others appear to have settled into an awkward mix of plan and market. Likewise, the number of political systems that bear resemblance to the authoritarian ways of the Soviet Union is as pronounced as the number of polities that have little in common with the old system. The region is rich in different outcomes in different issue areas. David Laitin has written that explaining these varied outcomes would qualify as "quintessential questions on the comparative political agenda."[1] Some of these outcomes fit social science theory derived from experiences in other contexts, whereas others challenge conventional understandings of social, political, and economic change.

In the decade since the collapse of the Soviet Union, scholars have come to realize that comparative political theory adds a great deal to our understanding of the great changes that have taken place in the former Soviet space. But although the similarities between the post-Soviet transition and those of Latin America, Europe, Asia, and Africa offer confirmation of some generalizations about change, the differences between the post-Soviet transition and others offer post-Soviet scholars the opportunity to challenge and revise long-held theories. Thus, the study of the former Soviet Union has not and should not simply borrow comparative politics theory and apply it haphazardly in an awkward attempt

---

[1] David Laitin, "Comparative Politics: The State of the Discipline," APSA Paper, August 2000, p. 3.

to explain transitional outcomes there. Rather, post-Soviet politics has served and should serve to further the agenda of comparative politics more generally. We hope that the group of authors and essays we have assembled here will reflect this empirical fact and normative mission.

THE BEGINNING OR THE END OF HISTORY?

An additional and related consideration that motivated our development of this collection of essays is one of time. We view the twentieth century as neatly bracketed by two seminal social experiments: the establishment of a socialist state in the Soviet Union beginning in 1917 and the demise of the Soviet state in December 1991. The first event – the Bolshevik Revolution – fundamentally altered the way states were organized and their interaction with each other. In reaction to this historical event, the social sciences also developed new theories and paradigms, including the study of comparative political systems, bipolarity in international relations, and Marxism, a school of thought that permeated western social sciences for nearly a half century.[2] The second event – the collapse of the Soviet Union – was no less consequential for world history. The event extinguished peacefully the fifty-year-old bipolar international system. The event also punctuated the end of communism as an ideological, political, and economic alternative to western democracy and capitalism. History, of course, did not end in 1991, but it did take a decisive turn away from concepts and regimes that were considered enduring and permanent just a decade earlier. Since the Soviet Union's collapse in December 1991, the post-Soviet world has gone through the twists and turns of tumultuous political, economic, and social change.

The consequences of the Soviet collapse for American social science, however, have been less dramatic than was the beginning of Soviet communism in 1917.[3] Explaining the end of communist regimes and international bipolarity should have been one of the fundamental research projects of the last decade. Surprisingly, it has not achieved such prominence. In the initial moments after the collapse of the USSR, non-Soviet specialists berated the field of Sovietology for failing to predict collapse.[4]

---

[2] Some will object to the suggestion that Marxist theory was in any way related to the rise of the Soviet Union. The correlation between the dissolution of the USSR and the decline in Marxist studies, however, is striking and robust.

[3] The event had dramatic consequences for Soviet and Russian social sciences.

[4] For one of the most scathing attacks, see Martin Malia, "From under the Rubble, What?" *Problems of Communism*, January–April 1992, pp. 89–106. See also the essays in Michael

Those noncommunist specialists focused on the future and promised to save the theoretically depraved subfield of Soviet-area studies. The "transitologists" were particularly imperial and messianic in promising to bring the good news of the word of their theoretical insights to Soviet-area specialists. As Karl and Schmitter wrote, "The neophyte practitioners of transitology and consolidology have tended to regard the implosion of the Soviet Union and the regime changes in eastern Europe with 'imperial intent.' These changes seem to offer a tempting opportunity to incorporate (at long last) the study of these countries within the general corpus of comparative analysis."[5]

The impact of this neocolonial challenge was profound within the Soviet – and soon to be named "post-Soviet" – field. Some scholars simply stopped publishing. Numerous young scholars interrupted their careers and postponed empirical inquiries to learn quantitative and game theoretic tools. The field of post-Soviet studies was effectively on probation before the rest of the social sciences community.

Strikingly, however, more than a decade later the integration of post-Sovietology into the mainstream of political science is far from complete. At the same time, the mainstream of social science – despite earlier promises of rescue – has done little to address the new problems introduced by the demise of the Soviet Union. With important exceptions, the more senior Soviet scholars have not adapted new theories and tools of

---

Cox, *Rethinking the Soviet Collapse: Sovietology and the Death of Communism and the New Russia* (London: Pinter, 1998); and the essays in Part 2 of the special issue of *The National Interest* called "The Strange Death of Soviet Communism: An Autopsy," No. 31, Spring 1993. For a comprehensive response, see George Breslauer, "In Defense of Sovietology," *Post-Soviet Affairs*, Vol. 8, No. 3 (July–September 1992), pp. 197–238.

[5] Philippe Schmitter with Terry Lynn Karl, "The Conceptual Travels of Transitologists and Consolidologists: How Far East Should They Attempt to Go?" *Slavic Review*, Vol. 53, No. 1 (Spring 1994), p. 177; and Philippe Schmitter and Terry Karl, "The Types of Democracy Emerging in Southern and Eastern Europe and South and Central America," in Peter Volten, ed., *Bound to Change: Consolidating Democracy in East Central Europe* (Boulder: Westview Press, 1992), p. 43. For "anticolonial" responses, see Valerie Bunce, "Regional Differences in Democratization: The East Versus the South," *Post-Soviet Affairs*, Vol. 14, No. 3 (1998), pp. 187–211; Valerie Bunce, "Should Transitologists Be Grounded?" *Slavic Review*, Vol. 54, No. 1 (Spring 1995), pp. 111–27; Roger Markwick, "A Discipline in Transition? From Sovietology to 'Transitology,'" *Journal of Communist Studies and Transition Politics*, Vol. 12, No. 3 (September 1996), pp. 255–76; Thomas Remington, "Regime Transition in Communist Systems: The Soviet Case," *Soviet Economy*, Vol. 6, No. 2 (1990); and Michael McFaul, "Revolutionary Transformations in Comparative Perspective: Defining a Post-Communist Research Agenda," in David Holloway and Norman Naimark, eds., *Reexamining the Soviet Experience: Essays in Honor of Alexander Dallin* (Boulder: Westview Press, 1996), pp. 167–96.

Introduction

social science to the study of their geographical terrain.[6] Younger scholars have adapted, but their research still struggles for attention in the mainstream of political science. Amazingly, the leading journal in political science, the *American Political Science Review*, has published no more than a handful of articles on postcommunism in the past ten years!

In addition, with a few exceptions, the more robust subdisciplines of political science have given relatively little attention to theory development regarding the extinction of communism and the emergence of postcommunism.[7] Peter Ordeshook may be the only major rational choice theorist to devote major attention to postcommunism, and he emerged from his inquiry thoroughly discouraged about the applicability of rational choice analysis to the questions that arise from this field. Others simply ignore the post-Soviet cases altogether as a way to protect the validity of their findings derived from other regional studies (including, most importantly, American-area studies). International relations theorists have devoted more time to explaining systemic change in the international system, but only slightly more. Since 1991 – the formative years in the birth of new formerly communist nations – states, economies, polities, and regional systems have both challenged and confirmed many of our assumptions about comparative politics and international relations. Yet social scientific inquiry about these new polities has remained marginal to the core of American political science.[8]

When the new cases from the postcommunist world of economic, political, and international change are analyzed, the dominant research method deployed has been to confirm or disconfirm extant theories. This research design is useful and important, as many of the chapters in this book

---

[6] Some exceptions include Timothy Colton, *Transitional Citizens: Voters and What Influences Them in the New Russia* (Harvard University Press, 2000); Tom Remington and Steve Smith, *The Politics of Institutional Choice: The Formation of the Russian State Duma* (Princeton: Princeton University Press, 2001); Philip Roeder, *Red Sunset: The Failure of Soviet Politics* (Princeton: Princeton University Press, 1993); and Valerie Bunce, *Subversive Institutions: The Design and the Destruction of Socialism and the State* (Cambridge University Press, 1999). Specialists in Eastern Europe did not have to 'adapt" as much, since they were always better versed in the theories of comparative politics and international relations than were those who study the Soviet Union.

[7] Exceptions include Juan Linz and Alfred Stepan, *Problems of Democratic Transition and Consolidation: Southern Europe, South America, and Post-Communist Europe* (Baltimore: Johns Hopkins University Press, 1996).

[8] Despite the virtual elimination of comparative economics as a subdiscipline at many major universities, the economists have devoted much more time and energy to understanding the transitional economies. Whole journals have been devoted to the subject, and major mainstream journals and leading economists have devoted space and time to the subject.

demonstrate. However, it can also be limited. Why, for instance, should a theory of federalism developed from an analysis of a stable, static case like the United States be used to explain the formation of center-regional relations in new states emerging from a collapsed unitary state? Why should theories of party development developed from analyses of nineteenth-century party systems in Western Europe be deployed to explain the original formation of interest group politics in twenty-first-century, postcommunist Russia? More generally, why should theories of equilibria be the bases of theory development about phenomena fundamentally out of equilibria?

BETWEEN AREA STUDIES AND PHYSICS

The fact that Soviet and post-Soviet studies have been on the defensive for the past decade at the same time that a serious infusion of new theories of change from comparative politics were lacking have seriously impeded the development of grand theories.[9] Instead of simply defending area studies or accepting full stop the aim of fitting research on this region into established theories, postcommunism needs to carve a middle ground of theoretically and empirically based research.

The original blow to the Sovietological field, in fact, should never have been accepted as a blow at all. Static and evolutionary models, like most theories in political science, dominated Sovietology before the collapse. Many theorists have posited that unexpected change cannot be, and therefore should not be, accounted for by theory. Kenneth Waltz has gone so far as to assert that theories should not even *aspire* to explain change because "a theory explains continuities. It tells one what to expect and why to expect it. Within a system, a theory explains recurrences and repetitions, not change."[10] Consequently, our most robust theories often seek to explain "nonevents" – why the rules of the U.S. Congress "make public policy stable and predictable when it might be expected to be arbitrary"[11]; why countries do not go to war even when the anarchy of the international system permits if not encourages them to do so; or why totalitarian

---

[9] Although perhaps focused on a different set of causes, David Laitin makes a similar observation about the field in his "Post-Soviet Politics," *American Review of Political Science*, Vol. 3 (2000), pp. 117–48.
[10] Kenneth Waltz, *Theory of International Politics* (New York: McGraw-Hill, 1979), p. 69.
[11] Robert Bates, "Macropolitical Economy in the Field of Development," in James Alt and Kenneth Shepsle, eds., *Perspectives on Positive Political Economy* (Cambridge: Cambridge University Press, 1990), p. 46.

and authoritarian political systems do not collapse even when they are inefficient. Explaining change to these systems in equilibrium – be it the Gingrich "revolution" in 1994, the collapse of the bipolar international system in 1989, or the collapse of the Soviet regime in 1991 – is beyond the domain of these static theories in *all* of these subdisciplines.

Yet, Soviet scholars have been held accountable. The "failure" to predict the Soviet collapse produced real self-doubt within the Soviet discipline. Amazingly, more than ten years after the collapse, scholars still do not even have a shared definition of what we have witnessed in the region. Russian change/continuity is an example of what exactly? Revolution or merely reform? Democratization or merely a transition to some yet unknown endpoint? Without some common understanding of the phenomenon in question, it remains difficult to develop explanatory theories.

Two intellectual responses have resulted. At one extreme, students of the region make the claim that Russia is unique. Theories developed to explain other countries do not apply to this riddle wrapped in a mystery inside an enigma.[12] And if they do apply, it will take decades before we know how to apply them. In the interim, observers of Russia are encouraged to collect data. At the other extreme, scholars try to demonstrate that Russia is similar to other countries and therefore theories derived from the study of these other countries can and must be applied to the Russian case. Because most theories in American social science have their origins in the study of the United States, these scholars usually end up applying models built around the American case – be it models of federalism, executive–legislative relations, or fiscal stability – to illuminate similar phenomena or expose dissimilar phenomena in Russia and the other new states of the former Soviet Union. This group of scholars tends to avoid grand theory and resist explaining the entire "case" of change, but focuses instead on smaller questions and puzzles.

The consequences of both of these research strategies is that hardly anyone is trying to explain the big picture of change in Russia, let alone the entire postcommunist region. This failure to "think big" – a failure to place change in Russia in its proper context, to seek to develop new theories about change rather than just borrowing old theories – is understandable, but nonetheless regrettable. Those clinging to the notion that the Russian case is sui generis risk being pushed to the margins of social science. But those carving the Russian case into small enough pieces to

---

[12] Stephen Cohen, *Failed Crusade: America and the Tragedy of Post-Communist Russia* (New York: Norton, 2000).

make the phenomena in question look generic also do an injustice to the magnitude and nature of the changes that we are witnessing in this part of the world.

Despite notable differences in context, Russian politicians should hope that their work today will produce an economy and polity that could be compared productively with stable systems in other countries. In the scholarly community, social scientists studying the region cannot forever be defined by one historical data point – the end of communism. Historians, not political scientists, use such markers to delineate their subfields. Yet, many of the essays in this book suggest that it is too early to subsume things Russian (or Uzbek) into the static models of mainstream political science. Rather, while the data are still "lying in the streets," scholars should be attempting to frame change in Russia and perhaps in other postcommunist countries as well as a dynamic, sometimes unique phenomenon nonetheless worthy of theorizing.[13]

This book makes the case for understanding postcommunist regime change as an analytically useful category, which should be considered comparable to but distinct from other kinds of regimes and/or regimes in transition. This is not to argue that other kinds and levels of theory should not be deployed to understand outcomes in and affected by these regimes. All the essays in this book are grounded in contemporary theoretical debates in the social sciences. However, importation of theories derived – whether inductively or deductively – from analyses of other kinds of regimes must take into account the specific features of the Soviet/Russian case and postcommunism more generally.

Two basic assumptions in tension with each other provide the basis for this argument. First, not all change is evolutionary.[14] Some changes, arguably many of the most important changes in regime development, are rapid and abrupt. Revolutions – the simultaneous change in the polity and economy – are the rarest but most transformative kind of regime change. Theories, models, and metaphors derived from static phenomena or evolutionary change, therefore – such as democratization, modernization, rational choice, or learning – are not adequate for explaining

---

[13] For more refined arguments as to why, see Valerie Bunce, "Should Transitologists be Grounded?"

[14] A corollary to this hypothesis is that states, regimes, and institutions are not constantly changing in an evolutionary manner to meet the needs and demands of their environments. Rather, they can remain static, to be changed only by *rapid*, revolutionary disruptions. See Stephen Krasner, "Approaches to the State: Alternative Conceptions and Historical Dynamics," *Comparative Politics* (1984), p. 216.

Introduction

revolutionary change. Incremental changes may have been influential, if not necessary, for precipitating revolutionary disruptions. But once this critical threshold has been reached, the kinds of outcomes to be predicted from revolutionary change are different from those that result from evolutionary change.[15]

The kind of change that has unfolded in the Soviet Union/Russia and perhaps in the entire former communist world stands as compelling evidence for this first hypothesis. The Russian state and the surrounding states from the former Soviet Union and Eastern Europe have undergone monumental political, economic, and social change in the past several years, rivaled only by the French Revolution or the Bolshevik Revolution in scope or consequence.[16] The old Soviet polity, consisting of a state subordinated to the Communist Party of the Soviet Union, was destroyed. In the vacuum, new political institutions are emerging in some states, including elected parliaments and executives, a separation of power between the legislature and the executive, and several political parties. Simultaneously, new patterns of autocracy are taking shape in other new states. The final endpoints of these political transformations are still uncertain. Likewise, the old Soviet command economy in which virtually all production and distribution were controlled by the party-state also has collapsed. In some new states, the old is being replaced by a new system based on private property, free prices, and market forces. In other new states, hybrid institutional arrangements between the state and market have consolidated. In all cases, however, *Soviet* communism is being replaced by various shades of new economic institutions. Theories developed to explain static events or evolutionary change, therefore, will be inadequate to explain these rapid and simultaneous transformations of both the polity and economy of Russia and other postcommunist states.

A second assumption is that history matters; change is path-dependent. The political and socioeconomic institutions that comprise a regime are the consequence of historical processes. As Robert Putnam cogently summarized,

Whatever other factors may affect their form, institutions have inertia and "robustness." They therefore embody historical trajectories and turning points.

---

[15] Barrington Moore, *Social Origins of Dictatorship and Democracy* (Cambridge, MA: Harvard University Press, 1966).
[16] Although much of the following discussion also pertains to other states of the former Soviet Union as well as the former socialist states of Eastern Europe, this essay focuses on Russia alone.

History matters because it is "path dependent": what comes first (even if it was in some sense "accidental") conditions what comes later. Individuals may "choose" their institutions, but they do not choose them under circumstances of their own making, and their choices in turn influence the rules within which their successors choose.[17]

Even during periods of revolutionary change when new rulers make a conscious attempt to break with the past, the path of transformation is still influenced by past decisions, institutions, and organizations of socioeconomic relations.

The Russian case and the universe of cases comprising changing communist regimes also offers confirmation of this second hypothesis. In particular, the mostly peaceful method of change has magnified the influence of the old on the new in these transformations. The peaceful process by which Russia has moved toward creating this new Russian polity and economy has left in place many formal and informal Soviet institutions. As Kenneth Jowitt has remarked,

any substantial analysis of democracy's and market capitalism's chances in Eastern Europe must interpret the maelstrom itself, and that means coming to analytical grips with the cultural, political, and economic "inheritance" of forty years of Leninist rule. For Western analysts to treat the Leninist legacy the way Leninists after 1948 treated their own East European inheritance – namely as a collection of historically outmoded "survivals" bound to lose their cultural, social, and psychological significance – would be an intellectual mistake of the first order.[18]

Not everything from the past, however, is consequential for the future. If it were, there would be no change. The analyst's task is not to assert the existence of a communist legacy. Rather, we must specify under what conditions certain practices from the past matter for contemporary outcomes and under what conditions legacies are unimportant. Theories of political and economic change that do not treat institutions and organizations constructed during the communist era as a potential independent variable – whether explicit or implicit – cannot explain or hope to aid the logic of change unfolding in these postcommunist regimes. Undoubtedly, the organization of communist totalitarian and posttotalitarian regimes influenced the beginning of transformation, the mode of transformation,

---

[17] Robert Putnam, *Making Democracy Work: Civic Traditions in Modern Italy* (Princeton: Princeton University Press, 1993), p. 8. See also Krasner, "Approaches to the State," p. 225.
[18] Kenneth Jowitt, *The New World Disorder: The Leninist Extinction* (Berkeley: California University Press, 1992), p. 286.

and the type of postcommunist consolidation to emerge in these instances of regime change.

ADVANCING SOCIAL SCIENCE RATHER THAN
DEFENDING TERRITORY

With these assumptions about rapid change *and* (however paradoxical) path dependency in mind, theorists about the postcommunist world should be prepared to contribute to broader social science theory without abandoning altogether those features (and thus theoretical arguments) unique to the postcommunist world. Some outcomes in postcommunist politics are consistent with extant theories in political science. Others are not. This simple observation about variation must be the starting point for theoretical inquiry in the postcommunist world. Old theories should be applied to new cases as a method of developing theory, but only if the champions of old paradigms are willing to listen, interpret, and argue with the results of these applications.

In organizing this volume, we did not aim to take stock of all predicted and curious outcomes in the postcommunist world over the last decade. Nor did we aspire to conduct a literature review of all the important work published on the post-Soviet experience.[19] We also did not seek to discuss every topic in postcommunism, nor did we ask twenty-seven scholars to write about twenty-seven cases of regime change.[20] Nor did we invite seven people to write specifically on a single issue like democratization, although the issues of transition and change are themes that run through all of the essays.[21]

Instead, we wanted to encourage comparison of what we think are central issues of the past ten years across the postcommunist space. We

---

[19] For such a review, see Laitin, "Post-Soviet Politics."
[20] For a survey of all topics related to Russia, see Archie Brown, ed., *Contemporary Russian Politics: A Reader* (Oxford: Oxford University Press, 2001). The best complete survey of all postcommunist regimes is in Adrian Karatnycky, Alexander Motyl, and Amanda Schnetzer, *Nations in Transit 2001: Civil Society, Democracy and Markets in East Central Europe and the Newly Independent States* (New York: Transaction Books, 2001).
[21] Excellent volumes organized this way include Richard Anderson, M. Steven Fish, Stephen Hanson, and Philip Roeder, *Postcommunism and the Theory of Democracy* (Princeton: Princeton University Press, 2001); Zoltan Barany and Robert Moser, eds., *Russian Politics: Challenges to Democratization* (Cambridge: Cambridge University Press, 2001); and Harry Eckstein, Frederic Fleron, Erik Hoffman, and William Reisinger, *Can Democracy Take Root in Post-Soviet Russia? Exploration in State-Society Relations* (Lantham, MD: Rowman & Littlefield, 1998).

assembled a distinguished group of authors with intimate knowledge of different aspects of the transition process and invited them to write about what they know best and what they have learned from the last ten years of tumultuous change in the former Soviet Union. At the same time, we believe that the topics discussed in this volume are also central to political science and thereby offer us a way to demonstrate the degree to which post-Soviet studies has not only integrated into the mainstream of comparative politics but also helped to shape theoretical debates. As a result, this book is a sampler, not an encyclopedia, of some of the most interesting theoretical and empirical work on postcommunism in the last decade.

SEVEN SAMPLES

In Chapter 1, Philip Roeder examines the triumph of nation-states in the postcommunist world at a time when the concept of the nation-state is under serious assault from the forces of globalization. Roeder notes that social science offers two approaches that might explain the success of these nation-state projects in the wake of the demise of the Soviet Union. The first is a nationalist argument regarding popular demands for self-determination. The second argument, derived from the international relations literature, posits that the nation-state triumphs as a result of international pressures that favor this institutional framework over a multinational alternative. Roeder argues, however, that neither of these approaches satisfactorily explains the postcommunist outcomes that he examines. He posits instead that the postcommunist transition to twenty-eight nation-states where nine states once stood resulted from "the failure of segmental political incorporation of ethnic groups by the former communist regime." Thus Roeder links the creation of new nation-states to the political institutions of the old regime – particularly that of ethnofederalism.

Roeder's chapter is notable not only for its grand historical sweep and fresh empirical data, but also for his careful assessment of the relative inadequacies of comparative social science explanations for the triumph of nation-states in the former Soviet bloc. In arguing for the influence of institutional legacies – like the segmental incorporation of ethnic groups into federations of homelands – Roeder properly emphasizes the importance of the communist institutional legacy in explaining unanticipated postcommunist outcomes.

Introduction

In Chapter 2, Michael McFaul moves the discussion from why nation-states emerged in the postcommunist context to the different types of regimes that have emerged to govern these new nation-states. The transition from communism in Europe and the former Soviet Union has only sometimes produced a transition to democracy. Since the crumbling of the Berlin Wall in 1989 and the collapse of the Soviet Union in 1991, twenty-eight states – most of them new states – have abandoned communism. But only nine have entered the ranks of liberal democracies as assessed by Freedom House. The remaining majority of new postcommunist states are various shades of dictatorships or unconsolidated "transitional regimes." Why did some states abandon communism for democracy, while others opted for authoritarian rule?

McFaul's chapter provides an answer. In endorsing actor-centric approaches that have dominated analyses of the third wave of democratization, he nonetheless challenges the central hypothesis of the earlier literature concerning the relationship between the mode of transition and the resulting regime type. His essay offers an alternative set of causal paths from *ancien regime* to new regime, which can account for both democracy and dictatorship as outcomes. In his view, situations of *unequal* distributions of power produced the quickest and most stable transitions from communist rule. In countries with asymmetrical balances of power, the regime to emerge depends almost entirely on the ideological orientation of the most powerful. In countries where democrats enjoyed a decisive power advantage, democracy emerged. Institutions of power sharing or checks and balances did not result from compromise between the *ancien regime* and democratic challengers. Rather, they only emerged if the hegemonic democrats chose to implement them. Ideas – democratic ideas embraced by powerful political actors – played a central role in the creation of postcommunist democracies. Conversely, in countries in which dictators maintained a decisive power advantage, dictatorship emerged. Between these two extremes were countries in which the distribution of power between the old regime and its challengers was relatively equal. Rather than producing stalemate, compromise, and pacted transitions to democracy, however, such situations in the postcommunist world resulted in protracted confrontation between relatively balanced powers. The regimes that emerged from these modes of transitions are not the most successful democracies, but rather unconsolidated, unstable, partial democracies.

Chapter 3, by Vladimir Popov, takes on the politics of postcommunist economic reform. Popov's masterful essay first explains why the economic performance in the states of the former Soviet Union was so poor compared to East European countries, China, and Vietnam. Popov argues that conventional explanations regarding the dynamics of economic output during transitions that are associated with the speed and depth of liberalization (measured by liberalization indices), and with the success or failure in macroeconomic stabilization (measured by the rates of inflation), do not hold.[22] After controlling for nonpolicy factors – such as the level of development, pretransition industrial structure, and trade patterns – the impact of liberalization becomes insignificant. However, variations in inflation rates and institutional capacities of the state (as measured by the change in the share of government revenues in GDP and/or by the ratio of the rule of law to the democracy index) remain important determinants of performance. According to Popov, these factors explain the vast majority of differences in GDP change in twenty-eight transition economies. Popov contends, therefore, that the debate between shock therapists and gradualists that dominated discussions throughout the 1990s was misguided. The crux of the debate – the speed of transition – turned out to be a secondary issue for later economic performance. However, gradualists and shock therapists alike overlooked the key variable – the strength of institutions.

In the second part of the essay, Popov focuses on factors influencing the choice of "good" and "bad" economic policies, examining in particular the rationale behind the "bad" economic policy choices. The argument here is that the political economy of transition imposed constraints, similar to those observed in Latin American countries, and resulted in an inefficient import substitution industrial strategy and macroeconomic instability, in Russia in particular.

At the start of the transition period, after the deregulation of prices, former socialist countries experienced a dramatic and quick increase in personal income inequalities and sectoral inequalities in the profitability of enterprises. Previously, under authoritarian regimes, the state had been strong enough to mitigate these inequalities by imposing a substantial burden of transfers on producers. Strong democratic governments in Central European countries were able to do both – to eliminate part of the subsidies and to finance the remainder overtly. In contrast, the weak democratic governments that emerged in the postcommunist era in many

---

[22] For a statement of these "conventional" arguments, see Anders Aslund, *Building Capitalism: The Transformation of the Soviet Bloc* (Cambridge: Cambridge University Press, 2001).

Introduction

of the successor states of the former Soviet Union were not in a position to maintain large-scale subsidies. Consequently, they had to choose between eliminating the bulk of all subsidies and finding alternative ways of financing these subsidies (e.g., import substitution-oriented price controls, inflationary financing, building up domestic and foreign debt, maintaining the overvalued exchange rate, driving foreign borrowing up and/or foreign exchange reserves down). The first choice was politically dangerous, the second economically inefficient. The inability to cut subsidies inherited from the era of central planning was the major reason for an import substitution industrial policy and macroeconomic instability – budget deficits, inflation, increased domestic and foreign indebtedness, and overvalued exchange rates. All of these factors, in Popov's view, eventually led to Russia's 1998 currency crisis – a crisis that affected the entire CIS region. Just as Roeder and McFaul note, lingering legacies from the Soviet era had real consequences for the emergence of new practices a decade later.

Chapters 4 and 5, by Kathryn Stoner-Weiss and Timothy Colton respectively, examine specific problems inherent to Russia's transition over the last decade and offer theoretical insight to transitional regimes more generally. Stoner-Weiss makes the claim that weak central state capacity in implementing policy has produced a decade of partial reforms at best, failed reforms at worst. She argues that the national government's inability to ensure reliable policy coherence and implementation across the eighty-nine constituent units of the Russian Federation has left it unable to deliver to society many basic goods and services guaranteed by the constitution and federal laws. This inability, in turn, is at least partially a consequence of the underinstitutionalization of the state and state-society relationships.

Stoner-Weiss argues that Russia is a particularly striking example of a more general problem in transitional contexts. In countries that are entering a time of great change (postrevolution or postcollapse), the promise and hope for a new or renewed state's abilities are great, and yet so often the state proves to be weak and incapable of improving or changing the lives of the people it governs. Sometimes, despite the best of intentions, new weak states make life even worse.[23] Under what conditions does this outcome occur? Stoner-Weiss uses the Russian case to present some general arguments about the cycle of weak state capacity in developing countries even in the face of relatively weak societies.

---

[23] Joel Migdal makes a similar point in his *Strong States and Weak Societies* (Princeton: Princeton University Press, 1988), p. xx.

Stoner-Weiss points out that recent scholarship in comparative political development has been primarily concerned with democratization and the construction of democratic institutions. However, with the tentative triumph of at least electoral (if not always liberal) democracy in many parts of the developing and post-Soviet world, the time has come to refocus our attention on the more difficult question of why some states have proven better able to govern than others.[24] Questions of state capacity and effectiveness are, of course, intimately linked with the larger issues of democratic consolidation and resilience bacause if new democratic states prove incapable of better delivering goods and services to their populations than their authoritarian predecessors, the danger of regime reversal will surely increase. As many third-wave democratizing states remain unable to fulfill the developmental promises they made at the start of their transitions, the issue to which we should turn now (or return) is not so much the *kind* of government in any particular state, but the *degree* of government.[25]

Stoner-Weiss's essay contributes to these debates in a number of ways. Employing Michael Mann's distinction between the despotic and infrastructural powers of states, she develops an assessment of the relative capacities of the Russian central state.[26] In doing so, Stoner-Weiss provides a more useful method for measuring state capacity that moves beyond the distorting dichotomy of "weak" and "strong" states. She argues that what is missing in Russia's "democratic transition" is sufficient infrastructural, rather than despotic, power to ensure state authority extends beyond the Kremlin walls. Using creative metrics and unique empirical data to measure "infrastructural power," Stoner-Weiss highlights how a weakly mobilized mass society in Russia (a legacy of the Soviet past) has allowed a small sliver of emergent economic interests engendered by the economic transition to effectively capture parts of the state – particularly at the regional level.

In Chapter 5, Timothy Colton examines in close detail a particularly weakly defined institution of Russian mass society – political parties. Colton begins by pointing out an obvious fact frequently ignored in

---

[24] For definitions of liberal and electoral democracy, see Larry Diamond, *Developing Democracy: Toward Consolidation* (Baltimore: Johns Hopkins University Press, 1999).
[25] Samuel Huntington, *Political Order in Changing Societies* (New Haven: Yale University Press, 1968).
[26] This distinction appears in Michael Mann's *The Sources of Social Power, Volume 1: A History of Power from the Beginning to A.D. 1760* (New York: Cambridge University Press, 1986).

Introduction

western analyses of Russia – the one great success story in Russian democratization has been the opening up of elections to elite competition and voluntary mass participation. Since independence in 1991, Russia has held seven national elections – three presidential and four parliamentary. Although none would perfectly satisfy a rigorous test of democratic integrity, in all of them barriers to entry have been relatively low, campaigning has been relatively free, and participation has been reasonably high. In other countries with similar electoral practices, one particular institution – the political party – has been crucial to the organization of democratic elections and the mobilization of popular support.

Colton's chapter seeks to evaluate Russia's emerging party system in comparative terms. The assessment reveals a paradox. At first glance, Russian parties seem poorly organized and ill-defined. Although party activity has been legal in Russia since the Soviet constitution was amended to permit the organization of opposition parties in March 1990 and the number of parties in Russia has proliferated at an amazing rate, Russia's parties still have a poor reputation in society. Citizens mistrust them in the aggregate and are highly critical of their thronging numbers, whereas commentary by experts and journalists is if anything more dismissive. At the same time, however, Russians turn out to vote in party-organized elections and, interestingly, often have positive attitudes toward one or two parties.

Motivated by a larger concern about state-society relations, Colton's chapter addresses popular orientations toward the party system and toward political parties in post-Soviet Russia. He gives particular emphasis to the emergence of feelings of partisanship, in the sense of psychological attachment or closeness to a favorite party, a phenomenon that may conceivably prove to be a precursor of party identification in the familiar form it has assumed in the older democracies. Drawing on panel-format surveys of the Russian electorate from 1995, 1996, 1999, and 2000, Colton describes and analyzes the extent of partisanship, trends in its extent and distribution, its apparent origins, and its effects on voting behavior and on mass engagement in transitional politics. His survey data suggest a modest falloff in partisanship in Russia from the mid-1990s – a puzzling trend with alarming undertones. Colton considers whether this diminution of partisanship represents a momentary setback for partisan development or the beginnings of a long-term reversal of the gains realized earlier. He concludes by drawing out wider implications for our general understanding of comparative electoral politics and the dynamics of regime change.

In Chapter 6, Valerie Bunce offers a comparative essay on how Russia's particular transition should compel democratization theorists to rethink old assumptions. Her chapter examines what Russia teaches us about democracy and democratization. Bunce's essay is structured around four issues. The first is the question of false negatives. That is, if the literature on revolution predicts far too many revolutions (the false positive problem), the recent literature on comparative democratization exhibits the opposite problem – too many false negatives. Put simply, the literature underpredicts incidents of democratization. In particular, Bunce argues that Russian democracy is highly improbable and surprisingly "stubborn" if, of course, flawed. This curious fact introduces several provocative questions. For example, is it easier to produce and sustain democracy than is commonly assumed? How many routes are there to democracy? Should we be making a clear theoretical distinction between "minimal" democracy and full-fledged democracy? This in turn introduces an important observation: how we define democracy determines the number of democracies we find.

Bunce goes on to argue that Russia's democratic flaws may also be the components that allow the Russian democratic system to endure. Most analysts presume that Russian democracy is delicate, given its flawed character, and that Russians and the rest of the world are in effect "lucky" that Russia has not yet experienced democratic breakdown. Drawing on insights from Joel Hellman's work, Bunce makes the opposite argument – that the flawed character of Russian democracy is precisely why it has endured.[27] In doing so, her chapter challenges an assumption, pervasive in the literature on comparative democratization, that there is a necessary and positive correlation between the quality of democracy and its sustainability and that flawed democracies, as a result, are more likely to break down than their more well-rounded, full-fledged counterparts.[28]

The third issue addressed in Bunce's sweeping essay is the intellectual contribution of communist analyses to the larger debate in comparative politics between those focused on the long-term or structural causes of democratization versus the more recent literature on "quick" democratization. In this field of comparative theorizing, these two bodies of work exist side by side, absent any interaction with each other. Bunce draws on the Russian case to build bridges between these two lines of argumentation.

---

[27] Joel S. Hellman, "Winners Take All: The Politics of Partial Reform in Post-Communist Transitions," *World Politics*, Vol. 50, No. 2 (January 1998), pp. 203–234.
[28] See, for example, Diamond, *Developing Democracy*.

The fourth and final theme that Bunce raises is the understudied relationship between the state and democratization. The key issues here include state capacity (as discussed in Stoner-Weiss's chapter) and the spatial settlement of the state – that is, the boundaries of political authority, such as relations among administrative units. Most of the literature on comparative democratization ignored the state question. Russia, according to Bunce, forces us to worry not only about "weak states," but also about porous boundaries and democratization as a spatial concept.

In the final chapter of the volume, James Goldgeier and Michael McFaul address Russia's relations with the West. Whereas the other chapters in this book deal primarily with theories in comparative politics, the chapter by Goldgeier and McFaul is concerned first and foremost with theoretical debates in international relations. Goldgeier and McFaul contend that the dominant paradigm in international relations – realism – has done a poor job of explaining Russia's relations with the West – and the United States in particular – since the collapse of the Soviet Union. In the immediate wake of the Cold War's end, scholars in the realist tradition predicted a return to great power balancing in Europe. Balancing has not occurred. The core powers – led by the United States – have moved to expand their zone of peace and prosperity eastward. And although Russia conceivably should (and often says it does) feel threatened by this eastern expansion, Moscow has generally pursued a policy of integration with the West rather than balancing against the West for the last decade.

To explain this inconsistency with realist predictions, Goldgeier and McFaul focus on regime change within Russia. While pursuing a policy of democratization at home, Russia also pursued a policy of cooperation with western democracies abroad. The same powerful interest groups in favor of economic and political liberalization domestically also supported cordial relations with the West and the United States in particular. These groups have not yet institutionalized their preferences: Russia is not a liberal democracy. But these groups have maintained their leading position in Russian politics. This distribution of forces within Russia in turn has acted to check the balancing impulses from other interest groups, even when confronted by western policies such as NATO expansion and the bombing of Serbia that appear antithetical to Russian national interests.

CONCLUSION

As we forewarned, this collection of essays does not represent either a comprehensive survey of all the intellectual currents in postcommunist studies or a geographical inventory of regime change or economic reform in the region. The volume does, however, demonstrate the theoretical richness of postcommunist studies. The chapters in this collection underscore the fact that the study of postcommunism is increasingly a valuable source of insights for the mainstream of comparative politics and the social sciences more generally. At the same time, this group of essays productively employs methods and theoretical approaches developed in other contexts without pretending that postcommunist cases look and act exactly like the older, more stable regimes from which mainstream social science theories were developed. In sum, this volume demonstrates that art is reflective of life: the social science of postcommunism, like postcommunist countries themselves, is alive and full of potential.

1

The Triumph of Nation-States: Lessons from the Collapse of the Soviet Union, Yugoslavia, and Czechoslovakia*

Philip G. Roeder

Today, twenty-eight nation-states founded on the principle that a nation has a right to a state of its own stand where, a little over a decade ago, nine states had vowed to replace nations with socialist internationalism. Fifteen Soviet, five Yugoslav, and two Czechoslovak successor states stand where previously there were three multinational unions. This postcommunist transition represented the second most intense burst of new states to enter the international system since 1815. This is curious because it took place at a time when nations and states, we are told, are under assault as never before from global forces. This development begs the question that I will address in this chapter – what accounts for the triumph of these nation-state projects rather than others?

The nation-state has two faces – as a community and as an institution – and social scientists have used two different approaches to explain its triumph. Students of nationalism emphasize the element of national community and commonly attribute the triumph of nation-state projects to the demand by peoples for states of their own. Alternatively, many students of international relations have stressed the institutional development of the state and attribute the triumph of the nation-state to international selection mechanisms that favor this institutional form over its multinational competitors: nation-states trump the multinational alternatives

---

* Many people contributed to this project. I especially thank Andrew Barnes, Sheri Berman, George Breslauer, Valerie Bunce, Timothy Colton, Tanisha Fazal, Stephen Hanson, Stephen Holmes, Jeffrey Kopstein, Michael McFaul, Kenneth Schultz, Gary Shiffman, Kathryn Stoner-Weiss, and Celeste Wallander for their comments on earlier drafts of this essay.

by their military prowess, economic efficiency, or international acceptance. Yet neither approach offers an entirely satisfactory account of the postcommunist transformation. Instead, in the postcommunist transition to nation-states and, particularly, the post-Soviet transition, new nation-states resulted from the domestic politics of state failure – specifically, from the failure of segmented states. Segmental institutions – particularly, ethnofederalism in the Soviet Union as well as Czechoslovakia and Yugoslavia – provided the organizational means, the incentives, and the opportunity for politicians to create new nation-states from the old multinational states. Rather than attributing the triumph of nation-states to culture (nationalism), national security (war-making capacity), economics (efficiency), or international acceptance, the segmental-institutions thesis attributes the triumph of nation-states to the political institutions of the old regime. This is one of the important lessons of the transition from communism; elements of this causal connection have been drawn out by Valerie Bunce, Carol Skalnik Leff, Ronald Suny, and myself.[1] I will argue in this chapter that the lessons of this institutional failure are still wider: With hindsight, it sheds light on the previous experience of state-creation in the age of nationalism. It suggests that this incubation of the nation-state in the segmental institutions of the multinational state may be the most common reason for the triumph of new states in the era of nationalism.

This essay is divided into three parts. The first examines the creation of new states since 1815 so as to place the experience of the postcommunist countries in perspective. This leads to the question addressed here – why specific nation-states have joined the international system. I round up the usual suspects – nationalism, war-making capacity, economic efficiency, and international acceptance – and interrogate each, but find that none can offer a credible accounting of the triumph of post-Soviet nation-states in particular and postcommunist nation-states more generally. In the second section, I present the case that the triumph of post-Soviet – as

---

[1] Valerie Bunce, *Subversive Institutions: The Design and the Destruction of Socialism and the State* (Cambridge: Cambridge University Press, 1999); Carol Skalnik Leff, "Democratization and Disintegration in Multinational States: The Breakup of the Communism Federations," *World Politics* 51 (January 1999), 205–35; Ronald Grigor Suny, *The Revenge of the Past: Nationalism, Revolution, and the Collapse of the Soviet Union* (Stanford: Stanford University Press, 1993); Philip G. Roeder, "Soviet Federalism and Ethnic Mobilization," *World Politics* 43 (January 1991), 196–232; and Philip G. Roeder, "Peoples and States after 1989: The Political Costs of Incomplete National Revolutions," *Slavic Review* 58 (Winter 1999), 854–82.

The Triumph of Nation-States

well as post-Czechoslovak and post-Yugoslav – nation-states was due in large part to the segmental institutions of the communist state. In a stylized model I point out the political dynamics that follow naturally on these institutional arrangements and then test this relationship with statistical evidence. Finally, I discuss the implications of this thesis for our understanding of nationalism and our histories of the nation-state more broadly.

COMMON EXPLANATIONS FOR THE TRIUMPH OF NATION-STATES

From 1816 to 2000, a total of 171 new or reconstituted states joined or rejoined the international system.[2] (See Table 1.) Decolonization of territories that had not been incorporated into the metropolis – that is, they remained separate as colonies or protectorates – created ninety-seven new states. Division of the metropolitan territories of states – including both secession of territories previously constituting part of the metropolis (e.g., Estonia and Slovakia) and the reconstitution of the rump metropolis (e.g., the Russian Federation or the Czech Republic) – accounted for an additional fifty-seven new states. Since 1815, the region that we now call the postcommunist states has been the stage for thirty-five of these fifty-seven successful secessionist and reconstituted states that have received international recognition.

The creation and reconstitution of states around the world took place throughout the entire 185 years after the Congress of Vienna, but as Table 1 shows, this process accelerated during the latter half of the twentieth century. It would be imprudent to make bold claims about the trends in secession, since it occurs in a few episodic bursts. Nonetheless, it is difficult to sustain the claim that this is a declining trend. Compared to earlier decades, the 1990s represent the second most intense period of transformation in the existing state system by creating new nation-states – second only to the 1960s.

All this begs a question: Why did these nation-states triumph while other state projects failed? For example, why is there now an Uzbekistan

---

[2] These figures are calculated from Kristian Gleditsch and Michael Ward, "A Revised List of Independent States since the Congress of Vienna," *International Interactions* 25 (1999), 393–413. In all instances I follow the list of Gleditsch and Ward except in the treatment of rump states – where the authors are inconsistent. Where states seceded from the metropolis, the reconstituted remainder is added to the list as a rump state (e.g., Russian Federation 1991).

TABLE 1. *New and Reconstituted States, 1816–2000*

a. by origin

Origin of State	(Examples*)	Number
Division of States		
– Post-colonial states	(Argentina 1816, Australia 1901, Zaire 1960)	97
– Post-secession states	(Estonia 1918 and 1991, Romania 1878)	51
– Rump states	(Czech Republic 1993, Russia 1991)	6
– Post-occupation states	(North Korea 1948, South Korea 1948)	6
Unification of Existing States	(Germany 1871 and 1990, Yemen 1990)	5
Newly Incorporated Territories	(Liberia 1847, Transvaal 1852)	6
TOTAL		171

b. by period

Period	New States	Rate (per year)	Post-Secession (percent)	Post-Colonial (percent)
Period I (1816–1900)	31	.365	41.9	38.7
Period II (1901–40)	26	.650	65.4	23.1
Period III (1941–85)	89	2.225	4.5	87.6
Period IV (1986–2000)	25	1.667	92.0	4.0
TOTAL	171			

* Examples indicate the year the state joined or rejoined the international system.
Source: Calculated from the list of states in Kristian D. Gleditsch and Michael D. Ward, "A Revised List of Independent States since the Congress of Vienna," *International Interactions* 25 (1999), 393–413. Codings of origins done by the author.

rather than a Bokhara, Turkestan, or Soviet Union? Why have some national projects, but only a few of the total number, succeeded at the expense of multinational empires and federations? Many students of nationalism attribute the triumph of nation-states to the demands by peoples for states of their own. So it is the distribution of support for a specific nation-state project within a population – often told in a story of the awakening of national identity – that explains the origins of specific nation-states. Yet, it is difficult to show that these factors actually account for the pattern of nation-states that exist today. Particularly in the post-Soviet triumph of nation-states – but also in the other postcommunist secessions – it is difficult to show that intense popular nationalism is the common thread that explains which successor states emerged from the collapse of the Soviet Union.

Alternatively, many students of international relations attribute the triumph of the nation-state to international selection mechanisms that favor the state over alternative forms of political organization, such as multiethnic empires and federations. For example, Robert Gilpin argues that "the nation-state succeeded because it was the most efficient form of political organization for the set of environmental conditions that developed in early modern Europe."[3] In his magisterial account of the dominance of the (prenational) state over its early modern alternatives, Hendrik Spruyt identifies the three potential advantages of the state emphasized by various analysts – its war-making potential, its economic efficiency, and its international acceptance.[4] The causal processes include survival among competing political forms and conscious emulation of successful forms. Yet, it is equally difficult to show that the new states perform better – either militarily or economically – than the federations they replaced. Whether one compares (1) multiethnic communist federations with the more homogenous unitary communist states, (2) the multiethnic communist federations with their postcommunist successor nation-states, or (3) the more heterogeneous postcommunist states with the more homogeneous postcommunist states, there is no pattern that suggests the greater fitness of nation-states. Moreover, the international community did not encourage the secession of nation-states; indeed, the leading powers tended to prefer preserving the multinational states.[5]

Nationalism

Nationalism, in the sense that I will use the term here, refers to a claim that a specified people should be self-governing within a separate territorially defined state.[6] The awakening of popular nationalism is frequently cited

---

[3] Robert Gilpin, *War and Change in World Politics* (Cambridge: Cambridge University Press, 1981), 116.
[4] Hendrik Spruyt, *The Sovereign State and Its Competitors: An Analysis of Systems Change* (Princeton: Princeton University Press, 1994.)
[5] One might object that the latter theories were not intended to explain the emergence of specific nation-states, and it is often difficult to extend the logic of these explanations to predict which among competing nation-state projects is likely to succeed, but a theory that fails to explain most occurrences of a phenomenon is, indeed, not very good.
[6] John A. Armstrong, *Nations Before Nationalism* (Chapel Hill: University of North Carolina Press, 1982); John Breuilly, *Nationalism and the State*, 2d edition (Chicago:

as a primary force leading to the creation of the postcommunist successor states.[7] Increasingly intense nationalism in the smaller union republics undoubtedly contributed to pressure for their independence.[8] Yet, the awakening of popular nationalism provides a less than compelling account for two reasons. First, even in the Baltic republics, where popular nationalism was most intense by 1991, it distorts a complex interaction to claim that popular nationalism led and inspired the acts of the union-republic governments that resulted in independent nation-states.[9] The relationship between popular nationalism and governmental actions was not unidirectional, but interactive. In the late 1980s, members of the Communist Party leadership opened the doors for popular nationalism that in turn supported their own expanding autonomy claims against Moscow. By these early actions, leaders of the union republics signaled to the public what was permissible to express and what was possible to achieve. As strategic politicians, these leaders were aware that their decisions to press for *glasnost* and *demokratizatsiia* would both tie and strengthen their hands.[10] In Estonia, for example, leaders of the union republic were instrumental in creating the Popular Front, which predictably increased public pressure for autonomy and in turn strengthened the leaders' hand in subsequent bargaining with Moscow. The declaration of sovereignty issued in November 1988 by Estonia's Communist Supreme Soviet escalated the demands in the public debate over the status of the union

---

University of Chicago Press, 1993); Ernst Gellner, *Nations and Nationalism* (Ithaca: Cornell University Press, 1983).

[7] Gail W. Lapidus, "From Democratization to Disintegration: The Impact of Perestroika on the National Question," in *From Union to Commonwealth: Nationalism and Separatism in the Soviet Republics*, edited by Gail W. Lapidus and Victor Zaslavsky (Cambridge: Cambridge University Press, 1992), 45–70. Also see Mark R. Beissinger, *Nationalist Mobilization and the Collapse of the Soviet State* (New York: Cambridge University Press, 2002); Ian Bremmer, "Post-Soviet Nationalities Theory: Past, Present, and Future," in *New States, New Politics: Building the Post-Soviet Nations*, edited by Ian Bremmer and Ray Taras (Cambridge: Cambridge University Press, 1997), 3–26.

[8] John B. Dunlop, "Russia: Confronting a Loss of Empire, 1987–1991," *Political Science Quarterly* 108 (Winter 1993–4), 603–34; Elizabeth Fuller, "How Wholehearted Is Support in Georgia for Independence?," *Report on the USSR* 12 April 1991, 19–20. In Moldova there was no solid majority in 1991 for any of the competing nation-state projects of the Soviet Union, Greater Romania, or an independent Moldova.

[9] Anatol Lieven, *The Baltic Revolution: Estonia, Latvia, Lithuania, and the Path to Independence* (New Haven: Yale University Press, 1993), 219–55; Rein Taagepera, *Estonia: Return to Independence* (Boulder: Westview Press, 1993), 127–214.

[10] On the relationship of tying one's hands and strengthening one's hands in bargaining situations, see Thomas C. Schelling, *The Strategy of Conflict* (New York: Oxford University Press, 1963), 22–8.

republic, which further strengthened the republic leaders in negotiations with Moscow.[11] The decision to hold fully competitive elections in early 1990 for the union-republic's Supreme Soviet with electoral rules that would limit the influence of enterprise managers loyal to Moscow had the foreseeable consequence of returning a legislature that would escalate demands for autonomy still further.

Second, despite the visible role of nationalism in the Baltic States, Georgia, and Armenia, it cannot explain the triumph of the other nation-states or the actual breakup of the Soviet Union. These five republics comprised less than 6 percent of the population of the Soviet Union and 1.3 percent of its land area. A strong center could have blocked their secession – as it had for decades. In the largest union republics that comprised over 90 percent of the Soviet population and land mass – and those most important for the Union's survival – nationalism played at most a small part in the creation of nation-states. For example, popular sentiment in the three countries that delivered the coup de grâce to the Soviet Union at Belovezhskaia Pushcha in December 1991 – Belarus, Russia, and Ukraine – was opposed to or ambivalent about secession. In the March 1991 Referendum on the renewal of the Soviet Union, 55 percent of the registered voters in Russia cast a "yes" vote that was widely interpreted as an endorsement for the Union; 58.6 percent of registered voters in Ukraine and 68.9 percent of registered voters in Belarus voted for the renewed Union. The "no" votes comprised only 20 percent, 23 percent, and 13 percent of the registered voters, respectively.[12] Even two years after the breakup of the Soviet Union, John Dunlop could describe Russians as "a people in quest of an identity," because Russians had not yet found a replacement for the idea that the Soviet Union was their nation-state.[13] In Ukraine, citizens were divided in their national identities and it remained ambiguous even after the referendum of December 1991 whether a majority favored secession and an end to the common-state

---

[11] "Deklaratsiia Verkhovnogo Soveta Estonskoi Sotsialisticheskoi Respubliki 'O suverenitete Estonskoi SSR,'" *Sovetskaia Estoniia*, 19 November 1988.

[12] United States, Commission on Security and Cooperation in Europe, *Referendum in the Soviet Union: A Compendium of Reports on the March 17, 1991 Referendum on the Future of the U.S.S.R.* (Washington, DC: U.S. Government Printing Office, 1991). On the ambiguity of the result in Ukraine, see Taras Kuzio and Andrew Wilson, *Ukraine: Perestroika to Independence* (New York: St. Martin's Press, 1994), 159.

[13] Dunlop (fn. 8), 603. Also see Mark R. Beissinger, "The Persisting Ambiguity of Empire," *Post-Soviet Affairs* 11 (1995), 149–84; Roman Solchanyk, "Ukraine, The (Former) Center, Russia, and 'Russia,'" *Studies in Comparative Communism* 25 (March 1992), 31–45.

embracing Ukraine and other union republics.[14] Even two years after independence, only a small majority (56 percent) of Ukrainians polled by Kiev's International Sociological Institute endorsed Ukraine's independence.[15] Alexander Motyl concludes that independence came "not because the nationalists tried harder or because they were stronger, but because the external conditions were right," and in these conditions it was the antinationalist Leonid Kravchuk who led the transition to independence.[16] Belarusian popular nationalism may have been weakest and support for the Soviet Union remained high in Belarus even after the breakup. A national referendum on May 14, 1995, recorded a 65 percent turnout and 83.3 percent support for restoration of Russian as an official language of the state and economic integration with Russia and 75.1 percent support for restoration of the Soviet-era symbols of the Byelorussian Soviet Socialist Republic.[17] Absent other causes, the multinational state could have survived the growth of nationalism in its smaller units in 1991.

In short, rising popular nationalism certainly accompanied the creation of new postcommunist nation-states, but it does not provide an entirely satisfactory explanation for why there is an independent Belarus, Tajikistan, and thirteen other new states. Similar observations have been made about the ambivalence of popular nationalism in the creation of some of the postcommunist nation-states in Eastern Europe. Indeed, the Czech and Slovak nation-states triumphed even though a solid majority of the population opposed this.[18] At best – and even this is highly contested by specialists on the Balkans – only in Yugoslavia and particularly in the secession of Slovenia and Croatia does popular nationalism give us much purchase on the triumph of specific nation-states over multinational states.

---

[14] Roman Solchanyk, "The Politics of State Building: Centre-Periphery Relations in Post-Soviet Ukraine," *Europe-Asia Studies* 46 (1994), 47–68; Paul S. Pirie, "National Identity and Politics in Southern and Eastern Ukraine," *Europe-Asia Studies* 48 (1996), 1096.
[15] *OMRI Daily Digest* 1 (10 July 1995).
[16] Alexander Motyl, *Dilemmas of Independence: Ukraine after Totalitarianism* (New York: Council on Foreign Relations, 1993), 23.
[17] On the failure of the Belorussian nationalist movement to mobilize the Belorussian population, see Beissinger (fn. 7), 252–7.
[18] Sharon L. Wolchik, "The Politics of Ethnicity in Post-Communist Czechoslovakia," *East European Politics and Societies* 8 (Winter 1994), 177. Also see Martin Butora and Zora Butorova, "Slovakia: The Identity Challenges of the Newly Born State," *Social Research* 60 (Winter 1993), 721–2.

War-Making Capacity

According to some students of international relations, war and war-making potential favored nation-states over the institutional alternatives such as dynastic states, empires, or multinational states and over alternative nation-state projects because the specific nation-states represent an optimal mix of expanded resource base and intense popular loyalty that is necessary for modern warfare.[19] According to Gilpin, empires fielded larger armies and city-states commanded more intense loyalty from their soldiers, but the nation-state trumped both of these by an optimal mix of size and loyalty found in mass, citizen armies.[20] There is some evidence that military fitness played a role in the triumph of postcommunist nation-states. First, military failure contributed to the collapse of the multiethnic states. Alumni of the Reagan Administration claim to have spent the Soviet Union to its death in an arms race that bankrupted the evil empire,[21] and President Vladimir Putin himself has acknowledged that excessive military spending contributed to the demise of the Soviet Union (*Reuters*, August 11, 2000). Second, the Soviet Union's losing war in Afghanistan certainly weakened the Soviet state by the end of the 1980s. Third, looking more broadly at all postcommunist countries, as the fifth row of figures in Table 2 shows, since communism homogeneous nation-states in fact maintain larger armed forces (on a per capita basis) than their heterogeneous neighbors. Yet, the difference between the heterogeneous and homogeneous states in Table 2 is small in magnitude and not statistically significant; the two groups are apparently drawn from a single distribution – the mean for each lies within one standard deviation of the other.

Indeed, three qualifications suggest that military fitness played at most a minor role in the transition to postcommunist nation-states. First, only in Yugoslavia did war play a direct role in the triumph of nation-states. Alternatively, actual war played no direct role in producing the breakup of either the Soviet Union or Czechoslovakia and conflicts in Abkhazia,

---

[19] Robert Gilpin, *War and Change in World Politics* (Cambridge: Cambridge University Press, 1981), 117–18; Charles Tilly, "Reflections on the History of European State-Making," in *The Formation of National States in Europe*, edited by Charles Tilly (Princeton: Princeton University Press, 1975), 3–83.
[20] Gilpin, ibid.
[21] Peter Schweizer, *Victory: The Reagan Administration's Secret Strategy That Hastened the Collapse of the Soviet Union* (New York: Atlantic Monthly Press, 1994).

TABLE 2. *Comparisons of Ethnically Homogeneous and Heterogeneous Communist and Postcommunist States*

	Unitary States			Multiethnic Federations		
Communist period:	Mean	(St Dev)	n	Mean	(St Dev)	n
1. Armed Forces (per 1,000 population)	11.70	(3.46)	6	12.76	(4.87)	3
2. Defense Expenditures (percent of GDP)	4.50	(3.33)	6	6.83	(4.50)	3
3. Economic Growth 1970–86 (change in per capita GDP)	41.11	(13.30)	4	46.38	(16.25)	3
4. Foreign Trade Growth, 1980–6 (change in dollar value)	1.92	(29.46)	4	−3.74	(29.04)	3

	Homogeneous States (Titular >85%)			Heterogeneous States (Titular <85%)		
Postcommunist period:	Mean	(St Dev)	n	Mean	(St Dev)	n
5. Armed Forces (percent of labor force)	1.77	(0.89)	9	1.21	(0.79)	18
6. Growth in GDP, 1990–8 (change in per capita GDP)	0.37	(2.84)	9	−6.28	(4.62)	17
7. Foreign Trade (percent of GDP)	33.95	(18.99)	8	24.57	(14.15)	15
8. Economic Liberalization (Scale = 1 to 5)	3.01	(0.45)	9	3.60	(0.63)	17
9. Average Tariff Rate (percent)	13.96	(5.36)	5	8.06	(4.11)	9
10. Foreign Direct Investment (percent of GDP)	1.66	(0.81)	9	1.93	(1.76)	12
11. Net Aid (percent of GDP)	2.18	(1.99)	9	3.66	(4.03)	16

Source: Data from International Institiute for Strategic Studies, *The Military Balance 1989–1990* (London: Brassey's, 1989); United Nations, *Statistical Yearbook 1988/89* (New York: United Nations, 1992); World Bank, *World Development Indicators 2000* (Washington, DC: World Bank, 2000); and Heritage Foundation, *Index of Economic Freedom* (Washington, DC: Heritage Foundation, 2000).

Chechnya, Nagornyi Karabakh, South Ossetia, and Transdniestria failed to produce new nation-states. That is, in most instances war was not a selection mechanism in any direct sense.[22] Moreover, with the waning of the fear of war in the period of *perestroika*, there is little reason to suspect that expectations of more efficient war making in the future were among the considerations that drove the secessionist movements. Second, looking at all postcommunist states, as the first two rows of figures in Table 2 show, in the communist period the multiethnic federations (the Soviet Union, Yugoslavia, and Czechoslovakia) were able to maintain larger armed forces (on a per capita basis) and shoulder a heavier defense burden (as a percentage of gross domestic product) than the more homogeneous unitary states. Yet, it would be rash to conclude that the multiethnic federations were more fit in military terms, because the differences between the two groups are not statistically significant. Third, the postcommunist successor states are distinctly less capable of defense than the communist metropolises they replaced and are able to bear a much smaller military burden than the metropolises bore. Indeed, the combined armed forces of the Soviet successor states in 1998 numbered 1,954,000, down 63 percent from the size of the Soviet armed forces in 1985; and combined defense expenditures in 1998 were down 83 percent from 1985 – a decline that cannot be attributed to improved efficiency.[23] In short, there is little basis for a claim that greater military prowess distinguished the more homogeneous unitary communist states from the multinational communist federations, the more homogeneous successor states from the multiethnic federations, or the homogeneous postcommunist states from the more diverse postcommunist states. Neither direct conflict among competing states nor emulation of states with greater military prowess can account for the triumph of the postcommunist nation-states.

Economic Performance

Students of international political economy have also claimed that states triumphed over empires because states are economically more efficient, leading to higher survival rates or to emulation of the more efficient

---

[22] The test of arms in Yugoslavia may have demonstrated the relative military fitness of outside powers, such as NATO, but not of the more homogeneous secessionist states.
[23] Calculated from data in International Institute of Strategic Studies, *The Military Balance 1999–2000* (London: Oxford University Press, 1999), 301–3. Defense expenditures are in constant 1997 prices.

by less efficient polities.[24] Yet it is difficult to demonstrate that relative economic performance accounts for the triumph of the postcommunist nation-states. Moreover, the economic losses associated with the system of nation-states may actually make nation-states less efficient than their multiethnic predecessors.

Sociological research on the cultural foundations of economic exchange and economic research on the size and number of states suggest that homogeneous nation-states may enjoy two economic advantages over ethnically plural societies. First, homogeneous nation-states may be more likely to develop political cultures that support market relations. Early sociologists such as Émile Durkheim stressed that a cultural environment of trust and solidarity is necessary for the contracting and exchange of the modern market, and J. S. Furnivall argued that this solidarity and trust is absent from ethnically plural societies.[25] Repeated surveys in the postcommunist states do point to an absence of solidarity between some ethnic communities.[26] Second, in ethnically diverse societies, government policies are more likely to lead to economic inefficiency, costly compensatory schemes, and administrative waste. In these societies, government finds it harder to identify policies that can be applied uniformly throughout society.[27] The greater heterogeneity of preferences may require compensatory schemes that buy the allegiance of ethnic communities whose median preference is far from the policy adopted by the government.[28] These payments represent an inefficient reallocation of wealth and carry increased administrative costs that can retard economic growth in diverse societies.[29] In support of these arguments, the sixth row of figures in Table 2 shows that since the end of communism, the homogeneous

---

[24] Douglass C. North, *Structure and Change in Economic History* (New York: W. W. Norton, 1981).
[25] J. S. Furnivall, *Netherlands India: A Study of Plural Economy* (New York: Macmillan Company, 1944).
[26] Rasma Karklins and Brigita Zepa, "Religious-Centered Multiethnic Societies: Multiple Identities and Ethnopolitics in Latvia," *American Behavioral Scientist* 40 (September 1996), 33–45; Stephen Shulman, "The Cultural Foundations of Ukrainian National Identity," *Ethnic and Racial Studies* 22 (November 1999), 1011–36; Mary E. McIntosh, Martha Abele MacIver, Daniel G. Abele, and David B. Nolle, "Minority Rights and Majority Rule: Ethnic Tolerance in Romania and Bulgaria," *Social Forces* 73 (March 1995), 945.
[27] Tilly (fn. 19), 79.
[28] Alberto Alesina and Enrico Spolaore, "On the Number and Size of Nations," *Quarterly Journal of Economics* 112 (November 1997), 1027–56.
[29] Andrew D. Austin, "The Price of Nationalism: Evidence from the Soviet Union," *Public Choice* 87 (April 1996), 1–18.

nation-states have experienced higher economic growth than the more diverse states, but this difference is not statistically significant.

Relative economic efficiency has made at most only a small contribution to the transition to postcommunist nation-states. As the third row of figures in Table 2 shows, in the last decade and a half prior to *perestroika*, the multiethnic communist federations were growing more rapidly than the more homogeneous unitary communist states, although the differences are not statistically significant. Most economic theory cautions that the potential gains of homogeneity must be weighed against the costs of smaller states: larger states lead to larger markets, greater division of labor, economies of scale, lower per capita cost of nonrival public goods, greater efficiency in taxation, less duplication of government costs (notably for defense and law enforcement), coordination of public goods (including transportation, communications, and standards), and lower per capita cost from uninsurable shocks.[30] A preponderance of evidence from the postcommunist transition to nation-states shows that gains in efficiency from homogeneity are, indeed, lost in smaller markets. The successor states do not perform better than the multiethnic metropolises they replaced. Division of the market came at a high price that compounded the costs associated with economic reform: In the first nine years of independence (1992–2000), the successor states "lost" the equivalent of 3.3 years of economic output (based on the 1990 level). The combined gross domestic product of the fifteen soviet successor states in 2000 was still down 37 percent from the gross domestic product of the Soviet Union in 1990.[31] In short, the multiethnic communist federations were not less efficient than either the unitary communist states or their successor states, and the more diverse postcommunist states are not significantly less efficient than their more homogenous post-communist neighbors.

International Acceptance

A third international selection mechanism is acceptance by the dominant powers. Three different reasons have been offered why the dominant powers might prefer nation-states to multinational alternatives, yet none

---

[30] Alesina and Spolaore (fn. 28); Bruno Dallago and Milica Uvalic, "The Distributive Consequences of Nationalism: The Case of Former Yugoslavia," *Europe-Asia Studies* 50 (1998), 71–90; Patrick Bolton and Gerard Roland, "The Breakup of Nations: A Political Economy Analysis," *Quarterly Journal of Economics* 112 (November 1997), 1057–90.

[31] Calculated from data in World Bank, *World Development Indicators* 2002 [CD-ROM version] (Washington, DC: World Bank, 2002).

successfully accounts for the post-Soviet transition to nation-states. First, due to its greater political stability, the nation-state is better able to make credible commitments and so other international actors are more likely to enter agreements with it.[32] Second, nation-states are more likely to open their economies to transnational transactions – in part because homogeneous states are likely to be smaller and in part because diverse states have more reason to fear that transnational interactions will empower their ethnic minorities at the expense of the state. Indeed, as the fourth row of figures in Table 2 shows, the more homogeneous unitary states of the late-communist period saw growth in the value of foreign trade from 1980 to 1986, while the multiethnic federations saw decline in the value of foreign trade. As the seventh row of figures shows, homogeneous postcommunist states were likely to engage in more international trade than their diverse postcommunist neighbors. Third, the international norm of self-determination favors new states that can claim to represent the will of a people.

Once again, the evidence of the postcommunist transition suggests that international acceptance in the ways outlined in the previous paragraph played at most only a small role in the triumph of nation-states. The international community did not rush to embrace the new nation-states at the expense of the multinational metropolises they replaced, and the international community has not embraced homogeneous nation-states more readily than their more diverse neighbors. For example, after communism the more homogeneous nation-states were not more fully integrated into the global economy than their more diverse neighbors. The differences in levels of trade are not statistically significant. As the eighth and ninth rows of figures in Table 2 show, the diverse states were actually somewhat more likely to liberalize their economies and to maintain lower tariff rates. The next two rows of figures also demonstrate that these diverse states were more likely to receive more foreign direct investment and aid from the advanced industrial democracies. None of these differences is statistically significant, however.

Moreover, the prevailing understanding of the right to national self-determination – upheld by the dominant powers – did not legitimize the claims of the secessionist states. As James Mayall notes,

The core of this conventional understanding [after 1945] was the belief that international society consisted of sovereign, i.e., independent states; that they formed

---

[32] Spruyt (fn. 4), 167–71.

a society because they recognize each others' sovereignty and what this entailed, namely their territorial integrity and right to manage their domestic affairs without outside interference; and that consequently the right of self-determination referred only to colonies.[33]

Hence, throughout much of the Cold War period, decolonization was virtually the only source of new states. The international community resisted recognition of secessions from existing states. The western states set a precedent for dealing with secession from the Soviet Union when they refused to recognize Lithuania as a sovereign state in March 1990, after its parliament voted to seek independence. Even as late as August 1, 1991, during his visit to Kiev, President George Bush urged the Ukrainians to reject "suicidal nationalism" and negotiate with Moscow to reform the Soviet Union.[34] Even more recently in Abkhazia, Chechnya, Karabakh, and Kosovo, among others, the international community has been unwilling to recognize claims to independence.

In sum, the four usual explanations for the triumph of nation-states leave us with a less than satisfactory account of the triumph of post-Soviet and postcommunist nation-states. Not nationalism, war-making capacity, economic efficiency, or international acceptance can explain the outcome without considering the role of domestic political institutions of the *ancien regime* – an explanation that also casts a new light on the usual suspects.

THE FAILURE OF SEGMENTAL INCORPORATION

The political institutions of segmental incorporation played a central role in the triumph of the post-Soviet nation-states.[35] The Soviet Union had responded to national diversity with segmental incorporation of ethnic groups in a federation of homelands and engaged its minorities as members of ethnically distinct subordinate states rather than members of a uniform citizenry. It is a pattern that was duplicated in Yugoslavia and Czechoslovakia. These three segmented states are the only ones to split

---

[33] James Mayall, "Sovereignty, Nationalism, and Self-Determination," *Political Studies* 47 (Special Issue 1999), 475.
[34] Motyl (fn. 16), 181.
[35] Roeder (fn. 1); Suny (fn. 1); Robert J. Kaiser, *The Geography of Nationalism in Russia and the USSR* (Princeton: Princeton University Press, 1994); Rogers Brubaker, *Nationalism Reframed: Nationhood and the National Question in the New Europe* (Cambridge: Cambridge University Press, 1996); Daniel S. Treisman, "Russia's 'Ethnic Revival': The Separatist Activism of Regional Leaders in a Postcommunist Order," *World Politics* 49 (January 1997), 212–49; and Bunce (fn. 1).

apart during the transition from communism. Among the twenty-two successor states spawned by the breakup of these three countries, six inherited some form of segmental institutions – Azerbaijan, Georgia, Russia, Tajikistan, Uzbekistan, and rump Yugoslavia. Four of these six – all but Tajikistan and Uzbekistan – have been plagued by civil wars between the new central governments and secessionist ethnic republics.[36]

The segmented state incorporates ethnic communities through separate territorial administrations – proto-nation-states within a common-state. Segmental institutions not only divided the territory of the common-state but also the populations associated with these into separate political statuses. Segmental incorporation of ethnic groups did not originate with the Soviet Union. Dynastic incorporation (such as the incorporation of Finland within the Russian Empire) united lands through the crown, but not a uniform polity. Modern overseas empires, such as the British Empire, typically refused to grant indigenous populations full citizenship within the metropolis, but made them subjects of the Crown through colonies and protectorates. Reservations for indigenous peoples in many settler societies, such as the United States, and multiethnic confederations, such as Canada under the British North America Act (1867), created or united proto-nation-states within a common-state.

The most important distinctions among segmented states concern the role of segment-states (like Ukraine) in the governance of the common-state (the USSR) and in their own self-governance, and the extent to which the various segment populations participate as equal citizens in the common-state. The larger the decision-making rights of the proto-nation-states within the common-state and the more unequal the citizenship rights of the various populations associated with these segment-states, the more the contacts of members of the cultural communities with the common-state are mediated through their own nation-states. The most important of these decision rights is the choice of the leaders of the segment. Once the leaders of segments are no longer accountable to the common-state, the probability of holding the segmented state together declines.

In some forms of segmented states, the government of the common-state becomes in essence an assembly of representatives of nation-states. This was perfected in the Soviet Union, where the collective presidency

---

[36] Of course, Tajikistan has suffered through a severe civil war, but the ethnic claims of the Pamiris and Gorno-Badakhshan autonomous *oblast* have played only a minor role in this.

(Presidium of the Supreme Soviet), the collective executive (Presidium of the Council of Ministers), and the Supreme Court all co-opted the chairmen of the corresponding bodies of the union-republic governments. Once union-republic governments were no longer dependent on Moscow for their tenure of office, the Soviet government became more like an international organization. Beginning in March 1990, the Soviet president conducted negotiations over the fate of the Soviet Union in a Council of the Federation composed of the leaders of the union republics.[37]

The reasons states resort to segmentation have included limits on state capacity to administer diverse societies, protection of the minority cultures from assimilation, and preservation of the privileges of the dominant community. Frequently, the design of segmental institutions is supposed to block the emergence of nationalist challenges that could divide the state. So, the Soviets rejected or abandoned schemes to create a Turkestan republic, Idel-Ural, or Mountain Republic because they might have created powerful units threatening the unity of the Soviet state; instead they created smaller nation-states, which they thought would be easier to control, like Uzbekistan, Tatarstan, and Chechnya.[38]

Segmental institutions had three unintended consequences that led to the unraveling of the communist federations: They provided ethnonational leaders with the means to back up their claims by punitive action against the leaders of the common-state. They established incentives for homeland leaders to press sovereignty claims against the common-state. They provided the opportunity for secession by weakening the common-state. In the end, these led to a fragile union that dissolved in a cascade of defections. In addition, segmental institutions became the prism through which nationalism and international acceptance did have an effect on the pattern of new nation-states.

Means – Proliferation of Institutional Weapons

Ethnonational challenges to existing states are more likely to succeed where leaders of the challenging community have the means to exert pressure on the leadership of the common-state. In the communist federations,

---

[37] *Pravda*, 16 March 1990. This type of co-optation is best known in the case of Yugoslavia's collective presidency.
[38] Ronald Wixman, *Language Aspects of Ethnic Patterns and Processes in the North Caucasus* (University of Chicago, Department of Geography, Research Paper No. 191, 1980), 126, 136–9.

segmental incorporation through homeland administrations provided this organization. In the Soviet federation, fifty-three of the territorial administrations of the Soviet Union were based on designated ethnic homelands, including fifteen union republics, twenty autonomous republics, eight autonomous *oblasts*, and ten autonomous *okrugs*. These policies were extended quite mechanically to the largest indigenous ethnic minorities – regardless of whether these had a well-developed sense of separateness or statehood. By 1988, ethnic homelands existed for all twelve of the largest ethnic groups, ten of the twelve next largest ethnic minorities (only the Germans and Poles were excepted), nine of the twelve next largest minorities (only the Bulgarians, Greeks, and Koreans were excepted), and for twenty-nine of the remaining sixty smaller ethnic groups. The policy of indigenization (*korenizatsiia*) drew national cadres into the political and administrative posts of the Communist Party and Soviet state in these territories.[39] Grey Hodnett's extensive data show that by the early post-Stalinist period (1955–72), in eleven of the fourteen non-Russian union republics indigenization had led to proportionate overrepresentation of the titular nationality in the leading posts of the Communist Party and state organs.[40]

The intended consequence of these segmental institutions was central control over ethnic communities, but the unintended consequence was the proliferation of institutional weapons that the leaders of the proto-nation-states could use against the common government. As Philip Selznick notes, decision rights can be weapons "used by a power-seeking elite in a manner unrestrained by the constitutional order of the arena within which the contest takes place" in order to change that constitutional order.[41] For example, in the Soviet Union control over scarce resources, such as grain or energy, or control over critical revenue sources gave homeland leaders the power to starve the common government into submission.[42] The power to veto or opt out of common policies gave homeland leaders the power to paralyze the common government, in order to induce it to

---

[39] J. V. Stalin, "The Policy of the Soviet Government on the National Question in Russia," in *Works* (Moscow: Foreign Languages Publishing House, 1953), 4:370–1.

[40] Grey Hodnett, *Leadership in the Soviet National Republics* (Oakville, Ontario: Mosaic Press, 1978), 101–3, 377–8; Ellen Jones and Fred W. Grupp, "Modernisation and Ethnic Equalisation in the USSR," *Soviet Studies* 36 (April 1984), 174.

[41] Philip Selznick, *The Organizational Weapon: A Study of Bolshevik Strategy and Tactics* (Glencoe: The Free Press of Glencoe, 1960), 2.

[42] Philip Hanson, "The Union Treaty: Embargoes or Surrender?," *Report on the USSR*, 28 June 1991, 15–16; John Tedstrom, "Soviet Fiscal Federalism in a Time of Crisis," *Report on the USSR*, 2 August 1991, 1–5.

concede. That is, segmental institutions gave these leaders the means to press claims for expansion of the rights of the nation-state – once motive and opportunity were present.

Motive – National Outbidding

Segmental incorporation of ethnic groups also established incentive structures that provided homeland leaders the motive to press more extreme national demands that culminated in a demand for sovereignty. Soviet federalism embedded the cadres of homelands within the all-union Soviet administrative hierarchy. By integrating the cadres into Party and state hierarchies, Soviet federalism made the "normal" politics of competitive appeals for resources the norm among ethnic elites as well.[43]

Once the leaders of each segment were accountable to local constituencies, segmental institutions encouraged national outbidding that led to an escalation of normal politics to claims for sovereignty. First, within homelands with autonomy to select their own leaders – whether undergoing democratization or not – politicians found that they could outbid one another with ever more extreme claims about what they would win at the central bargaining table.[44] This promised to expand the pie for all voters in the homeland at the expense of "aliens" outside the union republic. Thus, during the last two years of the Soviet Union, democratization of politics in the Baltic states, Georgia, and Moldova led to victories for politicians who claimed they would make their union republic's sovereignty a reality. Yet, even the autocratic leaders of other union republics, like Uzbekistan, began to press sovereignty claims. Sometimes this was also ethnic outbidding, as in Latvia, but oftentimes homeland leaders initially tempered their claims as claims on behalf of the sovereign rights of a civic nation – such as the nation of Kazakhstanis – made up of multiple ethnic groups within the union republic.[45] For example, in one of the first declarations

---

[43] Donna Bahry, *Outside Moscow: Power, Politics, and Budgetary Policy in Soviet Republics* (New York: Columbia University Press, 1987), 1–5; Howard L. Biddulph, "Local Interest Articulation at CPSU Congresses," *World Politics* 36 (October 1983), 28–52; Jerry F. Hough and Merle Fainsod, *How the Soviet Union Is Governed* (Cambridge: Harvard University Press), 510–17.

[44] Robert Hislope, "Intra-Ethnic Conflict in Croatia and Serbia: Flanking and the Consequences for Democracy," *East European Quarterly* 30 (January 1997), 471–94.

[45] Compare the "Deklaratsiia Verkhovnogo Soveta Latviiskoi Sovetskoi Sotsialisticheskoi Respubliki 'O Vosstanovlenii Nezavisimosti Latviiskoi Respubliki,'" *Sovetskaia Latviia*, 9 May 1990, with "Deklaratsiia 'O Gosudarstvennom Suverenitete Kazakhskoi Sovetskoi Sotsialisticheskoi Respubliki,'" *Kazakhstanskaia Pravda*, 28 October 1990.

of state sovereignty by an autonomous republic within Russia, the leaders of the Komi Republic based their claim to "state sovereignty" on the rights of the "people of Komi" and the Republic's commitment to preserve the "culture, language, traditions, and way of life [*byt*] of the people of Komi."[46] Ironically, the head of the Komi Republic – Yuri Alekseevich Spiridonov – who pressed these sovereign rights against the Russian state was not himself an ethnic Komi, but an ethnic Russian, and 58 percent of the "people of Komi" were ethnic Russians and only 23 percent were ethnic Komis.

Second, in the politics of the common-state, Segmental institutions provided homeland leaders an incentive to privilege their claims by framing them as claims on behalf of the sovereign prerogatives of their respective peoples. Such claims on behalf of the sovereign prerogatives of the homeland people took precedence over other claims, such as the claims from Russian provincial leaders. Homeland leaders who did not initially make sovereignty claims had to follow the leaders – lest their claims be disadvantaged. So, even in republics that failed to democratize, such as the Central Asian states, leaders of Communist Party machines had to promise their bureaucratic clienteles that they would wrench more power from Moscow. Once one republic had issued a sovereignty declaration, all the others had to follow.[47] Thus, as they sought to rewrite the constitution, the bargaining among leaders of republics in the Soviet Union became dominated by disputes over the powers of the autonomous homeland administrations that claimed sovereignty rooted in the rights of their respective peoples – much as in Czechoslovakia and Yugoslavia.[48] Politicians with other agendas that might cut across national issues – such as class or profession – had to frame their demands as national claims in order to gain access to the privileged centers of decision making.[49] In this institutional environment, all politics became international politics among nation-states claiming sovereignty.[50]

---

[46] "Deklaratsiia o gosudarstvennom suverenitet Komi Sovetskoi Sotsialisticheskoi Respubliki," *Krasnoe znamya* (Syktyvkar), 5 September 1990.

[47] Ann Sheehy, "Fact Sheet on Declarations of Sovereignty," *Report on the USSR*, 9 November 1990, 23–5. This was also true for the autonomous republics within the Russian Federation – see Daniel S. Treisman, *After the Deluge: Regional Crises and Political Consolidation in Russia* (Ann Arbor: University of Michigan Press, 1999), 203.

[48] See *Pravda*, 21–2 September 1989.

[49] Wolchik (fn. 18), 163. Also see John T. Ishiyama, "Representational Mechanisms and Ethnopolitics: Evidence from Transitional Democracies in Eastern Europe," *East European Quarterly* 33 (June 1999), 251–79.

[50] Suny (fn. 1); Katherine Verdery, "Nationalism, Postsocialism, and Space in Eastern Europe," *Social Research* 63 (Spring 1996), 79–83; Bogdan Denitch, *Limits and*

Opportunity – Withering Away of the Common-State

The opportunity for secession came with the weakening of the common-state, which resulted from the free-riding that segmental institutions encouraged and from the growing irrelevance of common policies. First, segmental incorporation encouraged leaders of each homeland to exploit the cooperation of others. That is, in a peculiar form of prisoner's dilemma, each leader had an incentive to free-ride on the cooperative behavior of the others; each had an incentive to increase her or his share of the political pie – such as withholding tax revenues owed to the common government – while others observed the rules and paid the price of maintaining the union.[51] Even if no leader had chosen to weaken the union, the cumulative effect of each following this logic of riding free would have been exactly that. Second, segmented states increased the likelihood that policies in the different ethnic communities would diverge, the communities would actually develop in different directions, their resulting needs and preferences would diverge, and common policies for the country as a whole would become increasingly irrelevant. The Communist Party in Czechoslovakia, the Soviet Union, and Yugoslavia had forced common policies on disparate communities, but once this unifying force weakened, the diverging development of republics made it more difficult to identify common policies that necessitated a common-state. In the transition from communism, political and economic changes progressed at different rates and in different directions in the separate ethnic homelands within the postcommunist federations, so that the policies of the common government became increasingly irrelevant.[52] It became harder to find policies that could address the needs of both an increasingly liberal and democratized Estonia as well as an increasingly illiberal, personalistic, and autocratic Turkmenistan. The central government responded by allowing more decisions to devolve onto the regions, but at some point the common government no longer had the means to enforce its will against secessionist governments.[53] Indeed, this is what the Belovezhskaia-Pushcha Agreements, signed by Russia, Ukraine, and Belarus, ratified; these did

---

Possibilities: The Crises of Yugoslav Socialism and State-Socialist Systems (Minneapolis: University of Minnesota Press, 1990), 78.

[51] Alvin Rabushka and Kenneth A. Shepsle, *Politics in Plural Societies: A Theory of Democratic Instability* (Columbus: Charles E. Merrill Publishing Company, 1972), 76.

[52] Bunce (fn. 1), 87–8.

[53] Michael Hechter argues that it was the imposition of direct rule after a period of indirect rule that produced the nationalist revolt. Yet, in all three communist federations the demand for sovereignty came after movement toward greater indirect rule. See Hechter's *Containing Nationalism* (New York: Oxford University Press, 2000).

not dissolve the Soviet Union, but simply confirmed that for all intents and purposes it had already disappeared. Communism did not cause the state to wither away; segmentation of the state did.

Process – Cascading Defections from the Union

In its last days, each segmented state became a brittle union and fell apart quickly. The process of cascading defections reflected the way that each secession affected the incentives and opportunities of all others. The first secession raised the cost of maintaining the union and lowered the costs of leaving for all others so that a second community passed its "tipping point."[54] This second secession changed these costs for all others so that a third passed its "tipping point," and so forth. For example, in late 1991, after the Baltic states had left the Soviet Union and as Georgia and Moldova appeared about to follow, Russia's reformist leaders found it harder to imagine remaining in a confederation in which they could be outvoted by the unreconstructed communists of the Turkic republics.[55] Similarly, in the former Yugoslavia, once Slovenia and Croatia indicated they would secede, Macedonia and Bosnia could not remain behind as junior partners in a Yugoslavia soon to be dominated by Serbia.[56]

To prevent this cascade of defections from the very beginning of the communist federations required centralized controls that were outside the segmental institutions. The communist Party Secretariat provided this through its *nomenklatura* powers that permitted the all-union general secretary to remove homeland leaders. The Soviet regime waged a continual battle against signs of nationalism among the homeland cadres – beginning with the struggle against *sultangalievism* in the 1920s. After 1960 the Soviet Communist Party leadership removed over a dozen union-republic first secretaries because they permitted regional differences to become ethnic issues. For example, in 1972 the Ukrainian and Georgian secretaries were both removed for "national narrow-mindedness" and overzealous promotion of local interests.[57] Once this control was

---

[54] Thomas C. Schelling, *Micromotives and Macrobehavior* (New York: W. W. Norton and Company, 1978), 101–2.

[55] Solchanyk (fn. 13), 42.

[56] V. Gagnon, Jr., "Ethnic Nationalism and International Conflict: The Case of Serbia," *International Security* 19 (Winter 1994–5), 130–66.

[57] Robert Conquest, *Soviet Nationalities Policy in Practice* (New York: Praeger, 1967); Teresa Rakowska-Harmstone, "The Dialectics of Nationalism in the USSR," *Problems of Communism* 23 (May–June 1974), 13.

removed – as soon as the communist systems became truly segmental with the introduction of union-republic control over its own leadership – the union began to unravel.

Why Did States Not Unravel Further?

Segmental institutions were also the prism through which nationalism and international acceptance influenced the pattern of nation-states that emerged from the demise of communism and, thus, help explain why the unraveling stopped with first-order homelands – the union republics. That is, the segmental-institutions thesis explains why provinces without a distinct ethnic basis, like Russia's *oblasts*, were unable to duplicate the strategy of ethnic leaders in first-order homelands; why second-order homeland leaders – that is, the leaders of autonomous republics, autonomous oblasts, and autonomous okrugs – were unable to carry this strategy to a successful conclusion; and why ethnopoliticians seeking to redraw the nation-state boundaries failed. Specifically, segmental institutions ensured that the claims on behalf of the first-order homeland administrations would not be trumped by competing national projects for alternative nation-states or for the common-state. Segmental institutions also served as a second "line in the sand" by which the international community could seek to contain the unraveling of sovereign states once the first line was no longer defensible.

A successful claim on behalf of a nation-state did not require strong popular nationalism, but it did require that other ethnopoliticians could not trump this claim by mobilizing the population on behalf of an alternative national claim – such as the Soviet Union or a division within the union republic. That is, the Soviet experience showed that politicians can successfully press claims on behalf of a nation-state not only where more of the population shares this national identity than other national identities, but also where the population has not yet developed any national identity or where the politicians can control the expression of the alternative identities. Segmental institutions provided the leaders of the proto-nation-states in the Soviet Union with claims that other ethnic entrepreneurs could not trump by mobilizing the population behind alternative popular appeals.

In the absence of a state of their own, popular and elite conceptions of the nation rarely coordinate. Prior to the communist period, many inhabitants of the Russian Empire were parochials without a well-developed identity that linked them to a people they thought had a legitimate right to a state of its own; indeed, like true parochials, many lacked even the concept of a state.[58] Elites offered competing projects for imagined states. For example, in 1917 competing ethnopoliticians in the Russian Empire advanced programs for statehood on behalf of the Muslims as a single people, the Turkic Muslims, regional amalgams such as Turkestan, nationalities such as the Kyrgyzes and Kazakhs, and smaller groupings such as the Greater Horde within the Kazakhs. All these competed with those members of ethnic groups who argued for subordinating ethnic differences in an all-Russian alliance of exploited classes.[59] In this period of competing national projects, identification with the groups that actually would become nation-states tended to be weak.

The Soviet institutions of segmental political incorporation coordinated elite and mass imaginations, but they tended to create dual identities and to make the homeland leaders the arbiters of conflicts between these identities. That is, segmental incorporation in the Soviet period did not simply forge nation-states, but, instead, privileged two national identities over others as the basis of statehood – Soviet and titular nationality – and gave both a reality.[60] In crafting the nationality into a nation-state, homeland leaders enjoyed a political monopoly – no one else was permitted to speak on behalf of the nationality. The homeland leaders institutionalized its monopoly over the public expression of identity, and under their direction the indigenization of leadership posts in these cultural institutions of the union republics was nearly complete. As Hodnett's figures for 1955 to 1972 show, in the union republics 412 of the 448 Communist Party propaganda secretaries, heads of Party propaganda and culture departments, ministers responsible for culture or education, and heads of

[58] Robert J. Kaiser, "Prospects for the Disintegration of the Russian Federation," *Post-Soviet Geography* 36 (1995); Suny (fn. 1), 29–76. See, for example, Teresa Rakowska-Harmstone, *Russia and Nationalism in Central Asia: The Case of Tadzhikistan* (Baltimore: Johns Hopkins University Press, 1970), 76–9. Compare Lucy Mair, *Primitive Government: A Study of Traditional Poltical Systems in Eastern Africa* (Bloomington: Indiana University Press, 1977); Eugen Weber, *Peasants into Frenchmen: The Modernization of Rural France, 1870–1914* (Stanford: Stanford University Press, 1976), 95–114.
[59] Serge A. Zenkovsky, *Pan-Turkism and Islam in Russia* (Cambridge: Harvard University Press, 1960); also see Ronald Grigor Suny, "Provisional Stabilities: The Politics of Identities in Post-Soviet Eurasia," *International Security* 24 (Winter 1999/2000), 139–78; and the discussion among Josh Sanborn, Scott J. Seregny, and S. A. Smith in *Slavic Review* 59 (Summer 2000), 267–342.
[60] Shirin Akiner, *The Formation of Kazakh Identity: From Tribe to Nation-State* (London: Royal Institute of International Affairs, 1995), 48–50. In this sense the Baltic nationalisms – forged in the period of independence – were different from most of the other nationalisms in the Soviet Union.

writers' unions and academies of sciences were drawn from the homeland's titular group.[61] The coordination of a common conception of the proto-nation-state was possible because the homeland leaders used their institutionalized monopoly of cultural life to silence competitors.[62] Creative professionals who sought to spread alternative projects for nation-states could not gain access to public forums; thus, their alternative imagined communities might gain currency only in small corners of the country among small circles of acquaintances.[63] For example, after seventy years of Soviet power in Central Asia, alternative national projects such as Turkestan could not compete with the official nationalisms of Kazakhs, Uzbeks, and the other titular nationalities.[64]

The stricture "national in form, socialist in content," however, meant that the homeland leaders also propagated a second imagined community with a right to a state of its own – the Soviet people. Indeed, as the constructivists have argued in other contexts,[65] most Soviet citizens possessed multiple identities that were invoked in different situations, but, in a pattern that is not common except in special institutional contexts, most also had at least two and sometimes three national identities – they believed they were members of both a Soviet state and a nationality-state such as Kyrgyzstan (and sometimes a Soviet state, a union-republic state such as Russia, and a nationality-state such as Tatarstan). For example, in a survey

---

[61] Hodnett (fn. 40), 90–1; Mark Popovsky, *Manipulated Science* (Garden City: Doubleday & Co., 1979), 118; Katherine E. Graney, "Education Reform in Tatarstan and Bashkortostan: Sovereignty Projects in Post-Soviet Russia," *Europe-Asia Studies* 51 (1999), 611–32.

[62] See, for example, Dietrich A. Loeber, "Administration of Culture in Soviet Latvia," in *Res Baltica*, edited by Adolf Sprudz and Armin Rusis (Leyden: A. W. Sijthoff, 1968), 133–45; Nicholas Vakar, *Belorussia: The Making of a Nation* (Cambridge: Harvard University Press, 1956), 150–1; Alex Inkeles, *Public Opinion in Soviet Russia: A Study in Mass Persuasion* (Cambridge: Harvard University Press, 1950); Peter Kenez, *The Birth of the Propaganda State: Soviet Methods of Mass Mobilization, 1917–1929* (Cambridge: Cambridge University Press, 1985).

[63] Timur Kocaoglu, "Muslim Chain Letters in Central Asia," *Radio Liberty Research Bulletin*, RL 313/83 (18 August 1983); Alexandre Bennigsen, "Mullahs, Mujahidin, and Soviet Muslims," *Problems of Communism* 33 (November–December 1984), 36–7; Ludmilla Alexeyeva, *Soviet Dissent* (Middletown: Wesleyan University Press, 1985), 31.

[64] Nancy Lubin, *Central Asians Take Stock: Reform, Corruption, and Identity* (Washington, DC: United States Institute of Peace, 1995), 18. Also see Martha Brill Olcott, "The Myth of 'Tsentral'naia Aziia,'" *Orbis* 38 (Fall 1994), 549–65.

[65] On multiple, situation-specific identities, see Nelson Kasfir, *The Shrinking Political Agenda: Participation and Ethnicity in African Politics* (Berkeley: University of California Press, 1976); Mary C. Waters, *Ethnic Options: Choosing Identities in America* (Berkeley: University of California Press, 1990).

conducted in Russia's republics after the breakup of the Soviet Union (November–December 1993), Timothy Colton and others found that a majority in each of twenty-one titular nationalities in sixteen republics – all but the Chechens of Chechnya – considered themselves representatives of both their republic and Russia, although they varied in the priority they placed on the republic or Russia.[66] This dual identity was evident in the last days of the Soviet Union. For example, on March 17, 1991, Ukraine's citizens were asked to vote on two referenda – one endorsing a new Union Treaty and another endorsing Ukraine's state sovereignty within a Union of Soviet Sovereign States; with 83.5 percent turnout, an overwhelming majority of the voters approved both questions.[67] Dual national identities also created the opportunity for cycling of popular majorities when citizens of union republics were asked at different times which polity they endorsed: In different contexts, citizens who thought of themselves as belonging to both a Soviet state and a national state would respond with seemingly contradictory answers.

Segmental institutions also privileged the homeland cadres in the reconciliation of conflicts between these dual national identities. For members of the titular nationalities in each homeland – particularly for those who spoke Russian poorly – their only point of contact with the Soviet state was through the indigenous cadres. Thus, Soviet policies placed the homeland cadres in the critical position to mediate between the halves of the dual Soviet-nationality identity. In this context, Moscow's attempt to trump the national claims of the union-republic leaders by mobilizing the Soviet identity among members of titular nationalities against the demands of their own union-republic leaders largely failed.[68] This also worked to the disadvantage of the leaders of provinces with populations drawn from the majority population of the union republic, leaders of second-order homeland administrations, and intellectuals with projects for new imagined communities – many of whom pressed national sovereignty claims that mimicked those of the union republics. For example, Russian governors pressed for a Urals Republic, Siberian Republic, Pomor'e Republic, and Primor'e Republic and in some instances buttressed these claims with

---

[66] Valerii Tishkov, *Ethnicity, Nationalism, and Conflict in and after the Soviet Union: The Mind Aflame* (London: Sage Publications, 1997), 261–4.
[67] That is, the lowest double positive percentage would result if 29.8 percent of the participants voted for the first referendum and against the second, 19.8 percent voted for the second and against the first, but 50.4 percent voted for both.
[68] Nils Muiznieks, "The Pro-Soviet Movement in Latvia," *Report on the USSR*, 24 August 1990, 19–24.

evidence that culture separated their people from other Russians.[69] Yet, the Russian government could mobilize the Russians of these "republics" (and even most second-order homelands, where Russians constituted the majority of the population) against these claims. Entrepreneurs with alternative national projects could not trump the claims of the union-republic leaders by mobilizing popular opposition.

The leaders of provinces and second-order homelands and the purveyors of alternative national projects were also typically at a disadvantage due to the coordinated efforts of the leaders of the first-order homelands and the international community. The territorial divisions within the segmented states became the focal point for the simultaneous resolution of two coordination problems – among ethnopoliticians and between ethnopoliticians and the international community.[70] Both limited the opportunities for alternative national projects. Among the leaders of the first-order homelands seeking to minimize conflicts with one another that might distract from their struggle to create independent states, acquiescence in the existing boundaries of the segmented state provided a conspicuous focal point that could avoid costly bargaining over the demarcation of state boundaries. Simultaneously, in the bargaining between ethnopoliticians wanting to dismantle a sovereign state and the international community seeking to avoid this, the existing boundaries of the segmented state provided an agreement to avoid the endless unraveling of sovereign states that the great powers feared. The convergence on the conspicuous solution did not represent a norm: When homeland leaders and international leaders justified the new borders, they appealed to principles of national self-determination[71]; the international community's norm against the use of violence to change the borders of existing states would have to be stretched to apply to this situation.[72] Neither homeland leaders nor the international community had an interest in articulating

---

[69] See, for example, *Izvestiia*, 30 March 1992, 26 January 1993, 3 July 1993; Peter Kirkow, "Regional Warlordism in Russia: The Case of Primorskii Krai," *Europe-Asia Studies* 47 (1995), 932–3.
[70] On focal points in coordination games, see Schelling (fn. 10).
[71] Martha Finnemore and Kathryn Sikkink, "International Norm Dynamics and Political Change," *International Organization* 52 (Autumn 1998), 892.
[72] Mark W. Zacher, "The Territorial Integrity Norm: International Boundaries and the Use of Force," *International Organization* 55 (Spring 2001), 215–50. In the United Nations Declaration of Principles of International Law Concerning Friendly Relations and Cooperation among States, UNGA res. 2625, 1970, this rejection of violence is coupled with the additional stipulation that principles of the declaration do not justify *any* action to facilitate secession or division of existing states.

the focal point (first-order divisions) into a norm, for this could have unleashed a wave of copycat claims to dismantle still other states. For the international community the boundaries of the first-order administrations became the best fallback position once the common-state could no longer be saved.[73]

Statistical Evidence

This argument inevitably begs the question of the endogeneity of segmental institutions – that is, whether the observed relationship between segmental institutions and nationalist challenges to the state may be simply spurious and the real cause is the demographic, cultural, or historical factors that give rise to both segmental institutions and nationalist challenges. Ethnic groups that are more likely to make nationalist challenges for demographic, cultural, or historical reasons may also for these same reasons be more likely to be recognized in segmental institutions. If these "deeper causes" are the real reason for ethnonational challenges, and segmental institutions contribute nothing to the likelihood of such challenges, we may have simply mistaken a symptom for a cause. Can we estimate the contribution that segmental institutions make to the likelihood of ethnonational challenges while controlling for the effect of demographic, cultural, and historical factors?

Part of the evidence against simple institutional endogeneity, discussed in a previous section, is that the designers of communist segmented states sought to minimize the centrifugal potential of segmental institutions by also recognizing groups less likely to press sovereignty claims, by dividing troublesome groups among separate homelands, and by amalgamating troublesome groups with loyal groups in new homelands. A second type of evidence that supports the segmental-institutions thesis is statistical. This can be approached in four different ways – all of which point to the same conclusion. First, we begin with the overwhelming correspondence between segmental institutions and the new nation-states. In the nine communist states in 1987, there were seventy-nine ethnic minorities that constituted at least 1 percent of the population or comprised

---

[73] S. Neil MacFarlane, *Western Engagement in the Caucasus and Central Asia* (London: Royal Institute of International Affairs, 1999), 4, 16. On the rejection of border changes by the late Soviet leadership, see Yegor Ligachev, *Inside Gorbachev's Kremlin* (New York: Pantheon Books, 1993), 172; Nikolai Ryzhkov, *Perestroika* (Moscow: Novosti, 1992), 203–4.

at least 100,000 individuals. Twenty of these were incorporated through first-order segmental institutions; nineteen of these twenty seceded – only the Montenegrins did not and, yet, they may soon leave the newly concocted Serbia-Montenegro state. Second, looking at this question from another perspective: The probability that any first-order administration would become a new nation-state was incalculably higher for homeland administrations than other units: There were 202 first-order administrations (provinces, districts, but excluding municipalities) in 1987 in the nine communist states; twenty-three of these were homeland administrations. All but one of the twenty-three homeland administrations (again, Montenegro is the exception) became new nation-states, none of the remaining 179 administrations did. Third, looking backward from the outcomes, all nineteen of the new nation-states had been first-order segmental administrations.

Fourth, looking more deeply into the processes that led to the creation of new nation-states, we can ask: Did these segmental institutions increase the likelihood of the crises with ethnic groups that preceded the breakup of the communist federations? In order to answer this question, I turn to a statistical procedure called logit analysis. The cases to be analyzed and compared (that is, the observations) include all major ethnic groups within the nine communist and twenty-eight postcommunist states.[74] The ethnic groups include all that constituted at least 1 percent of the country's total population in 1985 or, in the largest countries with a population over 10 million, that consisted of at least 100,000 members. The total number of cases in this analysis is 194.[75] The years covered are the decade from 1987 to 1996; this covers the last years of hegemonic Communist Party rule, the transition from communism, and the first years of postcommunist regimes.

In the logit analysis I use two dichotomous indicators (dependent variables) of an ethnonational crisis, in order to estimate the contribution

---

[74] The countries in this analysis are Albania, Armenia, Azerbaijan, Belarus, Bosnia, Bulgaria, Czechoslovakia/Czech Republic, Croatia, Estonia, Georgia, Hungary, Kazakhstan, Kyrgyzstan, Latvia, Lithuania, Macedonia, Moldova, Mongolia, Poland, Romania, Slovakia, Slovenia, Tajikistan, Turkmenistan, Ukraine, USSR/Russia, Uzbekistan, and Yugoslavia. The Czech Republic, Russia, and rump Yugoslavia are treated as continuations of Czechoslovakia, the Soviet Union, and Yugoslavia, respectively, so that USSR-Russia (1987–96) constitutes a single case as do Czechoslovakia-Czech Republic and Yugoslavia – Rump-Yugoslavia. The other successor states are separate cases with observations for the years of independence.

[75] The set of cases is derived from Iu. V. Bromlei, ed., *Narody mira: istoriko-etnograficheskii spravochnik* (Moscow: Sovetskaia Entsiklopediia, 1988).

of institutions to the probability of each type of event. The first indicator is the outbreak of an ethnonational crisis – a public dispute between the central government and members of an ethnic group over the latter's claim to expanded rights of self-governance (statehood) either for greater autonomy within the existing state or for independence outside it. These data are drawn from some 50,000 news reports from Radio Free Europe/Radio Liberty.[76] The second indicates the use of violence between forces of the central government and the ethnic group in one of these crises.[77] This involves instances of what Ted Robert Gurr classifies as rebellion or the Stockholm International Peace Research Institute classifies as an armed conflict in which the issue was the ethnic group's right to self-governance.[78] The proportion of dyads that experienced an ethnonational crisis during the decade was 39 percent; the proportion that experienced a violent crisis was 10 percent.

The dichotomous indicator of segmental political incorporation is an ethnic group with either a first-order or second-order autonomous homeland (such as a union republic or autonomous republic in the Soviet Union or a republic or autonomous province in Yugoslavia). To control for the demographic, cultural, economic, political, and historical factors that may be the true "deeper causes," the equations include five other independent variables: (1) the ethnic group's proportion of the country's total population,[79] (2) cultural distance – indicated by linguistic difference – between the ethnic group and the majority of the state,[80] (3) GDP per capita,[81]

---

[76] A crisis must involve a government response to a claim from an ethnic group; the government response must be at least a verbal acknowledgment of its existence.

[77] On the role of union-republic leaders in facilitating violence by nationalists, see Roeder (fn. 1) and Beissinger (fn. 7), 304.

[78] Ted Robert Gurr, ed., *Minorities at Risk Project* [Web site] (College Park: University of Maryland) <http://www.bsos.umd.edu/cidcm/mar>; Stockholm International Peace Research Institute, *SIPRI Yearbook: World Armaments and Disarmament*, annual editions (New York: Oxford University Press, 1987–98); Peter Wallensteen and Margareta Sollenberg, "Armed Conflict and Regional Conflict Complexes, 1989–97," *Journal of Peace Research* 35 (July 1998), 621–34.

[79] The independent variable is the minority's proportion of the country's total population in 1985. In these data, the largest minority in fact constitutes 40.6 percent of the country's population and the smallest constitutes less than 1 percent. (The proportion of the majority or titular group of a country is set to zero in the numerator, but not in the denominator. Thus, the lowest value is actually zero.)

[80] Cultural heterogeneity is operationalized as a dichotomous variable based on the native language of the ethnic group and the official language of the central government. When the two belong to the same linguistic phylum and group, they are classified as ethnically homogeneous dyads; otherwise, as diverse dyads.

[81] The measure of the state of the economy is the country's gross domestic product per capita. These data are measured in U.S. dollars at 1990 prices and are taken from United

(4) restrictions on political liberties,[82] and (5) a variable that indicates whether the ethnic group had previously enjoyed statehood or demanded this at some time in the twentieth century *prior* to the granting of autonomous status within one of the communist states.[33] This last variable is not collinear with the segmental incorporation variable. It yields a significant positive relationship only in the first equation (see Table 3). More importantly, even with the inclusion of this variable, the variable for segmental incorporation remains highly significant and robust.[84]

How much did segmental institutions increase the likelihood of ethnonational crises and violent crises?[85] For the "otherwise average" ethnic group,[86] the likelihood of an ethnonational crisis was sixty percentage points higher if the ethnic group was incorporated within the state through segmental institutions rather than uniform institutions. That is,

---

Nations, Department of Economic and Social Information and Policy Analysis, Statistical Division, *Statistical Yearbook*, annual editions (New York: United Nations, 1993–7).

[82] Democratization is operationalized by (1) the Freedom House's (1989) index of political liberties and (2) the inclusiveness of the regimes. Specifically, the Freedom House Index is weighted by the Proportion of Adults Registered to Vote and transformed so that it ranges from 7 (most democratic) to 1 (least democratic). The sources of data are Freedom House, *Freedom in the World: Political Rights and Civil Liberties*, annual volumes (New York: Freedom House, 1987–96) and International Institute for Democracy and Electoral Assistance, *Voter Turnout from 1945 to 1997: A Global Report on Political Participation* (Stockholm: IDEA, 1998).

[83] Sources of data are James Minahan, *Nations without States: A Historical Dictionary of Contemporary National Movements* (Westport: Greenwood Press, 1996); Richard Pipes, *The Formation of the Soviet Union: Communism and Nationalism, 1917–1923*, revised edition (New York: Atheneum, 1968).

[84] On a technical note: In tests that follow those reported in the text – tests that space does not permit me to show here – I attempted to disprove my results by examining the bias and robustness of the estimates. Specifically, the results I report here may mask a fundamental difference between the states of the former USSR and the other postcommunist states. Some of the included variables may be proxies for those excluded variables. I performed two diagnostic operations in both of the equations in order to see whether the results that I report might be spurious. First, I ran both equations with a dummy variable for the Soviet successor states. Second, I estimated the variance of coefficients in all equations using Huber's robust estimator with clustering by country. None of the tests change the magnitude or significance of the coefficient estimate for segmental institutions.

[85] This is a dichotomous variable that indicates whether the ethnic group within the specific ethnopolitical dyad has been granted a first-order or second-order autonomous region. These data are from Robert K. Furtak, *The Political Systems of the Socialist States* (Brighton: Wheatsheaf Books, 1986) and the annual editions of *The Europa World Yearbook* (London: Europa Publications, 1987–98).

[86] That is, all other variables are set to their mean values. The estimates of probabilities in the text and in Tables 3 and 4 are derived with the Clarify procedure developed by Gary King, Michael Tomz, and Jason Wittenberg and described by them in "Making the Most of Statistical Analyses: Improving Interpretation and Presentation," *American Journal of Political Science* 44 (April 2000), 341–55.

TABLE 3. *Probability and Logit Estimates: Ethnonational Crises*

	Ethnonational Crisis			Use of Violence		
	Maximum Change in Probability			Maximum Change in Probability		
Segmental political incorporation	59.7			31.3		
Minority's proportion of population	57.2			–		
Cultural distance	31.4			5.1		
Average gdp/capita (t-1)	45.3			33.5		
Restrictions on political liberties	–			–		
Previous statehood/ demand	38.6			–		
	Coefficient		(z)	Coefficient		(z)
Segmental political incorporation	2.859	***	(5.26)	4.134	***	(3.91)
Minority's proportion of population	7.391	*	(2.51)	6.062		(1.90)
Cultural distance	1.671	**	(3.10)	2.363	*	(2.53)
Average gdp/capita (t-1)	0.274	*	(2.07)	−0.900	**	(−3.10)
Restrictions on political liberties	0.116		(0.66)	0.206		(0.74)
Previous statehood/ demand	1.668	*	(2.22)	−0.185		(−0.27)
Constant	−4.760	***	(−3.98)	−4.031	*	(−2.30)
	n = 194			n = 194		
	χ^2 = 115.07			χ^2 = 36.76		
	Pseudo-R^2 = 0.452			Pseudo-R^2 = 0.296		

Significance: ***at .001 level; **at .01 level; *at .05 level.

the probability of an ethnonational crisis at least once during the decade involving an ethnic group that is otherwise typical except for its segmental incorporation was 77 percent; the likelihood for an ethnic group that was identical except for its incorporation through uniform institutions was only 17 percent. According to this estimate, segmental incorporation transformed one-in-six odds of a crisis into four-in-five odds. The likelihood that ethnonational conflict would turn violent was thirty-one percentage points higher for ethnic groups incorporated through segmental institutions than for ethnic groups incorporated under uniform

The Triumph of Nation-States

TABLE 4. *Probability (Percent) of Ethnonational Crises under Conditions of Prior Demands for Statehood and Contemporary Form of Incorporation*[*]

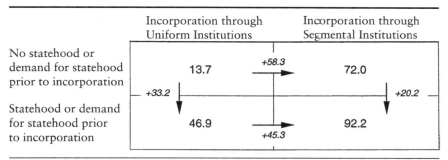

[*] Probabilities estimated from logit equation for Ethnonational Crises in Table 3.

institutions. The likelihood of escalation to violence was 32 percent for the former (segmental incorporation), but under 1 percent for the latter (uniform incorporation).

If we next vary both segmental incorporation and previous statehood or demands for statehood in the first equation, we get estimates of probabilities shown in Table 4. Ethnic groups that had previously enjoyed statehood or demanded statehood – prior to the institutionalization of segmental incorporation – were more likely to become engaged in crises as indicated by the increase in probabilities in the bottom cells. Yet, there was an additional and more substantial increase due to the effect of segmental incorporation shown by the probabilities in the right-hand cells. The apparent effect of segmental institutions is strong and not entirely due to other factors.

IMPLICATIONS

The post-Soviet and postcommunist transition to nation-states should lead us to rethink our explanations for the origins of nation-states. We have seldom had the opportunity to observe firsthand the creation of so many new states from old metropolises, and perhaps never have we had so many talented observers on the ground using the varied tools of social science at the moment of this transition. It might oversimplify the evidence from this transition to say "no segmental institutions, no new nation-states," but it is the single best explanation for the pattern of new nation-states created in the early 1990s. The Czechoslovak, Soviet, and Yugoslav successor states varied in the extent to which popular nationalism had developed prior to secession and enjoyed no uniform advantage in their war-making potential, economic viability, or international acceptance, but they all had been primary institutional building blocks of segmented polities. The segmental-institutions thesis states that it is the separate segment-states within a common-state – an arrangement that leads to the division of territories and their associated communities into separate political statuses – that has been essential to the success of projects to create new nation-states. This simple maxim also helps explain the national projects that failed. Ethnic groups without their own states within states, such as Romania's Transylvanian Hungarians, have failed in their aspirations for greater autonomy. National projects, such as the short-lived project for a Far Eastern Republic in Russia, have failed when pressed on behalf of regions without the resources of a segment-state and on behalf of populations that do not have a separate political status, but share a preeminent national identity with the common-state. In the final analysis, it was not simply multiethnic societies or federations that tore apart, but segmented states.

The findings presented in this essay underscore the fact that ethnic groups without segmental institutions were far less likely to press ethnonational claims and that none succeeded in gaining independence. The simple counterfactual claim implied by this is that had they been empowered by segmental institutions, they would have been far more likely to press such claims and more likely to succeed. This may explain, for example, why the diaspora communities of Slavs have been far less threatening to the unity of the successor states than had been predicted by many. More profoundly, however, the segmental-institutions thesis implies the counterfactual claim that if the boundaries of segmental institutions had been drawn differently, then a different set of national claims would have assaulted the common-states. This is not simply the "dogs that didn't bark," but the "dogs that weren't born." The decisions of the Soviet leaders did block the assimilation in larger nations of Tatar and Bashkirs; of Kazakhs, Kirgizes, and Karakalpaks; of Chechens and Ingushes; of Adygeis, Cherkesses, and Kabards; and of Balkars and Karachais, but promoted the assimilation of Batsbis, Mingrelians, and Svans by the Georgians or of the Ando-Dido and Archi peoples by the Avars.[87] There was little nationalism on behalf of the alternative imagined communities at the end of Soviet rule. Similarly, Latgalian nationalism that had produced political conflict within Latvia after World War I, including demands for a federal state that would give Latgale autonomy, had largely disappeared and certainly was not

[87] Wixman (fn. 38), 126, 174.

a strong political force dividing ethnic Latvians after seventy years of Latvian statehood.[88]

The story of nation-states born within segmental political institutions of the old regime actually is one that could be repeated about most of the new states created since 1815. It certainly describes many of the postcolonial states that emerged within concocted administrative boundaries such as Gran Colombia or Ubangi-Shari. It explains the strength of autonomy demands within feudal fiefdoms and homeland administrations that absolutist states failed to extinguish. For example, Michael Mann observes that within the Austro-Hungarian Empire, "virtually everywhere, nationalist movements focused on existing political units, provinces with distinct assemblies or administrations centered on old political units."[89] In almost all instances, new nation-states have emerged from the "administrative upgrade" of such segments. The exceptions are almost all instances in which outside powers intervened and imposed new national boundaries. The anomalies are odd instances such as the creation of Albania that are probably not exceptions to prove some rule.

The segmental-institutions thesis should also lead us to reexamine the relationship of nationalism to nation-states. First, the relationship of strong popular nationalism to the success of national projects is random – sometimes the consolidation of nationalism precedes success, but more often it accompanies or follows success. Strong nationalism certainly can contribute to success by increasing the leverage of secessionists over the common-state and ensures that their national claims against the common-state cannot easily be trumped by alternative national projects. Yet, in the absence of a nation-state, national identities seldom coordinate prior to the achievement of independence. The triumph of nation-states may appear to arise from awakening or reawakening nationalism, because that is the justification with which politicians clothe their projects for administrative upgrade.[90] The common thread in the triumph of

---

[88] Romauld J. Misiunas and Rein Taagepera, *The Baltic States: Years of Dependence 1940–1980* (Berkeley: University of California Press, 1983), 4; Andrejs Plakans, *The Latvians: A Short History* (Stanford: Hoover Institution Press, 1995), 103, 126–7; Georg von Rauch, *The Baltic States: The Years of Independence, Estonia, Latvia, Lithuania, 1917–1940* (London: C Hurst & Company, 1974), 37, 82–3; private communication with Rasma Karklins (28 December 2000).

[89] Michael Mann, "A Political Theory of Nationalism and Its Excesses," in *Notions of Nationalism*, edited by Sukumar Periwal (Budapest: Central European University Press, 1995), 49. Yet, Mann does advocate federalism for multiethnic states.

[90] Dmitry Gorenburg has taken me to task for underestimating the rationalism of Russia's ethnic leaders in "Regional Separatism in Russia: Ethnic Mobilisation or Power Grab?"

nation-states, however, is not national awakening; it is the failure of segmental institutions.

Second, and closely related to the previous point, the segmental-institutions thesis stresses the critical role that statehood plays in the origins of successful nationalisms. The fertile imaginations of intellectuals proliferate imagined communities. National projects abound in this world, but the experience of statehood – either independence or segmental autonomy – sets a few of these national projects apart. Statehood coordinates imaginations and empowers some national projects above others.[91] This suggests that nationalisms may be much more uniform around the world and through history than commonly believed. Students of nationalism have tended to view the type of nationalism that predominates in the region that is now the postcommunist world as somehow different from the original nationalisms that emerged in Western Europe. The segmental-institutions thesis suggests that it is not fundamentally so. Hans Kohn first argued that western nationalism, found in England, France, the Netherlands, Switzerland, and the United States, arose only after the formation of *de facto* nation-states, but eastern nationalism, found in central and eastern Europe as well as in Asia, arose prior to the consolidation of nation-states.[92] In this view, Eastern European and Eurasian nationalisms frequently challenge existing states and seek "to redraw the political boundaries in conformity with ethnographic demands."[93] Yet, most nationalism in the postcommunist states reflects the imprint of either earlier prenationalist nation-states (Hungary and Poland, for example) or pre-independence segmental institutions within multinational states (Macedonia, Moldova, and Tajikistan, for example). In this sense, successful eastern nationalism is much more like successful western nationalism than Kohn would have had us believe. Both originated as "nomenklatura" nationalism that the state then propagated among ever-widening circles of the population. In France, the conception of France emerged within the royal court, and as late as the early twentieth century the state was

---

Europe-Asia Studies 51 (1999), 245–74. My argument is actually agnostic on the issue of the sincerity of these leaders.

[91] Compare William F. S. Miles, *Hausaland Divided: Colonialism and Independence in Nigeria and Niger* (Ithaca: Cornell University Press, 1994), 42–59.

[92] Hans Kohn, *The Idea of Nationalism* (New York: Macmillan Publishing Company, 1945).

[93] Andre Liebich, "Nations, States, Minorities: Why Is Eastern Europe Different?" *Dissent* 42 (Summer 1995), 313–17.

still turning peasants into Frenchmen.[94] Successful eastern nationalism is also similar to what Benedict Anderson labels "Creole" nationalism: both emerged within "administrative units" among bureaucrats who came to imagine these segments of the state as "fatherlands," and these "absolutist functionaries" spread this sense of political solidarity to the broader population with the assistance of "provincial Creole printmen."[95]

Finally, the segmental-institutions thesis also has important implications for policy and constitutional design. It warns against the reliance on segmental institutions, such as ethnofederalism, in the management of ethnic conflict. It predicts that most national projects have little potential to challenge existing states because they lack the segmental political institutions that could coordinate national projects and that empower one project over others. The segmental-institutions thesis suggests that with early, prudent decisions, state leaders have considerable opportunity to avoid the costly nationalist challenges that have taken so many lives in the last decade. Yet, it predicts that such nationalist conflicts are likely to remain a problem precisely because states continue to create segmental institutions. Indeed, segmental institutions have become the international policy community's preferred solution to ethnic conflict around the world. A lesson of the Soviet Union and the other failed communist federations is that once segmental institutions coordinate national projects and empower one of these against the common-state, it becomes very difficult to turn back the clock and keep the common-state whole.

[94] Weber (fn. 58).
[95] Benedict Anderson, *Imagined Communities*, revised edition (London: Verso, 1991), 53; also compare Jeffrey Herbst, *States and Power in Africa: Comparative Lessons in Authority and Control* (Princeton: Princeton University Press, 2000), 58–109.

2

The Fourth Wave of Democracy and Dictatorship: Noncooperative Transitions in the Postcommunist World

Michael McFaul

The transition from communism in Europe and the former Soviet Union has only sometimes led to democracy. Since the crumbling of the Berlin Wall in 1989 and the collapse of the Soviet Union in 1991, twenty-eight mostly new states have abandoned communism. But only eight – the Czech Republic, Estonia, Hungary, Latvia, Lithuania, Poland, Slovenia, and just last year, Croatia – have entered the ranks of liberal democracies. The remaining majority of new postcommunist states are various shades of dictatorships or unconsolidated "transitional" regimes.

Why? Why did some states abandon communism for democracy, while others for authoritarian rule? Why are some states stuck in between?

The answers to these questions should be easy for political science. Simultaneous regime change in two dozen countries – all beginning from roughly similar places, but moving along very different trajectories over ten years – provides the perfect parameters to test extant theories and develop new hypotheses about regime change. Clear variation on the dependent variable with a finite set of independent variables offered up a unique laboratory to isolate causal patterns. A decade since the collapse of European communism, however, theory development regarding regime change has advanced only slightly. At the beginning of the decade, Adam Przeworski pointed to the inability to predict communism's collapse as a "dismal failure of political science." Yet, the paucity of plausible explanations for regime patterns in the postcommunist world ten years later stands as an even greater indictment.

This essay sketches an argument to explain regime changes in the postcommunist world. In endorsing actor-centric approaches that have dominated analyses of the third wave of democratization, this argument nonetheless challenges some of the central hypotheses of the earlier literature concerning the relationship between the mode of transition and the resulting regime type. This chapter offers an alternative set of causal paths from *ancien regime* to new regime, which can account for both democracy and dictatorship as outcomes. The transitions from communist rule to new regime types are so different from democratic transitions in the 1970s and 1980s that they should not be grouped under the same rubric of the third wave.[1] Instead, decommunization triggered a fourth wave of regime change to democracy *and* dictatorship.

One of the central claims of this earlier literature was that the mode of transition influenced the resulting regime type. It was hypothesized that democracy emerged as a result of transitional moments, in which the balance of power between supporters and opponents of the authoritarian regime was relatively equal and also uncertain. Because neither side had the capacity to achieve their first preferences through the use of force, they negotiated power-sharing arrangements with their opponents, which represented second-best outcomes for both sides. Often called "pacts," these power-sharing arrangements negotiated during transition then were institutionalized into a set of checks and balances in the new democracy. Significantly, ideas, norms, and beliefs played little or no role in these transition theories, leading to the famous phrase that a country could become a "democracy without democrats."

This pattern is not easy to discern in the postcommunist world. Most postcommunist transitions did not produce democracy, and even the successful democratic transitions did not follow the pacted path. Instead, situations of *unequal* distributions of power produced the quickest and most stable transitions from communist rule. In countries with asymmetrical balances of power, the regime to emerge depended almost entirely on the ideological orientation of the most powerful. In countries where democrats enjoyed a decisive power advantage, democracy emerged. Institutions of power sharing or checks and balances did not result from

---

[1] Chronologically, the postcommunist transitions occurred within the time span typically referred to as the third wave of democratization. The wave metaphor, however, connotes some relationship between cases, which is only weakly present. Transitions in democracy in Southern Europe and Latin America did not cause, trigger, or inspire communist regime change. The temporal proximity of these cases was more accidental than causal. As explored in detail in this essay, however, the fact that Southern Europe and Latin American transitions occurred first had significant path-dependent consequences for how we conceptualized and explained the postcommunist transitions. On waves, see Samuel Huntington, *The Third Wave: Democratization in the Late Twentieth Century* (Norman: University of Oklahoma Press, 1991).

compromises between the *ancien regime* and democratic challengers. Rather, they emerged only if the hegemonic democrats chose to implement them. Conversely, in countries in which dictators maintained a decisive power advantage, dictatorship emerged. In between these two extremes were countries in which the distribution of power between the old regime and its challengers was relatively equal. Rather than producing stalemate, compromise, and pacted transitions to democracy, such situations in the postcommunist world resulted in protracted confrontation. The regimes that emerged from these modes of transition are not the most successful democracies, but rather unconsolidated, unstable, partial democracies and autocracies.

To explore this alternative approach for explaining postcommunist regime change, this essay proceeds as follows. Section one outlines the basic tenets of the transitions literature that emerged from the analysis of Latin America and Southern Europe cases. Section two contrasts this earlier cooperative theory of regime emergence with a noncooperative model of regime change. Section three illustrates the analytical power of the noncooperative model for explaining regime change in the postcommunist world, highlighting the strong causal relationship between mode of transition and resulting regime type, but underscoring the weak resemblance this relationship bears to causal patterns identified in the earlier transitions literature. Section four examines cases that do not fit the theory outlined in section two. To account for these anomalous cases, two more factors must be added to the equation: the presence or absence of territorial disputes and proximity to the West. Section five concludes.

COOPERATIVE APPROACHES TO REGIME CHANGE

Inert, invisible structures do not make democracies or dictatorships; people do. Structural factors such as economic development, cultural influences, and historical institutional arrangements influence the formation of actors' preferences and power, but ultimately these forces have causal significance only if translated into human action. Individuals and the decisions they make are especially important for explaining divergent outcomes that result from similar structural contexts.

The importance of agency has figured prominently in theories of democratization for the past two decades. Dankwart Rustow's seminal article in 1970 first refocused the lens of inquiry on actors, and then the four-volume study edited by Guillermo O'Donnell, Philippe Schmitter, and Laurence Whitehead in 1986, *Transitions from Authoritarian Rule*, resurrected elites as the central drivers of regime change. This school posits that division within the ruling class begins the process of political liberalization, whereas strategic interaction between elites from state and society establishes the mode of transition and the kind of regime that then emerges. Elite groups are constructed as real actors with autonomous causal power to influence the course of regime change.[2]

Since these intellectual tracks were laid down, they have framed in large measure the thinking about regime change, pushing alternative theories, metaphors, and levels of analyses to the periphery of inquiry.[3] A single theory of transition has not been universally recognized by all working in this field, nor has an actor-centric theory of democratization been formalized.[4] Nonetheless, several hypotheses have gained wide acceptance.[5] Strikingly,

---

[2] Guillermo O'Donnell and Philippe Schmitter, *Transitions from Authoritarian Rule: Tentative Conclusions about Uncertain Democracies*, 4 (Baltimore: Johns Hopkins University Press, 1986); John Higley and Michael Burton, "The Elite Variable in Democratic Transitions and Breakdowns, *American Sociological Review* 54, no. 1 (February 1989) pp. 17–32; Terry Lynn Karl, "Dilemmas of Democratization in Latin America," *Comparative Politics* 23 (October 1990) no. 1, pp. 1–22; Adam Przeworski, *Democracy and the Market: Political and Economics Reforms in Eastern Europe and Latin America* (Cambridge: Cambridge University Press, 1991); Adam Przeworski, "The Games of Transition," in Scott Mainwaring, Guillermo O'Donnell, and J. Samuel Valenzuela, eds. *Issues in Democratic Consolidation: The New South American Democracies in Comparative Perspective* (Notre Dame: University of Notre Dame Press, 1993); and Josep Colomer, *Strategic Transitions: Game Theory and Democratization* (Baltimore: Johns Hopkins University Press, 2000). On an elite-centered approach to democratic breakdown, see Youssef Cohen, *Radical, Reformers, and Reactionaries: The Prisoner's Dilemma and the Collapse of Democracy in Latin America* (Chicago: University of Chicago Press, 1994); and Juan Linz, *Crisis, Breakdown, and Reequilibrium* in the series by Juan Linz and Alfred Stepan, eds., *The Breakdown of Democratic Regimes* (Baltimore: Johns Hopkins University Press, 1978).

[3] In the postcommunist world, the phenomenon in question might be more appropriately labeled something else besides democratization, such as revolution or decolonization. Illuminating adaptations of these alternative metaphors include Vladimir Mau and Irina Starodubrovskaya, *The Challenge of Revolution: Contemporary Russia in Historical Perspective* (Oxford: Oxford University Press, 2001); and Dominic Lieven, *Empire: The Russian Empire and Its Rivals* (New Haven: Yale University Press, 2001).

[4] Przeworski's *Democracy and the Market* comes the closest. See also Colomer, *Strategic Transitions*; and Cohen, *Radical, Reformers, and Reactionaries*.

[5] Because proponents of strategic theories of democratization do not universally recognize a single theory, it is difficult to argue with "transitology." In the last decade, many scholars have added useful theoretical caveats and important definitional adjectives to the earlier transitology canons. Space limitations do not permit discussion of all these innovations and nuances. Instead, the focus here is on the set of the core principles that define this literature as a paradigm in the study of regime change today. As Ruth Collier summarizes, "The 'transitions literature,' as this current work has come to be known, has as its best representative the founding essay by O'Donnell and Schmitter (1986), which established a framework that is implicitly or explicitly followed in most other contributions. Without

many of the postulates are very similar to institutional arguments being generated by rational choice theorists working in the positivist tradition.

In their quest to refute structural approaches, "transitologists" recognize very few prerequisites for democracy. Only one, as identified by Rustow, is salient: elites must have a common understanding of the borders of the state to proceed with crafting new rules for governing this state.[6] Beyond Rustow's one prerequisite, one of the principle theoretical contributions from the democratization literature on the third-wave concerns the causal relationship assigned to the mode of transition in determining successful and unsuccessful transitions to democracy. More ambitiously, some have even traced a causal relationship between the mode of transition and the type of democracy.[7] The theory is based on temporal path dependence; choices made at certain critical junctures influence the course of regime formation. The model – especially as developed by O'Donnell and Schmitter, Karl, Huntington, and Przeworski – identifies four choice-making sets of actors in the transition drama: soft-liners and hard-liners within the ruling elite of the *ancien regime*, and moderates and radicals among the challengers to the *ancien regime*.[8] Many modes of transition can result from the strategic interaction of these actors. Democracy by imposition – a path in which the moderates from the *ancien regime*

---

denying differences and subtleties, one could say that certain emphases within O'Donnell and Schmitter's essay have been selected and elaborated by other authors so that it is possible to aggregate various contributions and in broad strokes map out a basic characterization and set of claims in this literature as a whole." Ruth Collier, *Paths towards Democracy: The Working Class and Elites in Western Europe and Southern America* (Cambridge: Cambridge University Press, 1999), 5.

[6] Dankwart Rustow, "Transition to Democracy: Toward a Dynamic Model," *Comparative Politics* 2, no. 3 (April 1970) pp. 337–363. Others, including Karl, have highlighted a second precondition, the decline of a land-based aristocracy, an idea first discussed by Barrington Moore in *Social Origins of Dictatorships and Democracy* (Boston: Beacon Press, 1966). Because few communist countries had land-based aristocracies, this variable is not discussed in this essay.

[7] Terry Lynn Karl and Philippe Schmitter, "Modes of Transition in Southern and Eastern Europe, Southern and Central America," *International Social Science Journal* 128 (May 1991) pp. 269–284; Terry Lynn Karl and Philippe Schmitter, "Democratization around the Globe: Opportunities and Risks," in Michael Klare and Daniel Thomas, *World Security* (New York: St. Martin's Press, 1994); and Gerardo Munck and Carol Sklalnik Leff, "Modes of Transition and Democratization in Comparative Perspective," *Comparative Politics* 29 (April 1997) pp. 342–362.

[8] Huntington has different and more numerous categories – "standpatters, liberal reformers, and democratic reformers in the governing coalition, and democratic moderates and revolutionary extremists in the opposition." But there are close parallels to the O'Donnell and Schmitter labels. See Huntington, *The Third Wave*, 121.

dominate the terms of transition – has been most prevalent, but pacted transitions have received the most theoretical attention.[9] A democratic outcome is most likely when soft-liners and moderates choose to enter into pacts that navigate the transition from dictatorship to democracy.[10] If the transition is not pacted, it is more likely to fail.[11] In the earlier transitions literature, revolutionary transitions were considered most likely to produce nondemocratic outcomes. As defined by O'Donnell and Schmitter, democracy-enhancing pacts are interim arrangements between a "select set of actors" that seek to "(1) limit the agenda of policy choice, (2) share proportionately in the distribution of benefits, and (3) restrict the participation of outsiders in decision-making."[12] All three components are critical for success.

Agreements that limit the agenda reduce uncertainty about actors' ultimate intentions. A pact "lessens the fears of moderates that they will be overwhelmed by a triumphant, radical, majority which will implement drastic changes."[13] If property rights, the territorial integrity of the state, or international alliances are threatened by a revolutionary forces from below, then the hard-liners in the *ancien regime* will roll back democratic gains.[14] During the wave of democratization in Latin America and Southern Europe in the 1970s and 1980s, the simultaneous renegotiation of political and economic institutions rarely occurred, because "during the transition, the property rights of the bourgeoisie are inviolable."[15] The pursuit of economic and political reform was considered dangerous

---

[9] I am grateful to Terry Karl for this observation. On "transition from above" or "transformation" as the most common mode of transition to democracy, see Karl, "Dilemmas of Democratization in Latin America," 9; and Huntington, *The Third Wave*, 124.

[10] O'Donnell and Schmitter, *Transitions from Authoritarian Rule*; Karl, "Dilemmas of Democratization in Latin America"; Przeworski, *Democracy and the Market*; and Colomer, *Strategic Transitions*. A pact is not a necessary condition for a successful democratic transition, but enhances the probability of success.

[11] In facilitating the transition to democracy, pacts also can lock into place specific non-democratic practices, which in turn may over time impede the consolidation of liberal democracy. See Terry Lynn Karl, *The Paradox of Plenty: Oil Booms and Petro-States* (Berkeley: University of California Press, 1997), Chapter Five.

[12] O'Donnell and Schmitter, *Transitions from Authoritarian Rule*, 41.

[13] Daniel Friedman, "Bringing Society Back into Democratic Transition Theory after 1989: Pact Making and Regime Collapse," *East European Politics and Societies* 7, no. 3 (Fall 1993), 484.

[14] O'Donnell and Schmitter, *Transitions from Authoritarian Rule*, 27.

[15] Ibid., 69. See also, Huntington, *The Third Wave*, 170; and Adam Przeworski, "Some Problems in the Study of the Transition to Democracy," in Guillermo O'Donnell, Philippe Schmitter, and Laurence Whitehead, eds., *Transitions from Authoritarian Rule: Comparative Perspectives* (Baltimore: Johns Hopkins University Press, 1986), 63.

and destabilizing.[16] More generally, negotiations over contested issues in which the stakes are indivisible or the outcomes irreversible are more likely to generate irreconcilable preferences among actors than issues with divisible stakes and reversible outcomes.[17] Consequently, keeping such issues off the table was considered an important component of a successful transition.

Second, sharing proportionally in the distribution of benefits resulting from regime change provides both sides with positive-sum outcomes. Tradeoffs that may even include institutionalizing nondemocratic practices are critical to making pacts stick. As Daniel Friedman has written, "Negotiated transitions increase democratic stability by encouraging important interests to compromise on such basic issues as to whether new democratic institutions should be parliamentary or presidential, when to schedule the first free elections, and whether to grant clemency to human rights abusers or attempt to 'even the score.' Without compromises on such fundamental issues, powerful interest groups can have less incentive to cooperate with the new democratic regime."[18] In pacted transitions, no side achieves its optimal outcome, but all sides make relative gains over the nondemocratic past. From this perspective, "negotiations, compromises, and agreements" are central to making democracy.[19]

Finally, these theorists have placed special emphasis on limiting the role of radicals and the masses in the negotiation process. Pacted transitions are elite affairs; mobilized masses spoil the party. Jacobins must be sidelined to have success.[20] If they are part of the equation, then democracy is less likely to result.[21] As Karl posited in 1990, "To date, *no* stable

---

[16] Stephan Haggard and Robert Kaufman, "Economic Adjustment and the Prospects for Democracy," in Stephan Haggard and Robert Kaufman, eds., *The Politics of Economic Adjustment* (Princeton: Princeton University Press, 1992).

[17] See Elisabeth Jean Wood, "Civil War Settlement: Modeling the Bases of Compromise," unpublished manuscript (August 1999).

[18] Friedman "Bringing Society Back into Democratic Transition Theory after 1989," 483.

[19] Huntington, *The Third Wave*, 164.

[20] Giuseppe Di Palma, *To Craft Democracies: An Essay on Democratic Transitions* (Berkeley: University of California Press, 1990).

[21] Important challenges to this argument include Elizabeth Jean Wood, *Forging Democracy from Below: Insurgent Transitions in South Africa and El Salvador* (Cambridge: 2000); Grzegorz Ekiert and Jan Kubik, *Rebellious Civil Society: Popular Protest and Democratic Consolidation in Poland, 1989–1993* (Ann Arbor: University of Michigan Press, 1999); Nancy Bermeo, "Myths of Moderation: Confrontation and Conflict during the Democratic Transitions," *Comparative Politics* 29, no. 3 (April 1997) pp. 305–322; Alfred Stepan, *Democratizing Brazil* (Oxford: Oxford University Press, 1989); and Collier (fn. 5).

political democracy has resulted from regimes transitions in which mass actors have gained control even momentarily over traditional ruling classes."[22] In successful transitions from dictatorship to democracy in capitalist countries, trade unions, the left, and radicals more generally must not play a major role in the transition process, and only a limited role in the new political system that eventually emerges.[23]

Limiting the agenda of change, dividing proportionally the benefits, and marginalizing radicals and the masses are considered key components of a successful pact. But what causes pacts between moderate elites to materialize in the first place? Although not always explicitly stated, analysts of the third wave answer this question by examining the balance of power between the challenged and challengers. When the distribution of power is relatively equal, negotiated transitions are most likely. In summing up the results of their multivolume study, O'Donnell and Schmitter asserted that "political democracy is produced by stalemate and dissensus rather than by prior unity and consensus."[24] Philip Roeder has made the same claim in his analysis of postcommunist transitions: "The more heterogenous in objectives and the more evenly balanced in relative leverage are the participants in the bargaining process of constitutional design, the more likely is the outcome to be a democratic constitution."[25] When both sides realize that they cannot prevail unilaterally, they settle for solutions that provide partial victory (and partial defeat) for both sides. Democratization requires a stalemate – "a prolonged and inconclusive struggle."[26]

Przeworski has extended this argument to posit that *uncertain* balances of power are most likely to produce to the most democratic arrangements. "If everyone is behind the Rawlsian veil, that is, if they know little about

---

[22] Karl, "Dilemmas of Democratization," 8. See also Samuel Huntington, "Will More Countries Become Democratic?" *Political Science Quarterly* 99, no. 2 (Summer 1984), 6.
[23] Myron Weiner, "Empirical Democratic Theory," in Myron Weiner and Ergun Ozbudin, eds., *Competitive Elections in Developing Countries* (Durham: Duke University Press, 1987), 26; and J. Samuel Valenzuela, "Labor Movements in Transitions to Democracy," *Comparative Politics* 21 (July 1989) pp. 445–472. Even a study devoted to the role of the workers in democratization underscores the dangers of a too-mobilized society. See Dietrich Rueschemeyer, Evelyne Huber Stephens, and John D. Stephens, *Capitalist Development and Democratic Change* (Chicago: University of Chicago Press, 1992), 271.
[24] O'Donnell and Schmitter (fn. 2), 72. See also Huntington (fn. 1), 167.
[25] Philip Roeder, "Transitions from Communism: State-Centered Approaches," in Harry Eckstein Frederic Fleron, Erik Hoffman, and William Reisinger, eds., *Can Democracy Take Root in Post-Soviet Russia?* (Lantham: Roman and Littlefield, 1998), 209.
[26] Rustow (fn. 6), 352.

their political strength under the eventual democratic institutions, all opt for a maximin solution: institutions that introduce checks and balances and maximize the political influence of minorities, or, equivalently, make policy highly insensitive to fluctuations in public opinion."[27] Uncertainty enhances the probability of compromise, and relatively equal distributions of power create uncertainty.

This approach emphasizes the strategic process itself as the primary casual variable producing successful transitions.[28] As Roeder argues, "democracy emerges not because it is the object of the politicians' collective ambition but because it is a practical compromise among politicians blocked from achieving their particular objectives."[29] The dynamics of the strategic situation, not the actors and their preferences, produce or fail to produce democracy. As Levine excellently summarized, "democracies emerge out of mutual fear among opponents rather than as the deliberate outcome of concerted commitments to make democratic political arrangements work."[30] Moderate, evolutionary processes are considered good for democratic emergence; radical revolutionary processes are considered bad. Cooperative bargains produce democratic institutions; noncooperative processes do not.[31] "Democracy cannot be dictated; it emerges from bargaining."[32]

This set of arguments has a close affinity with positivist accounts of institutionalism that have emerged from cooperative game theory.[33] The

---

[27] Przeworski (fn. 2, 1991), 87.
[28] Roeder (fn. 25), 207.
[29] Ibid., 208. See also Philip Roeder, "Varieties of Post-Soviet Authoritarian Regimes," *Post-Soviet Affairs* 10 (January 1994), 62; and Colomer (fn. 2).
[30] Daniel Levine, "Paradigm Lost: Dependence to Democracy," *World Politics* 40 (April 1988), 379.
[31] See Hardin's review and then rejection of this approach in Russell Hardin, *Liberalism, Constitutionalism, and Democracy* (Oxford: Oxford University Press, 1999).
[32] Przeworski (fn. 2, 1991), 90.
[33] Hilton Root, "Tying the King's Hands: Credible Commitments and the Royal Fiscal Policy during the Old Regime," *Rationality and Society* 1, no. 2 (October 1989) pp. 240–258; Kenneth Shepsle, "Discretion, Institutions, and the Problem of Government Commitment," in Pierre Bourdeu and James Coleman, eds., *Social Theory for a Changing Society* (Boulder : Westview Press, 1991); Douglass North and Barry Weingast, "Constitutions and Commitment: The Evolution of Institutions Governing Public Choice in Seventeenth-Century England," *The Journal of Economic History* 49, no. 4 (December 1989) pp. 803–832; Kenneth Shepsle, "Studying Institutions: Some Lessons from the Rational Choice Approach," *Journal of Politics* 1, no. 2 (1989) pp. 131–149; and James Alt and Kenneth Shepsle, eds., *Perspectives on Positive Political Economy* (Cambridge: Cambridge University Press, 1990); and Barry Weingast, "The Political Foundations of Democracy and the Rule of Law," *American Political Science Review* 91 (June 1997) pp. 245–263.

crafting of new democratic institutions is framed as a positive-sum game, in which both sides in the negotiation may not obtain their most preferred outcome, but settle for second-best outcomes that nonetheless represent an improvement over the status quo for both sides. Uncertainty during the crafting of rules plays a positive role in producing efficient or liberal institutions.[34] These approaches to institutional emergence also emphasize the importance of shared benefits that result from new institutional arrangements. Above all else, institutions emerge from a bargain in which everyone gains.

A NONCOOPERATIVE MODEL OF TRANSITION

Actor-centric, cooperative approaches to democratization offer a useful starting point for explaining postcommunist regimes' transformations. Actors did cause regime changes in this part of the world, and because many of these actors claimed to be building democracy, the transitions to democracy literature offered a useful starting point and appropriate language for analyzing postcommunist transitions. Moreover, many of the democratic challengers in this region studied previous transitions (especially Spain) as models for their own countries. Some third-wave hypotheses do indeed apply to the postcommunist world. Rustow's emphasis on territorial clarity as a prerequisite for democratic transition is still salient. Although consensus about borders was not necessary to begin political liberalization processes in the communist world and some transitions have continued along a democratic trajectory without firmly settling borders issues, the resolution of major sovereignty contests was a precondition for new regime emergence for most of the region. Three multiethnic states – the Soviet Union, Czechoslovakia, and Yugoslavia – had to collapse before democratic or autocratic regimes could consolidate.

Further application of the third-wave hypotheses, however, begins to distort rather than illuminate this fourth wave of regime change. Most importantly, the preponderance of nondemocracies raises real questions about why postcommunist transitions should be subsumed within the third wave of democratization at all. In addition, the causal pathways of the third-wave transitions do not produce the "right" outcomes in the fourth-wave transitions from communist rule. In the former communist world, imposed transitions from above did not produce partial democracy,

---

[34] Geoffrey Brennan and James Buchanan, *The Reason of Rules* (Cambridge: Cambridge University Press, 1985), 30.

but dictatorship. Revolutionary transitions – the mode of transition thought to be least likely to facilitate democratic outcomes by third-wave theorists – actually produce the most stable and consolidated democracies in the postcommunist world. Balanced, stalemated transitions – those most likely to facilitate the emergence of democracy-enhancing pacts in Latin American and Southern Europe – have instead led to unstable regimes of the democratic and autocratic variety in the postcommunist world. In all three of these causal paths, negotiation, crafting, and compromise did not feature prominently. Even in the successful transitions to democracy in the postcommunist world, the three components of successful pacts played only a minor role in explaining regime change.

First, regarding limits on the agenda of change, earlier third-wave analysts celebrated the agenda-limiting function of pacts because these scholars presupposed that economic and political reform could not be undertaken simultaneously. The danger of multiple agendas of change frequently trumpeted in the earlier literature on democratization has not seen a clear empirical confirmation in the postcommunist world. Because communism bundled the political and the economic and the crumbling of communism occurred so rapidly, sequencing of political and economic change proved impossible. The reorganization of economic institutions did not necessarily undermine democratic transitions as many predicted at the beginning of the decade.[35] On the contrary, those countries that moved the fastest on economic transformation also have achieved the greatest success in consolidating democratic institutions.[36]

Second, the pacts literature assumed that the benefits of transition had to be divided and shared. In the postcommunist world, however, many of the contentious issues were not easily divisible. Empires are destroyed or retained; there are no successful models of third ways.[37] Likewise, there are few stable or efficient midpoints between a command economy and a

---

[35] The most theoretically rigorous prediction of failure was Przeworski (fn. 2, 1991).
[36] Joel Hellman, "Winners Take All: The Politics of Partial Reform in Post-Communist Transitions," *World Politics* 50, no. 1 (1998) pp. 203–234; Jean-Jacques Dethier, Hafez Ghanem, and Edda Zoli, "Does Democracy Facilitate the Economic Transition? An Empirical Study of Central and Eastern Europe and the Former Soviet Union," unpublished manuscript, World Bank (June 1999); *Transition Report 1999: Ten Years of Transition* (London: European Bank for Reconstruction and Development, 1999), Chapter Five; and Anders Aslund, *Building Capitalism: The Transformation of the Former Soviet Bloc* (Cambridge: Cambridge University Press, 2001).
[37] See the cases discussed in Stephen Krasner, ed., *Problematic Sovereignty: Contested Rules and Political Possibilities* (New York: Columbia University Press, 2001).

market economy.[38] In negotiations over borders or economy type in this region, the distribution of benefits has been highly skewed in favor of one side or the other. Even battles over political institutions resulted in skewed distributional benefits to the winners and did not produce compromise, benefit-sharing arrangements.

Third, the actors in these dramas were different from those scripted for leading roles in earlier models of democratization. Similar to earlier non-communist transitions, divisions existed between soft-liners and hard-liners in the *ancien regime*, but the splits played a much less significant role.[39] Instead, the degree of cooperation and mobilization within society was more salient, whereas the divides between moderates and radicals were less apparent.[40] The mass actors so damaging to democratization in third-wave analyses were instrumental to fourth-wave successes.

Fourth, the single most important condition for a successful pact – a stalemated balance of power – did not figure prominently as a causal force for democracy in the postcommunist world. As examined in the next section, pacts produced from stalemate played a role in only a small subset of successful democratic transitions. The mode of transition that most frequently produced democracy was an imbalance of power in favor of the democratic challengers to the *ancien regime*. Revolutionary movements from below – not elites from above – toppled communist regimes and created new democratic institutions. As feared by earlier writers on democratization, these mobilized masses often employed confrontational and uncooperative tactics. But such tactics promoted rather than impeded democratic change. When events such as elections or street demonstrations proved that the balance of power was in the opposition's favor, they imposed their will on antidemocratic elites. Communist rulers from the

---

[38] To be sure, market economies have incorporated aspects of the command economy such as state ownership and state control of prices over time, but without undermining the basic tenets of capitalism. Likewise, some command economies such as China have introduced market reforms gradually, but the process has undermined the command economy. The dispute over slavery is another instance in which a compromise solution benefiting both sides – those that advocated slavery and those that did not – was difficult to find.

[39] Only one reformist from the old regime, Mikhail Gorbachev, plays a central role in *all* the postcommunist transitions, as his reforms in the Soviet Union produce the opportunity for liberalization or new dictatorship in every country. There is no similar person or parallel dynamic in cases of democratization in Latin American and Southern Europe.

[40] A similar argument is made in Michael Bratton and Nicolas van de Walle, *Democratic Experiments in Africa: Regime Transitions in Comparative Perspective* (Cambridge: Cambridge University Press, 1997), 198–200.

old regime acquiesced to the new democratic rules because they had no power to resist.

Not all transitions from communism, however, resulted in democracy. A second mode of transition is when the distribution of power favors the rulers of the *ancien regime*, a configuration that results in autocracy. As is the case with the first path just described, the stronger side dictated the rules of the game to the weaker side. Only in this situation the stronger embraced autocratic ideas and preserved or reconstituted authoritarian institutions. Like the first path, and in stark contrast to situations in which the distribution of power was relatively equal, these imposed transitions from above reached a new equilibrium point rather quickly. In many cases, these regimes are just as consolidated as the liberal democracies. The logic of this kind of regime transition has no parallel in the third-wave literature, as regime change from dictatorship to dictatorship (albeit different kinds of dictatorships) was not part of the democratization research agenda.

In a third mode of regime change, when the distribution of power was more equally divided, the range of outcomes in the postcommunist world has been wider than liberal democracy. These strategic situations have produced pacted transitions leading to partial democracy, or protracted and oftentimes violent confrontations leading to either partial democracy, or partial dictatorship. A pacted transition resulting from a relatively equal distribution of power between the old and the new can be identified possibly in at least one postcommunist transition, Moldova, and perhaps in Mongolia as well. But other countries with similar power distributions such as Russia or Tajikistan did not produce pacts or liberal democracies. Instead, opposing forces in these countries fought to impose their will until one side won. The result of this "mode of transition" was partial, unstable democracy at best, civil war at worst.

That conflict can result from equal distributions of power should not be surprising. Analysts of the third wave focused on successful cases of democratization, deliberately ignoring unsuccessful cases. If all countries undergoing stalemated transitions are brought into the analysis, however, then the causal influence of this mode of transition becomes less clear. For instance, Angola has experienced stalemate between competing powers for decades, but no pacted transition to democracy has resulted. Equal distributions can compel both sides to negotiate, but they can also tempt both sides into believing that they can prevail over their opponents. As Geoffrey Blaney concluded in his analysis of international armed conflict, "War usually begins when two nations disagree on their relative strength and wars usually cease when the fighting nationals agree on their relative strength."[41] The same could be said about confrontation and reconciliation between competing forces within a domestic polity, especially during periods of revolutionary change when domestic anarchy begins to approximate the anarchy in the international system. In earlier analyses of democratization, uncertainty generated by relatively balanced forces facilitated the emergence of democratic institutions. In this reformulation, this same uncertainty produced the opposite effect – conflict. Conversely, the two other transition pathways had more certain distributions of power and therefore much less confrontation.

In all three modes of transition just described, noncooperative strategic situations usually produced institutions that favored one side or the other. The process is the opposite of "democracy without democrats." "Negotiation and compromise among political elites were [*not*] at the heart of the democratization processes."[42] In imposed transitions, one side took advantage of its more powerful position to craft institutions that benefited itself more than they benefit the weak. If the powerful adhere to democratic principles, then they imposed institutions that widely distribute the benefits of the new polity. Such decisions about institutional design were undertaken initially not out of obligation, compromise, or even interest, but out of a normative commitment to democracy. If the powerful believed in democratic principles, then they *imposed* democratic institutions. If the powerful believed in autocratic principles, then they imposed autocratic institutions.

The logic of these arguments bears a strong resemblance to realist or distributional accounts of institutional design.[43] The crafting of new institutions – democratic or otherwise – is framed as a zero-sum game, in which one side in the contest obtains its most preferred outcome, and the other side must settle for second-best and third-best outcomes. These institutions are not efficient; they do not enhance the welfare of all. But they are perhaps stable.[44] In transitions to democracies, the losers usually obtain second-best outcomes, but they too make relative gains over

---

[41] Geoffrey Blaney, *The Causes of War* (New York: The Free Press, 1973), 246.
[42] Huntington, *The Third Wave*, 165. The word "not" is inserted by this author.
[43] George Tsebelis, *Nested Games* (Berkeley: University of California Press, 1990); Stephen Krasner, "Global Communications and National Power: Life on the Pareto Frontier," *World Politics* 43 (1991) no.3, pp. 336–366; Jack Knight, *Institutions and Social Conflict* (Cambridge: Cambridge University Press, 1992); and Lloyd Gruber, *Ruling the World: Power Politics and the Rise of Supranational Institutions* (Princeton: Princeton University Press, 2000).
[44] Douglass North, *Institutions, Institutional Change, and Economic Performance* (Cambridge: Cambridge University Press, 1990).

the status quo ante.[45] In transitions to dictatorship, the losers' gains are much less substantial. The transition is not a bargain, but a confrontation with winners and losers. Although the social contract metaphor is often employed to describe constitutional emergence and stability, institutional arrangements that maximize everyone's utility are rare in the political world.[46]

The process of creating democracy (and dictatorship) outlined here is antithetical to the analytic and spiritual thrust of the literature on third-wave democratization. For democratic philosophers and political theorists, negotiation, bargaining, moderation, stalemate, and compromise are the stuff of successful democratic systems. Confrontation, violence, dictation, and hegemony are the enemies of liberal democracy. This approach for explaining regime change in the postcommunist world (and maybe elsewhere) also deliberately leaves out many components of earlier theories of democratization. For instance, the design of institutions is assigned little explanatory power regarding either regime emergence or regime stability. If powerful democrats draft the rules, it does not matter what electoral system is adopted, or whether a parliamentary or presidential system is erected.[47] Different kinds of democracy can work equally effectively and endure equally long. What matters most is that the powerful are committed to the democratic project.

CAUSAL PATHS OF POSTCOMMUNIST REGIME CHANGE

This alternative, noncooperative model for regime change offers a more comprehensive explanation of all postcommunist regime changes than the framework outlined by earlier analysts of third-wave transitions. By placing power and ideas at the center of analysis, and relaxing the primacy placed on negotiation and cooperation for a successful democratic transition, this model yields a different set of causal paths from communism to democracy and dictatorship. A distribution of power clearly in favor

---

[45] For elaboration of this argument, see Michael McFaul, *Russia's Unfinished Revolution: Political Change from Gorbachev to Putin* (Ithaca: Cornell University Press, 2001).
[46] Terry Moe, "The Politics of Structural Choice: Toward a Theory of Public Bureaucracy," in Oliver Williamson, ed., *Organization Theory: From Chester Barnard to the Present and Beyond* (Oxford: Oxford University Press, 1990).
[47] For evidence undermining the importance of these designs choices for consolidation worldwide, see Thorsten Beck, George Clarke, Alberto Groff, Philip Keefer, and Patrick Walsh, "New tolls and new tests in comparative political economy: The Database of Political Institutions," World Bank, unpublished manuscript, 2000.

TABLE 1 *Typology of Postcommunist Regimes*

	Dictatorships	Partial Democracies[49]	Democracies
Balance of Power for Challengers		Armenia Bosnia-Herzegovina Georgia	Croatia Czech Republic Estonia Hungary Latvia Lithuania Poland Slovakia Slovenia
Balance of Power Even or Uncertain	Tajikistan	Moldova Russia Ukraine Albania Azerbaijan Macedonia	Bulgaria Mongolia
Balance of Power for *Ancien Regime*	Belarus Kazakhstan Kyrgyzstan Turkmenistan Uzbekistan	Yugoslavia/Serbia	Romania

of democrats at the moment of transition has helped to produce liberal democracy ten years later. A distribution of power clearly in favor of the *ancien regime* dictators has yielded new forms of authoritarian rule a decade later. Both of these causal paths have resulted in stable regimes. In contrast, a balanced distribution of power has resulted in a range of outcomes well beyond the consolidated democracy outcome predicted by the earlier actor-centric literature on democratization. In contrast to the first two causal paths, countries that experienced this mode of transition are still relatively unstable ten years later.[48]

The construction of Table 1 required the use of crude estimates for the balance of power and the degree of democracy. Independent measures of

---

[48] Such regimes may be the norm rather than the exception in the world today. See Larry Diamond, *Developing Democracy: Toward Consolidation* (Baltimore: Johns Hopkins University Press, 1999).

[49] This label is deployed loosely to include all of those countries somewhere in between democracy and dictatorship. If dissected further, one might find electoral democracies, pseudodemocracies, partial democracies, quasi-autocracies, and competitive autocracies in this one residual category. Specifying the differences is an important intellectual task,

both variables are the best immunization from tautology. Quantitative measures taken roughly at the same time also help comparison. Consequently, the balance of power tripartite typology axis is based on the legislative elections that determined the composition of a state's/republic's legislature for the immediate transition period, roughly spanning 1989–92.[50] In most cases, these were the first multiparty legislative elections with at least some participation from the noncommunist opposition.[51] Within the Soviet Union, most of these elections took place in spring 1990. If the election produced a clear communist victory for the old ruling Communist Party or its direct successor – with victory defined as winning more than 60 percent of the vote – then the case is classified as a balance of power in favor of the *ancien regime*.[52] If the election produced a clear victory for noncommunist forces – with victory defined as winning more than 60 percent of the vote – then the case is classified as a balance of power in favor of the challengers. Cases in which neither communist nor anticommunist forces won a clear majority are classified as countries with equal balances of power. The tripartite typology on democracy is adapted from Freedom House measures.[53]

---

but is both beyond the scope and not central to the arguments of this essay. On the distinctions, see Diamond, ibid.; Jeffrey Herbst, "Political Liberalization in Africa after Ten Years," *Comparative Politics* 33 (2001) 331–358; Steven Levistky and Lucan Way, "Competitive Authoritarianism: Hybrid Regimes in Peru and Ukraine in Comparative Perspective," unpublished manuscript (2001); and David Collier and Steven Levitsky, "Democracy with Adjectives: Conceptual Innovation in Comparative Research," *World Politics* 49, no. 3 (April 1997).

[50] Steven Fish uses a similar method (with slightly different results), in his "The Determinants of Economic Reform in the Post-Communist World," *East European Politics and Society* 12 (1998). Polling data would add a nice complement to these election results, but unfortunately such data were not collected at the time.

[51] In certain cases, it is not so clear that the most temporally proximate election should be used, due to a speedy overhaul of the results within the next year or so. Albania and Azerbaijan are coded as more balanced cases and not clear victories from the *ancien regime* due to the tremendous change in the balance of power immediately following first votes. In Albania, the parliament elected in 1991 broke into discord. New general elections were held in March 1992 in which the democratic challengers (the PDS) won a two-thirds majority. In Azerbaijan, the Supreme Soviet elected in 1990 voted to disband after independence (in May 1992) in favor of a new National Assembly, which was then split equally between Communists and the Popular Front opposition group. Georgia is coded as a case in which the anticommunist challengers enjoyed overwhelming support due to the landslide victory of Zviad Gamsakhurdia in May 1991.

[52] CPSU party membership is not always a sufficient guide for coding "communist." In many cases, Popular Front leaders still were members of the CPSU. In these cases, these people are coded as anticommunist.

[53] Adrian Karanycky, ed., *Freedom in the World: The Annual Survey of Political Rights and Civil Liberties, 2000–2001* (New York: Freedom House and Transaction Books,

Imposition from Below: Hegemonic Democrats

The first transition path outlined above is most apparent in East Central Europe and the Baltic States. In some of these transitions, negotiations played an important role in starting liberalization processes and impeding potential authoritarian rollbacks. However, the dominant dynamic was confrontation, not compromise, between the old elite and new societal challengers. In most of these cases, societal mobilization was critical. It produced transitional leaders – Walesa, Havel, Landsbergis – who were not previously members of the elite and who only became important actors because of their widespread societal support. When the balance of power became clear, these new political actors, acting with the support of society, imposed their will on the weaker elites from the *ancien regime*, be they soft-liners or hard-liners. Although the process itself was not always democratic, the ideological commitment to liberal principles held by these transition victors pushed regime change toward democracy.[54] Democrats with power, not the process of transition, produced new democratic regimes. The process of regime transformation was revolutionary, not evolutionary.[55]

At first glance, both Poland and Hungary look like classic pacted transitions. Emboldened by Gorbachev's reforms and Poland's economic crisis, challengers to the Polish communist regime initially tiptoed toward political reform. At the beginning of the roundtable negotiations, the challengers did not have a firm assessment of the power distribution between

---

2001). Freedom House, however, uses different labels – free, partly free, and not free. Although imperfect, Freedom House ratings offer clear categories, if the degree of specificity needed is only three regime types. In contrast to the balance of power index, which is based on assessments from a decade ago, the Freedom House ratings used here are from 2000.

[54] Why were these challengers democrats, and not fascists or communists? Why did they have societal support in some places and not others? The explanation cannot simply be culture, history, or location as much of East Central Europe and the Baltic States also produced autocratic leaders with fascist ideas earlier in the century. A full exploration of the origins of democracy as the ideology of opposition at this particular moment in this region is beyond the scope of this chapter. As a preliminary hypothesis, however, it is important to remember the balance of ideologies in the international system at the time. The enemies of communism called themselves democracies. Therefore, the challengers to communism within these regimes adopted the ideological orientation of the international enemies of their internal enemies.

[55] In an argument in the same spirit as that advanced here, Bunce prefers the term "breakage" to distinguish transitions in the "east" from bridging transitions in the "south." See Valerie Bunce, "Regional Differences in Democratization: The East Versus the South," *Post-Soviet Affairs* 14, no. 3 (1998).

themselves and the *ancien regime*. First and foremost, Soviet power – always the chief constraint on all revolutionary change in the region – was now a variable, not a constant. The power of the democrats, however, was also uncertain. There had been no recent mass demonstrations and no free and fair elections that could provide measures of the power balance. Challengers responded to this ambiguity by seeking limited objectives and negotiations. The uncertainty about the balance of power also helped to fuel unrealistic expectations within the Polish communist elite, who believed that they could win a majority of seats if elections were held. The initial compromise reached was highly undemocratic. In the first elections in 1989, 35 percent of the seats in the Sejm were reserved for the communists and another 30 percent for their allies.

Yet, none of the concessions stuck. After Solidarity swept the elections for the contested seats, the balance of power between opposing sides became apparent, and thereby undermined the compromises that resulted from the roundtable negotiations. Poland has never again had a limited election in which only a portion of the seats was freely contested. Likewise, the roundtable concession that allowed Polish dictator Wojciech Jaruzelski to be elected president and the communists to maintain control over security institutions quickly unraveled. Once the election provided a better measure of the balance of power between the *ancien regime* and its challengers and after Gorbachev made clear that he would not intervene in Poland's internal affairs, the democratic winners began to dictate the new rules. In the long run, the Polish roundtable tried but failed to restrict "the scope of representation in order to reassure traditional dominant classes that their vital interests will be respected."[56] Importantly, these events also occurred in a relatively short amount of time, which did not allow enough time for the pacted institutional arrangements to become sticky.

The Hungarian experience more closely reflects the pacted transition model, but is still better understood as an imposition of democracy from below. Organized opposition to the communist regime was weaker in Hungary than in Poland, while soft-liners dominated the government. Membership in anticommunist groups numbered in the mere hundreds when negotiations began. Hungary's last opposition uprising was in 1956, compared to the more recent experience with opposition mobilization in Poland in 1980–1. Consequently, soft-liners from the *ancien regime* were

---

[56] Karl, "Dilemmas of Democratization in Latin America," 11.

in a much better position to craft a set of political reforms that protected their interests.[57] Hungarian communist officials secured their preferences regarding the electoral law, the creation of a presidency, and the timing of elections.

But these short-term advantages did not translate into long-term institutional legacies. During the turbulent months of the fall of 1989 and spring of 1990, the waning influence of communists in Hungary and the region became increasingly evident. Even before the first vote in March 1990, the old Communist Party already had become the new Hungarian Socialist Party, a renaming that occurred in most postcommunist countries when ruling elites realized that their old methods of rule were no longer viable. Yet, even this recognition of the changing power distribution did not help those from the *ancien regime*, as the renamed party captured only 8 percent of the popular vote in the party list vote, and won only one single-mandate district. Democrats won a massive electoral victory, an event that clearly revised balance of power between the old and the new. After this vote, the preferences of the powerful dominated all institutional changes, and quickly pushed Hungary toward liberal democracy.

In contrast to Poland and Hungary, the transitions in Czechoslovakia, Estonia, Latvia, Lithuania, and East Germany had no elements of pacting whatsoever. Instead, the mode of transition in these countries was openly confrontational. The challengers to the *ancien regime* were mass-based groups who had limited experience in public politics before 1989. Mass actors and confrontational tactics produced street demonstrations, strikes, and violent clashes with the authoritarian authorities – not roundtable discussions in government offices – which were the pivotal moments in these regime changes.

In Czechoslovakia, the confrontation between the state and society was open and dramatic. The leaders of the *ancien regime* did not discern the real distribution of power among the country's political forces. An organized democratic opposition did not exist prior to 1989, but grew exponentially during the November 1989 demonstrations. Cooperative negotiations between the communists and the street leaders never occurred, and the use of force against demonstrators was considered.[58] Pitted against a stronger force, the *ancien regime* eventually surrendered power. In the first free and fair elections in the country, the Communist

---

[57] Miklos Haraszti, "Decade of the Handshake Transition," *East European Politics and Societies* 13, no. 2 (Spring 1999), 290.
[58] The Central Committee wisely vetoed the idea on November 24, 1989.

Party won only 13 percent in both houses of parliament. The balance of power proved to be firmly on the side of the anticommunist challengers, who were then able to dictate changes to the country's regime without consulting old communist leaders.

In the Baltic republics, anti-Soviet groups sprouted during political liberalization in 1986–7, but elections in 1989 and 1990 were crucial to mobilizing anticommunist movements and demonstrating that the distribution of power between *ancien regime* and the challengers was in favor of the latter. In the 1990 elections, the anticommunist Sajudis won 80 percent of the parliamentary seats for the Lithuanian Supreme Soviet; the anticommunist Latvian Popular Front, the Latvian National Independence Movement, and candidates sympathetic to these two movements won 79 percent of the seats to the Latvian Supreme Soviet; and the Estonian Popular Front captured a solid majority of the contested seats for its Supreme Soviet. These elections did not result from or trigger negotiations with the *ancien regime* about power sharing or democratization.[59] Instead, all three republics unilaterally declared their independence and entered into a prolonged stalemate with Moscow. Instead of compelling moderates and soft-liners to compromise, this stalemate fueled confrontation. In January 1991, the Soviet government escalated the confrontation by invading Latvia and Lithuania with armed forces, killing over a dozen people. Demonstrations in defiance of the Soviet soldiers ensued. People assembled at the barricades and did not allow their leaders to negotiate. Polarization only ended after the failed coup attempt in August 1991 and the subsequent collapse of the Soviet Union. In the first post-Soviet elections in all three new states, the old Communist Party ruling elite made no significant showings.

In all of these cases, societal actors committed (to varying degrees) to democratic ideas enjoyed hegemonic power over their communist enemies and used this political power configuration to impose new democratic regimes and exclude the leaders of the *ancien regime* from the institutional design process. Some of these new regimes also implemented new antiliberal rules that restricted the franchise along ethnic lines. That such practices could occur further illuminates the basic dynamic of all of

---

[59] In Lithuania, the moderate Communist Party leader Algirdas Brazauskas tried to negotiate a transition and even split with the Soviet Communist Party. This factor, however, did not distinguish the Lithuanian transition from Latvia or Estonia in any appreciable way. In some respects, his appointment was the result of popular mobilization, making him the result of the shifting balance of power, not the cause.

these cases: hegemonic imposition of the new rules, rather than pacted negotiation.

Imposition from Above: Hegemonic Autocrats

Scholars of noncommunist transitions have noted that imposition from above is a common path toward democratization.[60] In the postcommunist world, this mode of transition has produced new kinds of dictatorship, not democracy. This second transition occurred in Kazakhstan, Kyrgystan, Turkmenistan, Uzbekistan, and Belarus.

The moment of transition from communist rule to authoritarian rule for these four Central Asian states is the same and well-defined – the four months between August and December 1991. Before the failed coup attempt in Moscow in August 1991 and the subsequent dissolution of the Soviet Union in December 1991, neither state nor societal leaders in these Soviet republics had pressed aggressively for independence. Nor were elections in 1989 and 1990 major liberalizing events in these republics. By 1991, some democratic groups had sprouted in Kazakhstan, Kyrgystan, and Uzbekistan. In the fall of 1991, however, the distribution of power in these countries still clearly favored the *anciens regimes*.[61]

At the beginning of regime change in these countries, analysts hoped/hypothesized that "pragmatic" leaders from above might be able to guide their countries along an evolutionary path to democracy. In Kyrgyzstan, the distribution of power in 1990 between reformers and conservatives was relatively more balanced than in other central Asian states, a situation that allowed Askar Akaev to be elected by a coalition of reformers and clan elites as the country's first president in August 1990.[62] Akaev took advantage of the failed coup attempt in Moscow in August 1991 to ratify his political power and legitimacy in October 1991, running unopposed and thus capturing 94.6 percent of the vote. For the first years of his

---

[60] Huntington, *The Third Wave*; and Karl, "Dilemmas of Democratization in Latin America."

[61] The leaders in these countries had to cut deals with regional leaders to maintain autocracy, but these pacts preserved continuity with the past, rather than navigating a path to a new regime. See Pauline Jones Luong, *Institutional Change through Continuity: Shifting Power and Prospects for Democracy in Post-Soviet Central Asia* (Cambridge: Cambridge University Press, 2002).

[62] Just over 50 percent of deputies in the Kyrgyz Supreme Soviet supported Akaev, allowing him to inch out the Communist candidate for the post. See Kathleen Collins, *Clans, Pacts, and Politics: Understanding Regime Transitions in Central Asia*, Ph.D. dissertation, Stanford University (December 1999), 193.

rule, he used his unchallenged authority to implement partial democratic reforms. Democratization from above stalled midway through the decade, however, as Akaev found autocracy more convenient. Like Akaev, Kazakh President Nursultan Nazarbaev also demonstrated tolerance toward a free press and independent political organizations soon after independence. As he consolidated his power, however, Nazarbaev has used his dictatorial powers to control the press and political parties, rig elections, and harass nongovernmental organizations. In Turkmenistan, former first secretary of the Communist Party and now president, Saparmurad Niyazov, never pretended to adhere to any liberal principles and instead crafted a "cult of the individual" dictatorship. In Uzbekistan, former first secretary of the Communist Party and now president, Islam Karimov, allowed only one falsified election in December 1991, in which he captured 86 percent of the vote.[63] In all of these countries, there was a deficit of powerful democrats at the transitional moment and therefore a deficit of democratic practices thereafter.

Belarus initially followed a similar path of autocratic imposition from above. Hard-liners dominated the *ancien regime* while the opposition, the Belarussian Popular Front, was weak. In the 1990 elections to the Supreme Soviet, the Communist Party of Belarus captured 86 percent of the seats while the Popular Front won less than 8 percent. In April 1991, strikes against the state demonstrated that society was capable of mass mobilization, and a few months later, the failed August 1991 coup undermined the legitimacy of the hard-liners in power, who had enthusiastically supported the coup leaders. A moderate, Stanislav Shushkevich, benefited from the failed coup attempt in August 1991. In contrast to more successful transitions to democracy, however, Belarus' first postcommunist leader was not a leader of the democratic opposition, but a reformer from within the system with almost no popular following. A divided elite allowed Belarus' first postcommunist vote for the presidency in June–July 1994 to be competitive, an opening cited in the third-wave democratization literature as positive for democratic emergence. Instead of creating an opportunity for a democrat to bubble up from society, however, the split in Belarus allowed an even more autocratic leader, Aleksandr Lukashenko, to emerge and win this election. Had a more powerful democratic movement emerged

---

[63] Karimov came to power before the Soviet collapse as a compromise between Uzbek clans. In Uzbekistan, the period of political instability occurred in the early Gorbachev years, but was over by the time of transition after Karimov had consolidated his political power. See ibid.

at the time, the trajectory of this transition might have been very different. The old hard-liners from the *ancien regime*, while initially wary of Lukashenko, quickly moved to work with the new leader in consolidating authoritarian rule.

Stalemated Transitions: Protracted Confrontation and Imposition

Unlike the first and second transition paths, which led to consistent, predictable regime types, the third postcommunist transition path – stalemated transitions – has produced radically different outcomes in the postcommunist world: electoral democracy in Moldova and Mongolia, fragile and partial democracies in Russia and Ukraine, and civil war followed by autocracy in Tajikistan. Transitions in which the balance of power between the *ancien regime* and its challengers was relatively equal have also been the most protracted and the least conclusive in the region. This result is the exact opposite of that predicted by earlier writers on third-wave democratization. Stalemated transitions were supposed to be most likely to produce both stable and liberal democracies.

Of all the postcommunist transitions, Moldova may be the closest approximation to a pacted transition.[64] Like every other regime change in the region, the Moldovan regime change began with an exogenous shock – Gorbachev's liberalizing reforms. These changes initiated from Moscow allowed for the emergence of nongovernmental groups, which eventually consolidated behind one umbrella organization, the Moldovan Popular Front (MPF). This MPF successfully combined nationalist and democratic themes, ensuring that militant nationalists did not dominate the anticommunist movement. In contrast to Poland, Hungary, or Lithuania, the opposition did not enjoy overwhelming support in society. On the contrary, the MPF won roughly a third of the seats to the Supreme Soviet in the spring 1990 elections, a percentage much closer to Democratic Russia's total in Russia than to the clear majorities captured by popular fronts in the Baltic Republics during elections at the same time.[65] The MPF's opponents in the *ancien regime*, however, were not communist stalwarts, but soft-liners seeking to cooperate with the opposition. When another

---

[64] Mongolia might be a close second. See M. Steven Fish, "Mongolia: Democracy without Prerequisites," *Journal of Democracy* 9, no. 3 (July 1998).
[65] William Crowther, "The Politics of Democratization in Post-Communist Moldova," in Karen Dawisha and Bruce Parrot, eds., *Democratic Changes and Authoritarian Reactions in Russia, Ukraine, Belarus, and Moldova* (Cambridge: Cambridge University Press, 1997), 293.

"external" factor – August 1991 – rocked the transition, old institutions quickly broke down, the Communist Party found itself in disarray, and elites from both state and society joined together to denounce the coup and declare independence. Although no formal pact was ever codified between them, soft-liners from the *ancien regime* and MPF moderates cooperated to craft a relatively smooth transition from communism to democracy. Presidential power changed hands peacefully through a very competitive election in 1996, and the balance of power in parliament has since shifted between left and right over the course of several elections. Relative stalemate, however, has not produced democratic consolidation. In 2000, Moldova became the first postcommunist country to alter the fundamental rules of the game of its political system by moving from a presidential system to a parliamentary democracy. This change was not negotiated but highly contentious, serving to destabilize rather than consolidate democratic institutions.

In several respects, the basic players and distribution of power between them in Moldova and Russia were similar. In response to Gorbachev's reforms, anticommunist political groups in Russia also formed and eventually coalesced into a united front – Democratic Russia. Elections in 1989 and 1990 and strikes in 1989 and 1991 helped to mobilize mass demonstrations against the *ancien regime*. New opportunities for nontraditional political action also attracted defectors and reformists from within the old ruling elite, including most importantly Boris Yeltsin. Within the Soviet state, soft-liners such as Alexander Yakovlev, Eduard Shevardnadze, and Gorbachev himself offered cooperative interlocutors for Russia's democratic challengers. Throughout the fall 1990 and spring of 1991, stalemate appeared to force both sides toward compromise.

Yet, the anticipated pact proved elusive. Soft-liners from the Soviet government and moderates from the Russian opposition attempted to negotiate new economic and political rules in the fall of 1990 under the rubric of the 500-Day Plan, but they failed. Again in the summer of 1991, they came very close to implementing another cooperative agreement, the "9 + 1 Accord," which would have delineated jurisdictional boundaries between the central state and the nine signatory republics. Before this agreement could be enacted, however, Soviet government hard-liners interrupted the negotiated path and instead tried to impose their preference for the old status quo through the use of force. Their coup attempt in August 1991 failed, an outcome that in turn allowed Yeltsin and his allies to ignore past agreements such as the "9 + 1 Accord" and pursue their ideas about the new political rules of the game including, first and foremost, Soviet dissolution. Yeltsin's advantage in the wake of the August 1991 coup attempt, however, was only temporary. Less than two years later, opponents to his reform ideas coalesced to challenge his regime. This new stalemate, which crystallized at the barricades again in September–October 1993, also ended in violent confrontation. Only after Yeltsin prevailed again in this standoff did he dictate a new set of political rules that the population ratified in a referendum. The regime to emerge subsequently was a fragile electoral democracy, which may not be able to withstand the authoritarian proclivities of Russia's new president.[66] A relatively equal distribution of power between the old regime and its challengers did not produce a path of negotiated change, but a protracted and violent transition that ended with imposition of an unstable electoral democracy.

Ukraine began the transition from communism with a balance of power between *ancien regime* and challengers similar to Russia. The failed coup attempt in August 1991 altered the political orientations of key players in Ukrainian politics. Like their Central Asian comrades, the leadership of the Ukrainian Communist Party, headed by Leonid Kravchuk, quickly jumped on the anti-Soviet bandwagon after the failed coup attempt as a way to stay in power. Overnight, Kravchuk became a champion of Ukrainian nationalism. He allowed for a referendum on Ukrainian independence in December 1991, which passed overwhelmingly. This nationalist reorientation of elites within the old ruling Ukrainian Communist Party helped to defuse the conflicts between friends and foes of the *ancien regime* that had sparked open confrontation in Russia in October 1993. Compared to Russia, Ukraine experienced a smoother transition from communism. At the same time, the prolonged domination of the old CPSU leaders has stymied the development of liberal democracy. Compared to cases in the Baltics and East Central Europe in which the democrats won overwhelmingly, broke with the past, dictated the new terms of the democratic polity, and have since produced stable regimes, Ukrainian democracy is still unstable and unconsolidated.

Tajikistan is an extreme example of a violent, confrontational transition resulting from a relatively equal distribution of power among the main political forces in the country. On the surface, the 1990 elections appeared to produce a solid victory for the communist *ancien regime*. In

---

[66] For elaboration, see the final two chapters of McFaul, *Russia's Unfinished Revolution*.

fact, however, a regionally-based split within the ruling elite developed as a result of political liberalization, which then deepened after Moscow's role in Tajik politics faded after the August 1991 coup attempt. Stalemate did not produce negotiations, but civil war.

In Tajikistan in the late 1980s, opposition groups coalesced around a mishmash of democratic, nationalistic, and religious ideas. Under the leadership of Khakhor Makhkamov, the state's response to these groups was at times cooperative and at times repressive.[67] After acquiescing to several liberal reforms guaranteeing the rights of social organizations and free expression, Makhkamov then used armed force to quell the so-called Islamic uprisings in February 1990, a move which helped to unite the democratic and religious strands of the opposition. The cleavage between state and opposition actors was more clan-based than ideologically motivated. For decades, the Khodjenti clan, with Moscow's support, had dominated political rule in Tajikistan. When challengers to Khodjenti hegemony consolidated and the distribution of power became more equal, especially after the failed August coup when Moscow's support was temporarily removed, the ruling elite could have opted to pact a transition and share power. Instead, they pushed to reestablish autocratic rule, first by rigging an election in favor of their new preferred leader, Rakhman Nabiyev, who in turn used his new office to crack down on opposition leaders and organizations. However, similar to his putschist counterparts in Moscow, Nabiyev overestimated the power of his clan and state. Opposition groups joined forces with frustrated leaders from other minority clans to resist old guard repression. Civil war ensued between relatively balanced foes.[68] By the end of the first year of independence, 50,000 people had been killed and another 800,000 displaced. Eventually, a settlement was brokered but the result for the regime was a new unstable autocracy, not democracy.

Although Moldova, Russia, Ukraine, and Tajikistan started the transition from communism with relatively equal distributions of power between *ancien regime* and challengers, all experienced a variety of transition paths, which in turn have influenced the formation of a variety of regime types. Other examples of each type can be found throughout the region, ranging from relatively democratic Bulgaria and Mongolia to less successful democratic transitions in Albania and Azerbaijan. In contrast

---

[67] Collins, *Clans, Pacts, and Politics*, 231.
[68] The defection of the Soviet 201st Motorized Rifle Division to the opposition's cause gave the opposition access to weapons that opposition groups in other republics did not enjoy.

to asymmetric power distributions producing impositions of dictatorship from above or democracy from below, many of the regimes that emerged from more balanced distributions of power are still unstable.

Strikingly, negotiation between the challenged and challengers played a causal role in determining regime type in only a few cases. The countries most successful in consolidating liberal democracy were some of the most confrontational transitions. Countries in which the distribution of power was relatively equal are neither the most successful democracies nor the most stable regimes. Although the mode of transition does appear to have a strong causal effect on the type of regime that emerges, the causal patterns in the postcommunist world bear little resemblance to the modalities identified in the third-wave literature.

What are the underlying causes of the balances of power and ideologies that produced these different modes of transition? Some "analysts" have asserted that the balance of power is best addressed as part of the outcome rather than a cause of the outcome.[69] The strong correlation between geography and regime type suggests that deeper structural variables might explain the regime variance without a careful accounting of balances of power and ideologies at the time of transition. Geography, as well economic development, history, culture, prior regime type, and the ideological orientation of enemies, most certainly influenced the particular balances of power and ideologies that produced democracy and dictatorship in the postcommunist world. Future research must seek to explain these transitional balances of power. However, this essay treats balance of power as an independent variable rather than a dependent variable for two reasons. First, this is the analytic setup of the earlier third-wave literature, which this chapter seeks to challenge. That this earlier literature posited different causal relationships for the same set of variables suggests that hypotheses from both theories are falsifiable and not tautological.

Second, the argument advanced in this essay is that these big structural variables only have path-dependent consequences in historically specific strategic settings.[70] The moment of transition for all of these cases (except perhaps Russia) was exogenous and therefore not caused directly by the

---

[69] Herbert Kitschelt, "Accounting for Outcomes of Post-Communist Regime Change: Causal Depth or Shallowness in Rival Explanations," unpublished manuscript (1999).
[70] The logic draws on the idea of punctuated equilibrium applied to institutional emergence in Stephen Krasner, "Approaches to the State: Alternative Conceptions and Historical Dynamics," *Comparative Politics* 16 (1984) pp. 223–246.

balance of power between friends and foes of the regime. The confluence of these forces that produced powerful democrats in Poland and powerful autocrats in Turkmenistan was only causally significant at a unique moment in time at the end of the twentieth century. After all, Poland had the same religious and cultural practices, nearly the same location, and the same enemies a century ago, but these factors did not interact to produce democracy then. Imagine even if Solidarity had succeeded in forging a pact with Polish communist authorities in 1981 in the shadow of Brezhnev's Soviet Union. The regime type to emerge would have had more institutional guarantees for the outgoing autocrats, whereas the legacies of such a pact might have persisted for a long time.

Nor do cultural and historical patterns or prior regime types correlate neatly with the pattern of regime variation in the postcommunist world. Countries with shared cultures and histories, such as Russia and Belarus or Romania and Moldova, have produced very different regimes since leaving communism, whereas countries with no common culture like Belarus and Uzbekistan have erected very similar regimes. More generally, the causal significance of the communist or even Soviet legacy is not uniform or postcommunist regime type. The very diversity of regime type within subregions of the former Soviet Union – Belarus versus Ukraine or Georgia versus Armenia – calls into question the causal significance of a shared communist history. Conversely, upon closer analysis, "similar" prior regimes also look very different. For instance, the degree of autocratic rule in communist Czechoslovakia more closely approximated the Soviet Union or Romania than Poland, Hungary, or Yugoslavia. Yet, a decade after decommunization, democracy in the Czech Republic is more similar to Poland, Hungary, and Slovenia than to Russia, Romania, or even Slovakia.

Decades from now, big structural variables like economic development, culture, and geography may correlate cleanly with patterns of democratization around the world and thereby provide more sweeping explanations. However, in the short span of only one decade, broad generalizations based on deep structural causes hide as much history as they uncover.

EXPLAINING ANOMALIES: BORDERS, LEADERS, AND THE WEST

The model positing a causal relationship between balances of power and ideologies at the time of transition and regime type a decade later can explain many cases in the region, but not every one. There are many boxes in the three-by-three matrix in Table 1 that should be empty but are not. Other factors must be introduced into the equation. First, the failure to meet Rustows's requisite of defined borders for the polity can impede democratic emergence indefinitely. Powerful challengers to the *ancien regime* can fail to establish democratic institutions if border issues linger. Second, over time, geographic location can override the causal influence of the initial mode of transition by offering neighboring state incentives to join the norm of the region.

Disputed Borders

The greatest number of cases defying the analytic framework outlined in this chapter are countries where the distribution of power was firmly in favor of the challengers yet the regime to emerge after transition was not fully democratic. This list includes Armenia, Bosnia-Herzegovina, Georgia, and, until last year, Croatia. These countries share one common problem that the more successful democracies in the region lacked – border disputes. To varying degrees, territorial debates sparked wars in the 1990s in all four of these countries. These territorial conflicts in turn empowered nationalist leaders with poor democratic credentials.

The actions of leaders, however, are not predetermined by geography. Ideas, leaders, and choice still play a role even in these cases. In Georgia, anti-Soviet sentiment fused with militant nationalism to produce Zviad Gamsakhurdia. In May 1991, Gamsakhurdia became Georgia's first democratically elected president by winning 85 percent of the vote. His nationalist ideas quickly fueled separatist movements among non-Georgian minorities and then civil war within the Georgian Republic. A change in leadership from Gamsakhurdia to the more democratic and less nationalistic Eduard Shevardnadze prevented the total collapse of the Georgian state and preserved some basic elements of a democratic regime in Georgia. Leadership changes, not a new consensus about borders, altered the course of regime change in Georgia. In Bosnia-Herzegovina, battles over borders produced ethnic war on a scale not witnessed in Europe in decades. No democratic leaders emerged to slow the violence until international forces intervened. Border disputes and ethnic conflicts in Croatia also helped to consolidate the political power of Franjo Tudjman, another antidemocratic nationalist. Since Tudjman's death, however, Croatia has moved quickly toward European integration and more democratic governance.

Armenia has moved in the opposite direction, away from democracy. After an initially peaceful transition to democracy, accelerated by the August 1991 coup attempt, Armenia's decade-long war with Azerbaijan over the Nagorno-Karabakh Republic has not only depleted the country's scarce resources, but also produced an alternative elite within the armed forces of those from the embattled republic. This elite in turn has articulated a less democratic conception of the Armenian regime. Under the leadership of Robert Kocharian, the former President of the Nagorno-Karabakh republic, this new elite forced Ter Petrosian to resign in February 1998. Since the palace coup and Kocharian's election as president in 1998 in a falsified vote, Armenia's regime has become increasingly authoritarian. Many factors have produced political crisis in Armenia, but the territorial dispute has been especially destabilizing.[71]

Leaders

A final set of cases that departs from the general argument of this chapter cannot be explained without bringing individual leaders into the equation. Kyrgystan's drift toward democratic rule in the early 1990s, Georgia escape from anarchy and civil war in the mid-1990s, and Belarus' deepening dictatorship in the later 1990s cannot be accounted for without introducing the leadership skills and ideological orientations of individuals in these countries.

Individuals can play an instrumental role in crafting the political institutions of a regime in transition. In stable institutional settings in which individuals choose from the same menu of choices over multiple iterations, the particular causal role of unique individuals is minimal. Preferences and power of leaders in stable institutional settings also should be easier to identify, and behavior easier to predict or explain. In stable settings, the preferences and power of social groups also should be relatively fixed, thereby constraining the leaders who represent these groups. In uncertain institutional settings, however, the causal role assigned to unique individuals should be greater. As Weber argued, "Charismatic rulership in the typical sense always results from unusual, especially political and

---

[71] Imagine the counterfactual. If Armenia was not at war over Nagorno Karabakh, then the military and intelligence services would not enjoy the prominence that they do and hard-liners like Kocharian would not have risen to power. Public opinion surveys in Armenia show that "providing for defense" is the issue in which the government enjoys its highest approval rating. See Office of Research, Department of State, "Armenians More Hopeful, Despite Killings," No. M-13-00 (February 11, 2000), 3.

economic situations... It arises from collective excitement produced by extraordinary events and from surrender to heroism of any kind."[72] When institutions break down, individuals have less information about the consequences of their actions or the intentions of other actors. They must make decisions under conditions of uncertainty, which may produce unintended results. In volatile institutional settings, the preferences and power of leaders become variables, not constants, especially when the collapse of previous institutions eliminates from the menu past preferences and alters the balance of power equation. For instance, when communist regimes collapsed, communism as an ideology was discredited, but new ideologies were both poorly understood and multiple, making coordination around them difficult. An effective leader who proposes a new ideological or normative orientation for the state and society can fill the void. The collapse of communism undermined (at least temporarily) the power of communist parties and their allies, while new groups were just forming in most postcommunist transitions, creating great uncertainty regarding the balance of power. Because the preference and the power of social groups also were rendered ambiguous by the transition, leaders of these groups were not as beholden or constrained by their constituents as leaders in more stable contexts. In these moments of institutional breakdown, we should assume that leaders have autonomy and the possibility to influence outcomes. Yet, as Weber also argued, we should expect leadership in such settings to be unstable and ephemeral, producing short-term zigs and zags in regime change, which may not necessarily have lasting effects.[73]

Tracing the causal role of individuals is fraught with complexities. But even a cursory tour of postcommunist transitions provides at least some evidence that leaders matter. Throughout Eastern Europe, charismatic leaders of societal movements provided important focal points for anticommunist mobilization. Lech Walesa in Poland and Vaclav Havel in Czechoslovakia were catalysts of mobilization. The magnitude of their contribution, however, is harder to assess given the overwhelming support for democracy in those countries.

In Central Asia, the unique role that Kyrgyz president Askar Akaev played in steering his country *initially* toward democracy is more apparent

---

[72] Max Weber, *Economy and Society*, edited by Guenther Roth and Claus Wittich, II (Berkeley: University of California Press, 1978), 1121.

[73] Depending on how charisma was routinized, Weber also argued that it could be deployed for authoritarian or democratic projects. For elaboration and application to contemporary regimes changes, see Michael Bernhard, "Charismatic Leadership and Democratization: A Weberian Perspective," ms, January 1998.

against the backdrop of more authoritarian regimes in the region. In Kyrgyzstan, the distribution of power in 1990 between reformers and conservatives was relatively more balanced than in other Central Asian states, a situation that allowed Akaev to be elected by a coalition of reformers and clan elites as the country's first president in August 1990.[74] Akaev did not provoke open confrontation with the sizable minority of *ancien regime* holdovers, but he also did not negotiate with them a new set of constitutional rules for governing Kyrgyzstan that might have benefited both sides. Instead, he took advantage of the failed coup attempt in August 1991 to ratify his political power and legitimacy in October 1991. He ran unopposed and captured 94.6 percent of the vote, an indication of the distribution of power in the Kyrgyz polity. He then used his mandate to impose his preferences for reforms, many of which were *initially* pro-market and pro-democratic. One democrat with a lot of power appeared to fuel democratization in Kyrgyzstan for the first years of independence.

In the Caucasus and the Slavic states, charismatic leaders also have played crucial roles in pushing their countries either toward democracy or dictatorship. In Georgia, the return of Eduard Shevardnadze to local politics initially reversed the autocratic tendencies of Gamsakhurdia. In contrast, the return to power of Heydar Aliev in Azerbaijan (like Shevardnadze, also a former First Secretary of the Communist Party of the Soviet Union) had the exact opposite effect, pushing Azerbaijan along a more autocratic route, after an initial period of more open politics.[75] In Russia, Yeltsin's militant anticommunism compelled him to adopt democracy as the most effective opposition ideology. Although his commitment to democratic principles proved dubious over time, his leadership did push Russia along a democratic trajectory.[76] Had a militant nationalist such as Vladimir Zhirinovsky gained control of Russia's anticommunist movement in the early 1990s, the weak Russian democratic polity might be an unambiguous dictatorship. This counterfactual is arguably approximated by Belarus under Lukashenka, a dictator who has openly praised Hitler.

---

[74] Just over 50 percent of deputies in the Kyrgyz Supreme Soviet supported Akaev, allowing him to inch out the Communist candidate for the post. See Collins, *Clans, Pacts, and Politics*, 193.
[75] Azerbaijan Civic Initiative, *Final Report on the October 11, 1998 Azerbaijan Presidential Election*. 1998.
[76] On Russia's democratic shortcomings that resulted from Russia's confrontational transition, see Michael McFaul, "What Went Wrong in Russia? The Perils of a Protracted Transition," *Journal of Democracy* 10, no. 2 (April 1999).

Lukashenka's charismatic style and mobilizing skills were key in transforming Belarus into one of the most autocratic regimes in the region, a prediction that few would have made at the beginning of the decade. Such a turn was not predetermined by deep historical or socioeconomic legacies. The absence of leadership can also be central. In Tajikistan, for instance, the dearth of strong, charismatic leaders allowed the stalemated transition to collapse into civil war.

It is still too early to know whether the role of leaders has long-term path-dependent effects. In countries such as Croatia and Serbia, the fall of autocrats has translated into new openings for democratic development. In the long run, the effects of these dictatorships may not be as consequential as other factors such as European integration. The limited impact of leadership in the long run, however, could translate into greater autocracy in nonwestern neighborhoods. In these regions, alternative regime types to democracy are both present and popular, whereas western models are remote.[77] Since 1995, Kyrgyzstan has drifted toward the regional norm of autocratic rule. Similarly, Georgian democracy has lost ground in the last few years. The original democratic impulses of Akaev and Shevardnadze do not seem to have produced long-term democratic institutions. Once Shevardnadze leaves power, democratic erosion in Georgia could accelerate even faster. In comparison to Georgia and Kyrgyzstan, democratic institutions in Russia erected in part due to Yeltsin are more robust, but even there, leadership change at the top has produced democratic erosion. None of these three leaders – Akaev, Shevardnadze, or Yeltsin – successfully translated their charismatic influence into stable democratic institutions. In sum, regime variations within regions that looked important at the moment of transition appear to be less important today. In the long run, regional convergence – be it democracy in Eastern Europe or dictatorship in Central Asia and the Caucasus – appears underway.

The West

Democratic overachievers comprise a third category of cases anomalous to the general model outlined above, a category that includes Romania and Bulgaria, two countries which started the transition from communism with leaders from the *ancien regime* with high degrees of power.

---

[77] Francis Fukuyama, "The Primacy of Culture," *Journal of Democracy* 6, no. 1 (January 1995), 11.

In Romania, anticommunist societal mobilization destroyed the *ancien regime*, but did not take the next step of filling the void with new societal leaders and organizations. After only two weeks of popular revolt, the Romanian dictatorship – the most totalitarian in the region – collapsed in December 1989. Nicolae Ceausescu, the Romanian leader, was killed and the Romanian Communist Party banned. There were no pacts, no negotiations, no compromises. After the Ceausescu regime perished, however, a phantom political organization, the National Salvation Front (NSF), rushed to fill the political vacuum. Quasi-dissidents, poets, and societal leaders initially allied with the NSF, but it gradually became clear that former communist officials had created this front as a means of staying in power. After "people power" destroyed the last communist regime, communist apparatchiks motivated by their own interests and not committed to democratic norms dominated the first postcommunist regime. In Bulgaria, the break with the *ancien regime* was less dramatic, but the resilience of the old guard was comparable. In the early 1990s, the prospects for Bulgarian and Romanian democracy were grim. A decade later, however, both of these countries have made progress toward consolidating liberal democracies.

Democratic consolidation in both countries has benefited from proximity to the West. Throughout the postcommunist world, there is a positive correlation between distance from the West and regime type.[78] Closeness to the West certainly does not explain regime type at the moment of transition. Before the fall of Milosevic, Serbia's dictatorship was much closer to Berlin than Georgia's electoral democracy, and autocratic Belarus is closer to the West than semidemocratic Russia. Over time, however, the pull of the West has helped weaker democratic transitions in the West become more democratic. Conversely, initially successful transitions to democracy farther from Europe such as Armenia or even Kyrgyzstan have had less success in consolidating. Neighborhoods matter. And it is not Christianity, education, or economic development that provides the causal push toward democracy, but location. Initially uncertain regimes in Bulgaria and Romania have become increasingly more democratic over time as these countries aggressively have sought membership in western institutions such as the European Union and NATO. Leaders in Romania and Bulgaria have real incentives to deepen democracy, because both countries have a reasonable chance of joining these western institutions. After a lost

---

[78] See Jeffrey Kopstein and David Reilly, "Geographic Diffusion and the Transformation of the Post-Communist World," *World Politics* 53 (October 2000) no.1, pp. 1–37

decade, Croatian and Serbian democracy now seem poised to benefit from European integration.

CONCLUSION

This chapter has outlined an actor-centric theory of transition that challenges many of the principle assumptions of the earlier actor-centric literature on third-wave democratization. Temporally, these regime changes occurred at the same time as other third-wave transitions. Yet, the causal mechanisms at play were so different, and the regime type so varied, that the postcommunist experience might be better captured by a different theory and a separate label – the fourth wave of regime change. (Why should the emergence of dictatorship in Uzbekistan be subsumed within the third wave of *democratization*?)

Furthermore, the approach outlined and the cases discussed in this chapter call into question the historical place of third-wave transitions in the development of theories about democratization more generally. Democratic imposition from below in which confrontation is the mode of transition is not a new phenomenon unique to the postcommunist world. On the contrary, democratic revolutions have tradition and include some of the most important case studies in democratization. Certainly, the American and French transitions were not pacted transitions. Rather, they were protracted, confrontational, armed struggles in which the victors then dictated the new rules of the game.[79] In several respects, France's violent, uncertain, and decades-long "transition" from autocratic rule looks more similar to Russia's ongoing transformation than Spain's negotiated path. Likewise, externally imposed regime changes, such as the democratic transitions in Germany, Austria, and Japan, involved no pacting or negotiation. Decolonization, which played no role in the third wave, has featured prominently in both the fourth wave discussed here as well as the second wave.[80] In the long stretch of history, the successful transitions from communism to democracy may look more like the norm, whereas the "pacted transitions" and "transitions from above" in Latin America and Southern Europe may look more like the aberration.

---

[79] Bruce Ackerman, *We the People: Transformations*, 1 (Harvard: Harvard University Press, 1998). To be sure, negotiations between liberal and anti-liberal (slave owning) elites in the United States helped to produce partial democratic institutions. These compromises, however, were not negotiated with moderates from the British *ancien regime*.
[80] Huntington, *The Third Wave*, 112.

Yet, negotiated transitions with alternative causal modes did occur in Latin America, Southern Europe, Africa, Asia, and perhaps Moldova. They must now be explained in a new historical context in which nonpacted, revolutionary transitions from below occurred both before and after. The next generation of democratization theory must seek to specify more precisely the conditions under which pacts can facilitate democratization and the conditions under which pacts are inconsequential. In other words, the third and fourth waves must be fused to generate a comprehensive theory of transitions. In addition, without abandoning agency altogether, this research agenda should attempt to push the causal arrow backward in order to account for the factors that produce different modes of transition in the first place. A comprehensive theory of transition will include both structural and strategic variables. In the postcommunist cases, the different historical responses to Soviet imperialism most certainly influenced the balance of power between friends and foes of the *ancien regime* at the time of transition. Ideological polarization between the democratic United States and communist Soviet Union during the Cold War also framed the normative choices about regime change made by revolutionaries and reactionaries. At the same time, prior regime type – that is, communism – did not play the negative or uniform role on democratization that many predicted.[81] The true causal significance of the transition moment can only be fully understood when the deeper causes of these modes are fully specified. This essay has argued that the balance of power and ideologies at the time of transition had path-dependent consequences for subsequent regime emergence. Yet the importance of these contingent variables can only be determined if their causal weight can be measured independently of deeper factors that cause and impede democracy.[82] Whereas democratization theorists have devoted serious attention to isolating causal links between mode of transition and regime consolidation, much less

---

[81] Przeworski, *Democracy and the Market*; Ken Jowitt, *The New World Disorder: The Leninist Extinction* (Berkeley: University of California Press, 1992); and Grzegorz Ekiert, "Democratization Processes in East Central Europe: A Theoretical Reconsideration," *British Journal of Political Science* 21 (July 1991), 288.

[82] Every independent variable can become the dependent variable of another study. In journal articles especially, as Michael Taylor has argued, the "explanatory buck has to stop somewhere." Michael Taylor, "Structure, Culture and Action in the Explanation of Social Change," *Politics and Society* 17 (1989), 199. To escape tautology and claim causal significance of more proximate variables, however, requires the researcher to demonstrate that the independent variables selected are not endogenous of more important prior variables, but that they have some *independent* causal impact.

attention has been given to the causes of transition paths in the first place.[83]

The project of constructing a general theory of democratization may very well fail. The causes of democratization in Poland may be distinct from the causes in Spain, let alone those most prominent in France. This essay's emphasis on temporal path dependence implies that different historical contexts may create unique factors for and against democratization. The unique patterns generated by the fourth wave of regime change in the postcommunist world suggest that the search of a general theory of democratization *and* autocratization will be a long one.

---

[83] Recent studies that have pushed the causal arrow back one step include Wood, *Forging Democracy from Below*; Valerie Bunce, *Subversive Institutions: The Design and Destruction of Socialism and the State* (Cambridge: Cambridge University Press, 1999); Barbara Geddes, "What Do We Know about Democratization after Twenty Years?" *Annual Review of Political Science* 2 (1999), 115–44; Alexander Motyl, *Revolutions, Nations, Empires: Conceptual Limits and Theoretical Possibilities* (New York: Columbia University Press, 1999); Grzegorz Ekiert, *The State against Society: Political Crises and Their Aftermath in East Central Europe* (Princeton: Princeton University Press, 1996); and Bratton and van de Walle, *Democratic Experiments in Africa*.

3

Circumstances versus Policy Choices: Why Has the Economic Performance of the Soviet Successor States Been So Poor?*

Vladimir Popov

INTRODUCTION

After the Soviet Union collapsed in December 1991 and market reforms were initiated, the economic performance of the successor states was more than disappointing. By the end of the 1990s, output (GDP) fell by about 50 percent compared to the highest prerecession level of 1989 (see Fig. 1). Investment dropped even more, income inequalities rose greatly so that real incomes declined dramatically for the majority of the population, and death rates increased by about 50 percent with a concurrent decline in life expectancy. In Russia output fell by 45 percent in 1989–98; suicide rates, crime rates, and murder rates skyrocketed; and death rates increased from 1 percent in the 1980s to 1.5 percent in 1994 and remained at this higher level thereafter, which was equivalent to over 700,000 additional deaths annually (see Fig. 2). Over a period of several years, such population losses are comparable to the impact of World War II on Soviet society.

By way of comparison, during the Second World War national income in the USSR fell by only 20 percent in 1940–2, recovered to its 1940 level in 1944, fell again by 20 percent in 1944–6 during the conversion of the defense industry, but exceeded its 1940 level by nearly 20 percent by 1948. In some of the former Soviet states that were affected by military conflicts (Armenia, Azerbaijan, Georgia, Moldova, Russia, and Tajikistan), GDP in 2000 was only 30 to 50 percent of its pretransition levels; in Ukraine, even

---

* Some sections of this essay are based on my article "Shock Therapy versus Gradualism: The End of the Debate (Explaining the Magnitude of the Transformational Recession)," *Comparative Economic Studies* 42, No. 1 (Spring 2000).

Circumstances versus Policy Choices

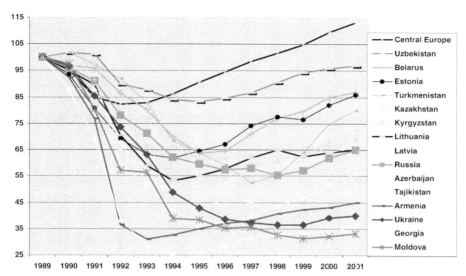

FIGURE 1. GDP change in FSU economies, 1989 = 100%

without the military conflict GDP fell by nearly two-thirds (see Fig. 1). By way of another comparison, in East European (EE) countries the reduction of output continued for two to four years and totaled 20 to 30 percent, whereas in China and Vietnam there was no transformational recession at all – on the contrary, from the very outset of reforms economic growth accelerated.

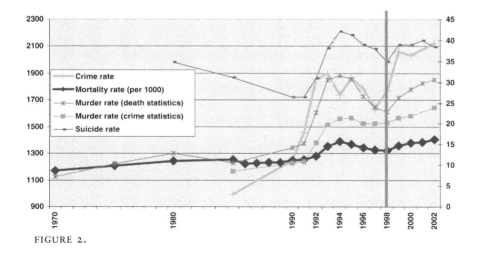

FIGURE 2.

Post factum, the reduction of output that occurred in the former Soviet Union (FSU) during the 1990s should be considered as an exceptional case in world economic history. Never and nowhere, to the best of my knowledge, has there occurred such a dramatic decline in output, living standards, and life expectancy in the absence of extraordinary circumstances such as wars, epidemics, or natural disasters. Even during the Great Depression (1929–33), GDP in western countries on average fell by some 30 percent and by the end of the 1930s recovered to its prerecession levels.

Why has the reduction of output and incomes in the FSU been so deep and so long? To what extent was this collapse caused by the initial conditions and circumstances (i.e., predetermined and unavoidable), and to what extent was it "man-made" (i.e., the result of poor economic policy choices)? If it is the wrong economic policy that is primarily responsible for the collapse, future historians may refer to the transition of the FSU as the biggest man-made economic disaster ever.

The ubiquitous feeling is that "things went terribly wrong" and that with different policies, most of the misfortunes that struck the former Soviet republics in the 1990s could have been avoided. After all, most other transition economies did better than the FSU states, and it is difficult to accept the idea that the exceptional length and depth of recession in post-Soviet states was predestined and inevitable. When it comes to the discussion of particular policies, however, there is much less agreement. The question as to why the FSU had to pay a greater price to reap the rewards of economic transition is answered differently by those who advocate shock therapy than by those who support gradual reforms. Shock therapists argue that much of the cost of reforms in the FSU can be attributed to the inconsistencies of policies followed, namely to the inability of the governments and the central banks to fight inflation in the first half of the 1990s. In contrast, the supporters of gradual transition argue exactly the opposite, blaming the attempt to introduce a conventional shock therapy package in Russia in particular for all the disasters and misfortunes of the transition period. A number of studies were undertaken to test whether fast liberalization and macrostabilization pays off and finally leads to better performance.[1] To prove the point, the authors of one study

---

[1] Jeffrey D. Sachs, The Transition at Mid-Decade, *American Economic Review* 86:2 (1996), pp. 128–33; Martha De Melo, Ceydet Denizer, and Alan Gelb, "Patterns of Transition from Plan to Market," *World Bank Economic Review* 3 (1996), pp. 397–424; Stanley Fisher, Ratna Sahay, and Carlos A. Vegh, "Stabilization and Growth in the Transition

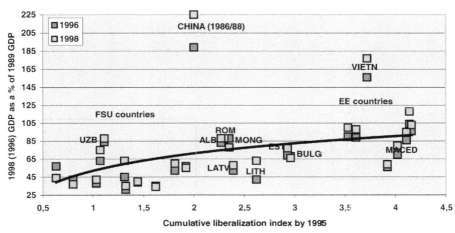

FIGURE 3. Liberalization and output change

regressed output changes during transition on liberalization indices developed in De Melo et al. (1996) and by the European Bank for Reconstruction and Development (published in its Transition Reports) – inflation and different measures of initial conditions. The conventional wisdom was probably best summarized in the 1996 World Development Report (WDR) *From Plan to Market*, which basically stated that differences in economic performance were associated mostly with "good and bad" policies, in particular with the progress in liberalization and macroeconomic stabilization. "Consistent policies, combining liberalization of markets, trade, and new business entry with reasonable price stability, can achieve a great deal even in countries lacking clear property rights and strong market institutions" was one of the major conclusions of the WDR.[2]

At first blush, there seems to be a positive correlation between liberalization and performance (see Fig. 3). However, a more careful consideration reveals that the link is just the result of sharp difference in

---

Economies: The Early Experience," *Journal of Economic Perspectives* 10 (2) (1996) pp. 45–66; A. Åslund, P. Boone, and S. Johnson, "How to Stabilize: Lessons from Post-Communist Countries," *Brookings Papers Econom. Activity* 1 (1996), pp. 217–313; P. Breton, D. Gros, and G. Vandille, "Output Decline and Recovery in the Transition Economies: Causes and Social Consequences," *Economics of Transition* 5 (1) (1997), pp. 113–30; A. Berg, E. Borensztein, R. Sahay, and J. Zettelmeyer, "The Evolution of Output in Transition Economies: Explaining the Differences," IMF Working Paper, May 1999; Stanley Fisher and Ratna Sahay, "The Transition Economies after Ten Years," paper presented at the AEA meeting in Boston, January 2000.

[2] *From Plan to Market: World Development Report* (NY: Oxford University Press, 1996), p. 142.

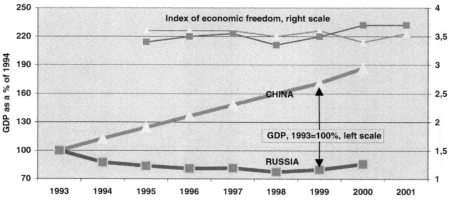

FIGURE 4. Indices of economic freedom and GDP growth in Russia and China

the magnitude of the recession in EE countries, as a group, and FSU states, also as a group (see Fig. 3). Within these groups any correlation is much weaker, not to mention China and Vietnam, which are outliers. The Chinese index of economic freedom (measured on a scale of 1 to 5 by the Heritage Foundation) was about the same in recent years as the Russian one, but the performance of the two countries differed markedly (see Fig. 4). To add insult to injury, out of the top four performers in the FSU (see Fig. 1) only one (Estonia) is the champion of liberalization, whereas the other three (Uzbekistan, Belarus, and Turkmenistan) are among the worst procrastinators with regard to economic reforms and the endurance of authoritarian regimes.

Overall, attempts to link differences in output changes during transition to the cumulative liberalization index and to macrostabilization (rates of inflation) have not yielded impressive results. Studies that tried to take into account a number of initial conditions (repressed inflation/monetary overhang before deregulation of prices, trade dependence, black market exchange rate premium, number of years under central planning, urbanization, overindustrialization, and per capita income) found that in most cases liberalization becomes insignificant.[3]

---

[3] Martha De Melo, Denizer Cevdet, Alan Gelb, and Stoyan Tenev, "Circumstance and Choice: The Role of Initial Conditions and Policies in Transition Economies," the World Bank, October 1997; Berta Heybey and Peter Murrell, "The Relationship between Economic Growth and the Speed of Liberalization during Transition," *Journal of Policy Reform* 3 (2) (1999); Gary Kruger and Merek Ciolko, "A Note on Initial Conditions and Liberalization during Transition," *Journal of Comparative Economics* 26 (4), pp. 618–34; V. Popov, "Shock Therapy versus Gradualism: The End of the Debate (Explaining the Magnitude of the Transformational Recession," *Comparative Economic Studies* 42,

The alternative explanation for the collapse of output in the FSU, adopted in this chapter, is that the speed of reform *per se* (shock therapy versus a more gradual transition) did not matter a great deal. The unique magnitude of the recession was caused primarily by three groups of factors: First, by greater distortions in the industrial structure and external trade patterns on the eve of the transition; second, by the collapse of state and nonstate institutions, which occurred in the late 1980s and early 1990s and resulted in chaotic transformation through crisis management instead of organized and manageable transition; and third, by poor economic policies, which basically consisted of macroeconomic instability and import substitution, regardless of whether the reforms were gradual or radical.

In the first approximation, the economic recession that occurred in FSU states was associated with the need to reallocate resources in order to correct the industrial structure inherited from the centrally planned economy (CPE). These distortions include overmilitarization and overindustrialization, perverted trade flows among former Soviet republics and Comecon countries, and the excessively large size and poor specialization of industrial enterprises and agricultural farms. In most cases these distortions were more pronounced than in Eastern Europe, China, and Vietnam, that is, the larger the distortions, the greater the reduction of output. The transformational recession was caused by an adverse supply shock similar to the one experienced by western countries after the oil price hikes in 1973 and 1979, and similar to postwar recessions caused by the conversion of the defense industries.

An additional reason for the extreme depth of the transformational recession was associated with the institutional collapse, and here the differences between EE countries and the FSU are striking. The adverse supply shock in this case derived from the inability of the state to perform its traditional functions – to collect taxes, constrain the shadow economy, as well as to ensure property and contract rights and law and order in general. Naturally, the state's inability to enforce rules and regulations did not create a business climate conducive to growth and resulted in increased costs for companies.

It is precisely this strong institutional framework that should be held responsible for both the success of gradual reforms in China and shock therapy in Vietnam, where strong authoritarian regimes were preserved

---

No. 1 (Spring 2000); Vladimir Popov, "Reform Strategies and Economic Performance of Russia's Regions," *World Development* (May 2001), pp. 865–86.

and institutions of central planning were not dismantled before new market institutions were created; and for the relative success of radical reforms in EE countries, especially in Central European countries, where strong democratic regimes and new market institutions emerged quickly. And it is precisely the collapse of a strong state and institutions that started in the USSR in the late 1980s and continued in the successor states in the 1990s that explains the extreme length, if not the extreme depth, of the FSU transformational recession.

To put it differently, the reforms initiated by Soviet leader Mikhail S. Gorbachev failed not because they were gradual, but because of the weakening of the state's institutional capacity. Similarly, Boris Yeltsin's reforms in Russia, as well as economic reforms in most other FSU states, were so costly not because of attempted shock therapy, but due to the collapse of the institutions needed to enforce law and order and carry out a manageable transition.

Finally, performance was of course affected by economic policy. Given the weak institutional capacity of the state – that is, its poor ability to enforce its own regulations – economic policies could hardly be "good." Weak state institutions usually imply import substitution and populist macroeconomic policies (subsidies to noncompetitive industries, budget deficits resulting in high indebtedness and/or inflation, overvalued exchange rates), which have a devastating impact on output. On the other hand, strong institutional capacity does not lead automatically to responsible economic policies. Examples range from the USSR before it collapsed (strong import substitution and periodic outbursts of open or hidden inflation) to such post-Soviet states as Uzbekistan and Belarus, which seem to have stronger institutional potential than other FSU states, but do not demonstrate better policies (macroeconomic instability, for instance).

It turns out that the FSU transition model (with the partial exceptions of Uzbekistan, Belarus, and Estonia) is based on the unfortunate combination of unfavorable initial conditions, institutional degradation, and inefficient economic policies such as macroeconomic populism and import substitution.

INITIAL CONDITIONS

Why were the speed and magnitude of economic liberalization not the paramount influences on economic performance? According to initial expectations, economic reforms were supposed to yield a "marketization dividend" leading to the greater efficiency of resource allocation and enabling increased output even with the same amount of resources. Losses in allocative efficiency in the centrally planned economies, as compared to market economies, existed mostly in the form of low capital productivity: in particular, higher capital accumulation ratios in these countries were needed to achieve growth rates similar to those of market economies.[4] In the market economy, higher growth rates could be achieved with lower investment/GDP ratios. Besides, on the eve of transition there were expectations of the "peace dividend" – an increase in living standards resulting from the conversion of the huge Soviet defense industry, that is, reallocation of resources from military to nondefense use. Why were these expectations not realized? Oher factors emerged that greatly outweighed the expected efficiency gains from liberalization in the short and medium run, such as the strong adverse supply shock that resulted from dramatic changes in relative prices after their deregulation and after the opening of the previously closed FSU centrally planned economies. Under the new price ratios (higher for resource products, lower for finished goods in general) there emerged a huge sector of noncompetitive enterprises that had previously functioned only because of implicit price subsidies. The reallocation of labor and capital to relatively efficient enterprises and industries in the emerging markets with poor regulatory frameworks proved to be a longer and much costlier process than expected. It led to the collapse of outputs in the most inefficient industries, but did not result in the compensating increase of output in relatively competitive industries. In 1998, at the trough of the Russian transformational recession, outputs in the least efficient light industry and heavy engineering were at a level of only one-tenth and one-third of the prerecession peak, respectively; whereas in the more competitive fuel and energy, steel, and nonferrous metal industries output did not fall below half or even three-quarters of the prerecession level. The greater were the distortions inherited from the period of central planning, the larger was the sector requiring restructuring under the new conditions, and the deeper was the transformational recession. I have attempted to calculate at least some quantifiable distortions – in industrial structure (industry/services/agriculture and the share of defense expenditure) and in trade patterns (trade exposure, trade among socialist

---

[4] Nickolai Shmelev and Vladimir Popov, *The Turning Point: Revitalizing the Soviet Economy* (NY: Doubleday, 1990), ch. 3; V. Popov, "Investment in Transition Economies: Factors of Change and Implications for Performance," *Journal of East-West Business* 4, No. 1/2, pp. 47–98; V. Popov, "Investment, Restructuring and Performance in Transition Economies," *Post-Communist Economies*, No. 3 (1999).

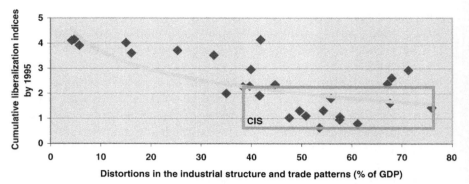

FIGURE 5. Liberalization indices and distortions in industrial structure and trade patterns

countries, and trade within the FSU) – by comparing the indicators for the CPEs before transition with the same indicators for similar size and GDP per capita market economies.[5] This revealed that the magnitude of the recession in transition economies is linked to the pretransition distortions (see Fig. 5). Together with such variables as the impact of wars (dummy) and GDP per capita before transition, these distortions explain 60 percent of the variations in GDP change in 1989–96 for twenty-eight transition economies, including China and Vietnam. In fact, it is readily apparent from Fig. 5 that for the FSU states, distortions on average were greater than in East European countries – in the first approximation it appears that this is one of the reasons for the poorer performance of FSU countries.

Recessions caused by supply-side factors may occur in centrally planned economies even without market-type reforms. Notable recent examples of the latter are of course Cuba and North Korea, which experienced a reduction of output in the early 1990s due to external shocks resulting from the decline of direct and indirect (through barter trade arrangements) subsidies from the Soviet Union. The CPE, provided that the planners follow appropriate policies, is known for its ability to adjust to external shocks (to quickly reallocate resources during wars, for instance), for which the Cuban case provides further support. Faced with the reduction of Soviet assistance in the magnitude of 20 percent of GDP, Cuban planners managed to limit the decline of output to about 40 percent of

[5] Popov, 2000.

GDP for a period of four years. Since 1994 the Cuban economy is growing again, a better record than in most FSU economies.[6]

Similarly, a supply-side recession may occur in a market economy, the recent major examples of adverse supply shocks being the energy price hikes of 1973 and 1979. The prolonged decline of Finland's GDP in the early 1990s (from 1989 to 1993 it plummeted by 12.5 percent, while the unemployment rate increased from 4 percent to 18 percent) may be an even better example, although the breakdown of bilateral clearing arrangements with the Soviet Union that contributed to recession was not its main cause.[7]

To rephrase, there is strong evidence that the recession experienced by most of the postcommunist economies was in essence a supply-side phenomenon that could have been dealt with either under central planning (no market reforms), a mixed plan-market system (gradual transition of Chinese type), or a predominantly market environment (shock therapy – immediate transition to the market). Differences in economic performance in postcommunist countries during transition appear to be associated predominantly not with chosen reform paths, but rather with the magnitude of initial distortions in industrial structure and trade patterns, and with the initial level of economic development. The impact of the speed of liberalization appears to be limited.[8]

Things are starting to change, however, and recently observed improvements in capital efficiency in some postcommunist countries should be attributed to the impact of transition. China and Vietnam managed to accelerate the rates of growth during the reform period without increasing investment/GDP ratios, whereas Poland maintains reasonable growth rates with a lower share of investment in GDP than before transition. In fact, a different theoretical framework is needed to explain differences in the performance of transition countries in the second half of the 1990s.

By the end of the 1990s, many countries were already recovering from the transformational recession, so the model of the supply-side recession

---

[6] Adjustment to similar external shock in North Korea was much less successful: although the supply shock was less pronounced than in Cuba (about 10 percent of GDP), the GDP decline continued for seven years (1990–6), exceeding 20 percent and leading to hunger.

[7] J. Kiander and P. Vartia, "The Great Depression of the 1990s in Finland," *Finnish Economic Papers*, No. 1 (1996), pp. 72–88.

[8] In addition to pretransition distortions there are, of course, other initial conditions that influenced the course of the transformation. They are too numerous to list here and range from market and private property experience before the transition to the size of monetary overhang on the eve of deregulation of prices.

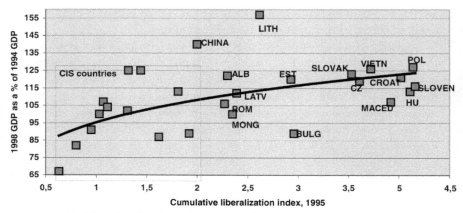

FIGURE 6. Liberalization index by 1995 and performance in 1994–98

(the greater the distortions in the industrial structure and trade patterns, the larger the reduction of output) is no longer applicable. Regressing output change in 1994–8 on the same variables that proved to be important for explaining the magnitude of the recession produces some strong, but negative, results. In short, the same regression equation that worked for the periods of 1989–96 and 1989–98 does not work at all for the period of 1994–8. The distortions coefficient has the "wrong" sign, T-statistics deteriorate sharply, and about two-thirds of the variations in growth rates remain unexplained.[9] On the contrary, the impact of liberalization becomes stronger and more statistically significant. The positive link between liberalization and performance can be observed in Fig. 6 even if two groups of countries – EE and Commonwealth of Independent States (CIS) – are considered separately.

In a sense, this is exactly the kind of negative result that supports the conclusions drawn earlier for the 1989–96 period. By mid-1990, the supply-side recession was over or coming to an end in most countries, and the theory that could explain reasonably well the performance during the collapse of output is no longer relevant. The process of economic growth that had already begun in most transition economies had little to do with the adverse supply shocks resulting from price, exchange rate, and trade liberalization. Accumulated distortions in industrial structure and in trade patterns – remnants of the planning past that were so important for explaining performance during the transition period – are no

---

[9] Popov, 2000.

longer relevant, as almost by definition they can affect only the process of the reduction of output, not the process of economic growth. In fact, although data for four years are insufficient to draw conclusions, poor regression results for 1994–8 period may mean exactly that. Likewise, the standard growth accounting exercise yields strange results. If carried out for transition economies in the first half of the 1990s,[10] the transformational recession model fails to explain data pertaining to the postdecline period.

The new economic dynamics of the transition economies (the growth process unfolding in most of them in the second half of the 1990s) could probably best be described in the framework of the conventional growth theory (production functions), where both – institutional capacities and the level of liberalization – will play a nonnegligible role. The economic growth theory deals with the change in potential GDP, whereas the supply shock model explains the temporary deviations of the actual output from potential.

There are at least two stylized facts, however, that are not explained by the supply-side recession scheme. First, in most FSU countries the reduction of output was not limited to particular industries, but occurred virtually across-the-board (with the exception of the trade and financial sectors in all states and the oil-and-gas industry in Uzbekistan). Whereas the adverse supply shock resulting from the change in relative prices can explain the reduction of output in noncompetitive industries, it does not shed light on the output collapse in relatively efficient and competitive industries. Second, in some FSU countries, Russia included, distortions were not much higher than in EE countries, but the reduction of output was considerably higher. But in China and Vietnam[11] there was no reduction of output at all, although distortions in these countries were no lower than in Albania, Mongolia, and some EE countries. If regression equations that account for initial conditions are used only to predict economic performance (GDP change), it turns out that China and Vietnam performed much better than expected; EE and Baltic states on average did not do

---

[10] Nauro Campos, "Back to the Future: The Growth Prospects of Transition Economies Reconsidered." William Davidson Institute Working Paper No. 229, Ann Arbor, April 1999.

[11] Although Vietnamese industry, excluding constantly and rapidly growing oil production, experienced some downturn in 1989–90 (−6 percent in 1989 and 0 percent in 1990), agricultural growth remained strong so that GDP growth rates virtually did not fall (5–6 percent a year). See M. Montes, "Vietnam: Transition as a Socialist Project in East Asia." Working Paper No. 136, UNU/WIDER, 1997.

so well, but still a bit better than expected; whereas most CIS states did much worse than expected.[12] Differences among particular FSU countries are also meaningful: poorly performing Russia was the country with one of the lowest levels of distortions in the FSU (about 40 percent of GDP), whereas the best-performing countries in post-Soviet space (Uzbekistan, Belarus, and Estonia) had very high distortions (51–71 percent of GDP).

To account for these stylized facts, it is necessary to expand the analysis by bringing another important factor into the picture – marked deterioration of the institutional capacity of the state in most FSU countries. Poor FSU economic performance during transition was influenced by the institutional collapse that aggravated the supply shock associated with pretransition distortions. The failure of the state to provide public goods in essence forced enterprises to increase spending to compensate for the lack of law and order (according to the anecdotal evidence, 20 percent of the personnel of the Russian banks in the mid-1990s consisted of guards!), which was equivalent to another supply shock. To what extent did the decline of the institutional capabilities contribute to worse economic performance in FSU countries, and what were the reasons for the institutional collapse?

INSTITUTIONS

For the purposes of this analysis, I consider only state institutions and define the institutional capacity of the state as its ability to enforce its own rules and regulations (regardless of relative merit). Thus, increases in the crime rate or in tax avoidance (shadow economy) are obvious manifestations of declining compliance with the existing regulations and a dwindling institutional capacity of the state. A good proxy for measuring institutional capacity of the state in the short and medium term is the financial strength of the government – the share of state revenues in GDP. Although much has been said about "big government" and high taxes in former socialist countries, by now it is obvious that the downsizing of the government that occurred in most CIS states during transition went too far. This argument has nothing to do with the long-term considerations of the optimal size of the government in transition economies – it is true that in most of them, government revenues and expenditure as a share of GDP are still higher than in countries with comparable GDP per capita.

---

[12] Popov, 2000. Op. cit.

Circumstances versus Policy Choices

But whatever the long-term optimal level of government spending should be, the drastic reduction of such spending (by 50 percent or more in real terms) cannot lead to anything but institutional collapse.

In general, from all points of view, the dynamics of government expenditure during transition are more important to successful transformation than even the speed of reforms. Keeping the government big does not guarantee favorable dynamics of output, as government spending has to be efficient as well. However, a sharp decline in government spending, especially for the "ordinary government,"[13] is a sure recipe for the collapse of institutions.

When real government expenditure falls by 50 percent or more – as it did in most CIS and Southeast European states in a short period of time – there is no opportunity to compensate for the decrease in the volume of financing by the increased efficiency of government spending. As a result, the ability of the state to enforce contracts and property rights, to fight crime, and to ensure law and order in general falls dramatically.

Thus, the story of the successes and failures of transition is not really the story of consistent shock therapy and inconsistent gradualism. The major plot of the postsocialist transformation "novel" is the preservation of strong institutions in some countries (but very different in other respects – from Central Europe and Estonia to China, Uzbekistan, and Belarus) and the collapse of these institutions in others. At least 90 percent of this story is about government failure (strength of state institutions), not about market failure (liberalization).[14]

Before the initiation of transitions in former socialist states, not only were government regulations pervasive, but also the financial power of the state was roughly the same as in European countries (government revenues and expenditure amounted to about 50 percent of GDP). This allowed the state to provide the bulk of public goods and extensive social

---

[13] Expenditure for "ordinary government" that is, total government outlays excluding defense, subsidies, investment, and debt servicing. See Barry Naughton, "Economic Reform in China: Macroeconomic and Overall Performance," in ed. D. Lee, *The System Transformation of the Transition Economies: Europe, Asia and North Korea* (Seoul: Yonsei University Press, 1997).

[14] The recognition of the fact that the previous debate about the speed of reforms was misfocused and misguided because it ignored the crucial role of institutions is part of the new conventional wisdom or "post-Washington consensus." Josef Stiglitz, "More Instruments and Broader Goals: Moving toward the Post-Washington Consensus," WIDER Annual Lecture, WIDER/UNU, 1998; "Whither Reform? Ten Years of Transition," World Bank's Annual Bank Conference on Development Economics, Washington, D.C., April 28–30, 1999.

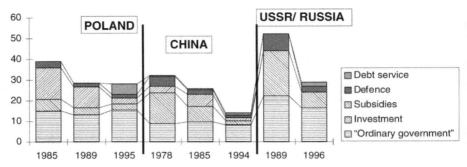

FIGURE 7. Government expenditure, % of GDP

transfers. During the transition, however, tax revenues as a proportion of GDP decreased markedly in most countries. Central European countries and Estonia managed to arrest the decline, while most CIS states experienced the greatest reduction. Exceptions within CIS prove the rule: Uzbekistan and Belarus, that is, exactly those countries that are known for proceeding with slow reforms are also believed to have the strongest state institutions among all CIS states.[15] The Ukrainian example, on the other hand, proves that it is not the speed of reforms *per se* that really matters: a procrastinator, it nevertheless did worse than expected, arguably due to poor institutional capabilities (trust in political institutions in Ukraine is markedly lower than in Belarus).

Three major patterns of change in the share of government expenditure in GDP,[16] which generally coincide with the three major archetypes of institutional developments and (even broader) with three distinct "models" of transition, are shown in Fig. 7. Under **strong authoritarian regimes** (China), cuts in government expenditure occurred at the expense of defense, subsidies, and budgetary-financed investment, while expenditure for "ordinary government" as a percentage of GDP remained largely

---

[15] The decline in government revenues as a percentage of GDP in these countries was less pronounced than elsewhere in CIS (Fig. 9).

[16] Data for China (*The Chinese Economy: Fighting Inflation, Deepening Reforms. A World Bank Country Study*, Washington, DC: World Bank, 1996), Russia (Goskomstat), and Poland (Rocznik Statystyczny 1990, Warszawa; and data from Institut Finansow provided by G. Kolodko) do not include off-budget funds, which are very substantial in all three countries and are used mostly for social security purposes. Defense expenditure are from official statistics, i.e., lower than western estimates, which is likely to lead to overstatement of spending for investment and subsidies at the expense of defense outlays. For USSR/Russia, investment and subsidies are shown together.

unchanged.[17] Under **strong democratic regimes** (Poland), budgetary expenditure, including those for "ordinary government," declined only in the pretransition period, but increased during transition itself. Finally, under **weak democratic regimes** (Russia), the reduction of the general level of government expenditure led not only to the decline in the financing of defense, investment, and subsidies, but also to the downsizing of ordinary government, which undermined and in many instances even led to the collapse of the institutional capacities of the state.

Although in China total budgetary expenditure and that for "ordinary government" are much lower than in Russia and Poland, they were sufficient to preserve the functioning institutions as the financing of social security from the government budget was traditionally low. In Russia, however, although expenditure for ordinary government seems to be not that much lower than in Poland, the pace of their reduction during transition exceeded that of GDP. To put it differently, given the various patterns of GDP dynamics, in Poland "ordinary government" financing grew by about one-third in real terms in 1989–95/6 (and in China it nearly doubled) whereas in Russia it fell by about three times! The Russian pattern of institutional decay proved to be extremely detrimental for investment and for economic performance in general.

Normally in market economies there is a positive correlation between the level of taxation, the share of government revenues in GDP, and the size of the shadow economy: if taxes are excessive, economic agents tend to avoid taxation through underground activity, including nonreported barter operations.[18] In transition economies, the opposite is true: the lower are state revenues, the larger is the shadow economy (see Fig. 8).[19] In fact, there was a nearly one-to-one crowding out effect: for every one percentage point of the reduction of the share of state revenues in GDP, the share of the shadow economy increased by one percentage point. To

---

[17] Naughton, 1997. Op. cit.
[18] Stephen Gardner, *Comparative Economic Systems* (NY: The Dryden Press, 1988), p. 24.
[19] To put it differently, the Laffer curve apparently is not applicable for macroeconomic comparison of western countries, as higher tax rates result in higher tax revenues despite the increase in shadow economy (tax avoidance). In transition economies, at least in those where institutions are weak, shadow economy growth (whether caused by higher tax rates or not) is so substantial that it more than counterweights possible increases in revenue collection. Similar results were reported for a larger group of sixty-nine countries – higher tax rates were associated with less unofficial activity (Eric J. Friedman, Simon Johnson, Daniel Kaufmann, and Pablo Zoido-Lobaton, "Dodging the Grabbing Hand: The Determinants of Unofficial Activity in 69 Countries," Fifth Nobel Symposium in Economics. Stockholm, September 10–12, 1999).

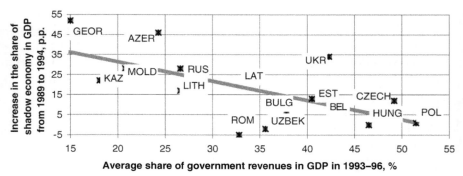

FIGURE 8. Government revenues and shadow economy, % of GDP, 1989–96

put it differently, the dynamics of the share of government revenues in GDP in transition economies is a fairly accurate measure of the ability of the state to enforce rules and regulations. The decline in government revenues is obviously correlated with performance (see Fig. 9), but it is not correlated with other variables.

After adding the decline in government revenues variable to the ones that characterize initial conditions (level of development and distortions) and external environment (war dummy variable), the explanatory power of the regression increases to 75 percent with excellent T-statistics (twenty-eight observations). And it is quite remarkable that the inclusion of liberalization variables at this point does not improve the regression statistics. Factoring in inflation enables an improvement of the explanatory power to 85 percent. The correlation coefficient rises further up to 92 percent, if other indicators of the institutional capacities, such as the

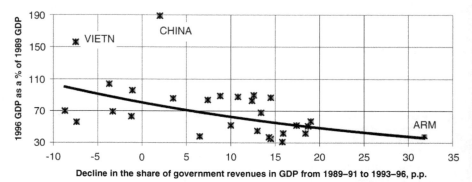

FIGURE 9. Change in GDP and in the share of government revenues in GDP

Circumstances versus Policy Choices

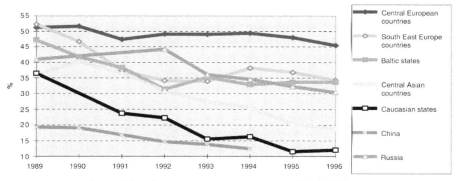

FIGURE 10. Consolidated government revenues as a % of GDP

share of shadow economy, are used, although the number of observations in this case is only seventeen because of lack of data.[20]

There was only one group of transition economies where the share of state revenues in GDP remained relatively stable during transition – Central European countries (see Fig. 10). Outside Central Europe there were only four countries where the share of government revenues in GDP did not fall markedly – Belarus, Estonia, Uzbekistan, and Vietnam. The first three are also the top three performers in the FSU region, whereas Vietnam's performance is second to only that of China. It is noteworthy that Belarus and Uzbekistan, commonly perceived as procrastinators, nevertheless show better results than more advanced reformers.[21] On the other hand, this is the alternative explanation of the Estonian success in economic transformation as compared to most CIS states and to neighboring Baltic states: the usual interpretation focusing on the progress in liberalization may overlook the impact of strong institutions.

According to the EBRD Transitions Report 1999, the quality of governance in the transition economies, as it is evaluated by companies themselves, is negatively correlated with the state capture index (percentage

---

[20] Popov, 2000. Op. cit.
[21] The alternative explanation for the relatively strong performance of Uzbekistan and Belarus is the lack of restructuring associated with the continuation of the large-scale subsidization of the inefficient production. At one point, the argument goes, these countries will have to bite the bullet and cut subsidies, which will lead to the temporary reduction of output. For a survey of the literature, see J. Zettelmeyer, "The Uzbek Growth Puzzle," IMF Staff Papers 46, No. 3 (September/December 1999); G. Taube and J. Zettelmeyer, "Output Decline and Recovery in Uzbekistan: Past Performance and Future Prospects," IMF Working Paper No. 98/132 (1998); M. Spechler, "Hunting the Central Asian Tiger," *Comparative Economic Studies* 42, No. 3 (Fall 2000).

of firms reporting significant impact from sales to private interests of parliamentary votes and presidential decrees). The relationship seems to be natural – the less corrupt is the government, the better the quality of governance. What is even more interesting is that both the quality of governance (positively) and the state capture index (negatively) are correlated with the change in share of state expenditure in GDP. Countries like Belarus and Uzbekistan fall into the same group with Central European countries and Estonia – with a small reduction of state expenditure as a percent of GDP during transition, good quality of governance, limited bribery, a small shadow economy, and low state capture index.[22]

Finally, there is a difficult question: what determines the institutional capacity of the state and under what particular conditions does this capacity deteriorate or improve? Institutions are usually considered as exogenous – at least in the short and medium term – and there are few studies offering clues to the patterns of the institutional decay. There is an extensive literature, however, on the interrelationship between economic growth and democracy.[23] Democracy is said to undermine investment (because of populist pressure for increased consumption) and to block "good" economic policies and reform because the governments in democratic societies are exposed to pressures from particularistic interests. Autocratic regimes are believed to be better suited than democratic regimes to oppose pressures for the redistribution of income and resources coming from the poor majority of the population.[24] Taiwan, South Korea, Chile, and China are usually cited as examples of autocracies that were successful in implementing liberalization and reform. It has been noted that cases of successful simultaneous economic and political reforms are

---

[22] Joel Hellman, Geraint Jones, and Daniel Kaufmann, "How Profitable Is Buying the State Officials in Transition Economies?" – *Transition, The Newsletter about Reforming Economies* (April 2000), p. 8–11.

[23] For a survey, see Adam Przeworski and Fernando Limongi, "Political Regimes and Economic Growth," *Journal of Economic Perspectives* 7, No. 3 (Summer 1993), pp. 51–69; S. Afontsev, "Economic Transformation in the Mirror of Political-Economic Analysis," *Rossiya XIXI*, No. 3 (1999), pp. 49–83 (in Russian); Adam Przeworski, Michael E. Alvarez, José Antonio Cheibub, and Fernando Limongi, *Democracy and Development: Political Institutions and Well-Being in the World, 1950–1990* (Moscow: Cambridge University Press, 2000); "Human Development Report 2002: Deepening Democracy in a Fragmented World," UNDP, 2002; Vladimir Popov, *Democracy and Development* (Moscow: Mimeo, 2003).

[24] A. Alesina and D. Rodrik, "Distributive Politics and Economic Growth," *Quarterly Journal of Economics* 109, No. 2, (May 1994), pp. 465–90.

relatively rare[25] and that introducing voting in postcommunist countries may be detrimental economically.[26]

Taiwan, South Korea, Chile before the late 1980s, and China until now are usually cited as examples of autocracies that were successful in implementing liberalization and reform. But, as A. Sen points out, "we cannot really take the high economic growth of China or South Korea in Asia as 'proof positive' that authoritarianism does better in promoting economic growth – any more than we can draw the opposite conclusion on the basis of the fact that Botswana, the fastest-growing African country (and one of the fastest growing countries in the world), has been an oasis of democracy in that unhappy continent."[27] However, it should be noted that whether Botswana should be classified as a democracy is questioned by researchers.[28] The same party has ruled the country since it gained independence in 1966, and we do not know for sure whether it would yield power if faced with a defeat at the polls. Nevertheless, Freedom House gives Botswana very high scores when evaluating political rights.

On the other hand, Olson[29] argued that autocracies can be predatory because there is no one to control the autocrat. He also believed that the populist problem of democracies can be dealt with by introducing constitutions that require supermajorities for certain government actions. Sen argues that comparative studies now available suggest that there is no relation between economic growth and democracy in either direction and that all major famines occurred under authoritarian, not under democratic regimes.[30] A survey of eighteen studies[31] produced mixed results – the sole pattern that one can discover in these findings is that most studies published after 1987 find a positive link between democracy

---

[25] S. Cheung, "The Curse of Democracy as an Instrument of Reform in Collapsed Communist Societies," *Contemporary Economic Policy* 16, No. 2 (April 1998), pp. 247–9.
[26] M.D. Intriligator, "Democracy in Reforming Collapsed Communist Economies: Blessing or Curse?" *Contemporary Economic Policy* 16, No. 2 (April 1998), pp. 241–6.
[27] Amartya Sen, "Human Rights and Asian Values: What Lee Kuan Yew and Lee Peng Don't Understand about Asia," *The New Republic* 217, No. 2–3 (July 14, 1997).
[28] Przeworski et al., 2000. Op. cit.
[29] Mancur Olson, "Autocracy, Democracy and Prosperity," in Richard J. Zeckhauser, *Strategy and Choice* (Cambridge: MIT Press, 1991), pp. 131–57.
[30] Amartya Sen, "The Value of Democracy," *Development Outreach*, Summer 1999. Ellman (Michael Ellman, "The 1947 Soviet Famine and the Entitlement Approach to Famines," *Cambridge Journal of Economics*, forthcoming) challenges this point by referring to the lack of famines in the authoritarian USSR after 1947 and to the Sudan famine that occurred under the democratic regime in 1985–9.
[31] Przeworski and Limongi. Op. cit.

and growth, whereas earlier studies, although not different in samples or periods, generally found that authoritarian regimes grew faster. There are conflicting studies of the impact of democracy on growth in transition economies – Fidrmuc (2002)[32] reports a moderate negative initial and direct effect, which is counterweighted by a positive indirect effect (democratization facilitates economic liberalization, which in turn is good for growth). On the contrary, Popov (2000) and Castaniera and Popov (2001)[33] find that there is a negative effect of democratization under the poor rule of law on economic performance and do not find any positive effect of liberalization on growth at least in the first ten years of transition.

A recent Human Development Report (UNDP, 2002), entitled *Deepening Democracy in a Fragmented World*, states that "political freedom and participation are part of the human development, both as development goals in their own right and as means for advancing human development" (p. 52). It argues that there is no tradeoff between democracy and growth and that democracies in fact contribute to stability and equitable economic and social development. Rodrik (1997)[34] does not find much of the correlation between democracy and economic growth for 1970–89 after initial income, education, and the quality of governmental institutions are controlled for, but provides evidence that democracies have more predictable long-run growth rates, produce greater stability in economic performance, handle adverse shocks much better than autocracies, and pay higher wages. These findings are very much in line with Przeworski et al. (2000): whereas there is no substantial difference in long-term growth rates, democracies appear to have smaller variance in the rates of growth than autocracies (fewer growth miracle stories, but also fewer spectacular failures), higher share of labor in value added, and lower share of investment in GDP.

However, usually the research on economic consequences of democracy looks at *levels of democracy* rather than at *changes in these levels*. The data collected by the Freedom House for the period since 1972 for

---

[32] Jan Fidrmuc, "Economic Reform, Democracy and Growth during Post-Communist Transition." CEPR Discussion Paper No. 2759, 2002.
[33] V. Popov, 2000, Op. cit.; Micael Castaniera and Vladimir Popov, "Framework Paper on the Political Economy of Growth in Transition Countries," EERC working paper, 2001. See <http://www.gdnet.org/pdf/425_Casta-Popov.pdf.> and <http://orion.forumone.com/gdnet/files.fcgi/425_Casta-Popov.pdf.>
[34] Dani Rodrik, "Democracy and Economic Performance," paper for a conference in South Africa (<http://ksghome.harvard.edu/~.drodrik.academic.ksg/demoecon.PDF>). December 1997.

over 180 countries make it possible to evaluate the impact of changes in democracy, that is, democratization per se, on economic and social development. It appears that the impact is different for developed and developing countries, especially when the strength of the rule of law is taken into account: for developing countries with poor rule of law, greater democratization in 1975–99 was associated with lower growth rates.[35]

Here, one more link between democracy and growth is suggested. It seems to be extremely important in postcommunist countries: democratization under a poor tradition of rule of law leads to institutional collapse, which undermines economic growth. In the absence of a rule-of-law tradition, it is easier to guarantee property and contract rights, to enforce state regulations, and to maintain order in general with the authoritarian rather than with the democratic regime (lawless order). The immediate results of democratization in the absence of a rule-of-law tradition are greater corruption, poorer enforcement of regulation, and higher crime rates.[36]

Using the terminology of political science, it is appropriate to distinguish between strong authoritarian regimes (China, Vietnam, and Uzbekistan), strong democratic regimes (Central European countries), and weak democratic regimes (most FSU and Balkan states – see Fig. 7). The former two are politically liberal or liberalizing, that is, protect individual rights, including those of property and contracts, and create a framework of law and administration. The latter regimes, although democratic, are politically less liberal because they lack strong institutions and the ability to enforce law and order.[37] This gives rise to the phenomenon of "illiberal democracies" – countries where competitive elections are introduced before the rule of law is established. Whereas European countries in the nineteenth century and East Asian countries recently moved from first establishing the rule of law to gradually introducing democratic elections (Hong Kong is the most obvious example of the rule of law without democracy), in Latin America, Africa, and currently in CIS countries democratic political systems were introduced in societies without the firm rule of law.

---

[35] V. Popov, *Democracy and Development* (Moscow: Mimeo, 2003).
[36] Triesman argues that the current degree of democracy, despite theoretical arguments, has no significant impact on the level on corruption; only a long exposure to democracy limits corruption. Daniel Triesman, "The Causes of Corruption: A Cross-National Study," Fifth Nobel Symposium in Economics. Stockholm, September 10–12, 1999.
[37] F. Zakharia, "The Rise of Illiberal Democracies," *Foreign Affairs* 76, No. 6 (November/December 1997), pp. 22–43.

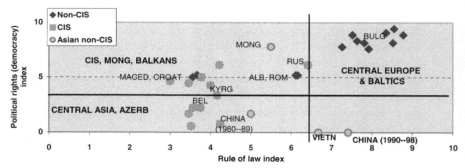

FIGURE 11. Indices of the rule of law and political rights (democracy), 0–10 scale; higher values represent stronger rule of law and democracy

Authoritarian regimes (including communist), while gradually building property rights and institutions, were filling the vacuum in the rule of law via authoritarian means. After democratization occurred and illiberal democracies emerged, they found themselves deprived of old authoritarian instruments to ensure law and order, but without the newly developed democratic mechanisms needed to guarantee property rights, contracts, and law and order in general (see upper left quadrant in Fig. 11). It is no surprise that this had a devastating impact on investment climate and output.[38]

As Fig. 12 suggests, there is a clear relationship between the ratio of rule-of-law index on the eve of transition to democratization index, on the one hand, and economic performance during transition, on the other, although the positive correlation for authoritarian countries is apparently different from that for democracies. To put it differently, democratization without strong rule of law, whether one likes it or not, usually leads to the collapse of output. There is a high price to pay for early democratization, that is, introduction of competitive elections of government before the major liberal rights (personal freedom and safety, property, contracts, fair trial in court, and so on) have been well established.

---

[38] The democracy index is taken from Freedom House (<http://www.freedomhouse.org/rankings.pdf>), but inverted and calibrated so that complete democracy coincides with 10 and complete authoritarianism with 0. The rule-of-law index is taken from N. Campos, "Context Is Everything: Measuring Institutional Change in Transition Economies," Prague, August 1999); and for China, Vietnam, and Mongolia from *International Country Risk Guide*, 1984 to 1998, and calibrated so that 10 corresponds to the highest possible rule of law.

Circumstances versus Policy Choices

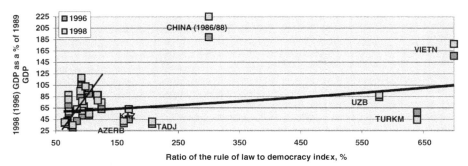

FIGURE 12. Ratio of the rule of law to democracy index and output change

If the rule of law and democracy indices are included in the basic regression equation, they have predicted signs (positive impact of the rule of law and negative impact of democracy) and are statistically significant, which is consistent with the results obtained for larger sample of countries. If the ratio of the rule of law to democracy index is included in the basic regression for output change, the results are impressive: nearly 80 percent of all variations in output can be explained by only three factors – pretransition distortions, inflation, and the rule-of-law-to-democracy index. If a liberalization variable is added, it turns out to be not statistically significant and does not improve the model's fit. At the same time, the ratio of the rule of law to democracy index and the decline in government revenues are not substitutes, but rather complement each other in characterizing the process of the institutional decay. These two variables are not correlated and improve the goodness of fit, when included together in the same regression, to 88 percent – a better result than in regressions with either one of these variables. The liberalization index, when added to the same equation, only deteriorates the goodness of fit, is not statistically significant, and has the "wrong" sign.[39]

To sum up, after allowing for differing initial conditions, it turns out that the fall in output in transition economies was associated mostly with the poor business environment resulting from institutional collapse. Liberalization alone, when it is not complemented with strong institutions, cannot ensure good performance. The best performance during transition was exhibited by countries with low distortions and strong institutions (China, Vietnam); the worst performance by countries with high distortions and weak institutions (CIS) – see Table 1. Moreover, the process

---

[39] Popov, 2000. Op. cit.

TABLE 1. *Main factors affecting performance*

Institutions/Distortions	Weak institutions	Strong institutions
High distortions	CIS	Central Europe
Low distortions	Albania, Mongolia	China, Vietnam

of the collapse of output in transition economies is best described by the supply-side recession model, where the key determinants are initial conditions and the strength of institutions, while the impact of liberalization is hardly noticeable. It follows that the debate about the speed of the liberalization (shock therapy versus gradualism) was to a large extent misfocused, whereas the crucial importance of strong institutions for good performance was overlooked.

Institutional capacities in turn depend to a large extent on the combination of the rule of law and democracy: the data seem to suggest that both authoritarian and democratic regimes with a strong rule of law can deliver efficient institutions, whereas under a weak rule of law authoritarian regimes do a better job in maintaining efficient institutions than democracies. In brief, the record of illiberal democracies in ensuring institutional capacities is the worst, which predictably has a devastating impact on output. The most efficient institutions are found in countries with the strong rule of law maintained either by democratic (Central Europe, Baltics) or authoritarian regimes (China, Vietnam). The least efficient institutions are in illiberal democracies combining poor rule of law with democracy (CIS, Balkans, Mongolia). Less democratic regimes with weak rule of law (Central Asia, Azerbaijan, Belarus) appear to do better than illiberal democracies in maintaining institutional capacity (see Fig. 11; Table 2).

POLICIES

Policies as opposed to institutions can be changed in a relatively short period of time and obviously affect performance. Here I consider economic

TABLE 2. *Main factors determining the institutional capacity*

Rule of law/Democracy	Weak rule of law	Strong rule of law
More democratic	CIS, Mongolia, Balkans	Central Europe, Baltics
Less democratic	Central Asia, Azerbaijan, Belarus	China, Vietnam

policies not associated with liberalization and privatization per se (which was discussed previously), that is, policies other than those aimed at the transformation of the CPE into a market economy. Such policies naturally include macroeconomic policy (as macroeconomic stability is needed in any type of the economy) and industrial policy in the broad sense (i.e., subsidies and other preferences to particular industries and openness of the economy to foreign competition). The suggested definition is certainly a simplifying scheme, as policies to deregulate prices or to privatize state enterprises are labeled as liberalization whereas policies to strengthen property rights or to build a stable banking system are classified as institution building. The point of this classification, however, is not to argue about definitions, but to separate (1) policies that are specific to the transition economies (marketization) from policies that are common for every market economy, and (2) policies with immediate (fast) impact on performance (industrial and macroeconomic policy) from policies which yield results only in the distant future (institution building).

The record of FSU countries with respect to macroeconomic stabilization and industrial policy is poor. Inflation remained high in the CIS states for a number of years in the first half of the 1990s and rematerialized several years later, after the 1998 currency crisis in Russia. It has already been largely documented that high inflation (over 40 percent a year) invariably tends to reduce growth performance.[40] Because inflation was and still is important in quite a number of countries, it deserves a detailed analysis as a phenomenon of persistent clear-cut suboptimal policy.

In turn, the impact of industrial policy on growth may be different. On the one hand, there is the example of East Asian countries that were subsidizing strong and competitive export-oriented sectors and were relying on export as a locomotive of economic growth: in China, for instance, the share of export in GDP increased from 5 percent in 1978 to 23 percent in 1994, while the GDP itself was growing at an average rate of about 10 percent. On the other hand, there are much less appealing examples of import-substitution industrialization (ISI) – subsidization of weak, noncompetitive industries. Soviet industrialization of the 1930s and beyond became a major isolationist import-substitution experiment: from that time on, the share of export in Soviet GDP did not increase until large scale fuel sales abroad started in the 1970s. The huge perverted industrial

---

[40] Michael Bruno and William Easterly, "Inflation Crisis and Long-Run Growth," unpublished paper, World Bank, 1995; Michael Bruno, "Does Inflation Really Lower Growth?" *Finance & Development* (September 1995).

structure created without any regard to costs and prices of the world market proved to be stillborn and nonviable in 1992, when it finally faced foreign competition after half a century of artificial isolation. One can also cite the examples of "the champion of isolationism" – North Korea – and other socialist countries, of many developing countries of socialist orientation that were creating their own heavy industries following the advice and using the assistance of the Soviet Union, of India (where the share of export in GDP remained frozen at a level of 6 percent from the 1950s to the 1980s), and many Latin American countries. The worse case of subsidization is the one that is aimed at import substitution (support of weak, inefficient industries) and is carried out through price controls, as subsidization in this case is not transparent and stimulates suboptimal allocation of resources. In CIS countries, subsidies continue to be much more important than in EE and especially in western countries, and price distortions are still very pronounced. In 1997, for example, effective electricity tariffs in FSU countries (and in many EE countries) were 1–4 U.S. cents per kWh (only in Poland, Latvia, Hungary, and Slovenia was it 6 cents and higher) as compared to 8 cents in the United States and 14 cents in fifteen European Union countries on average (EBRD Transition Report 1998, p. 43).

Baltic states, refusing to join the CIS, started to pay world-level prices for Russian fuel and energy right after the collapse of the Soviet Union, whereas prices for fuel exports to "near abroad" (CIS) increased to 75 percent of the world price for gas (40 percent for oil and coal) in 1994, and to about 70–80 percent in 1995. In Russia, however, after the deregulation of prices in January 1992, domestic fuel and energy prices were controlled directly and later indirectly (though export quotas and export taxes). Although they were allowed to increase from 3–5 percent of the world price level in January 1992 to 30–40 percent of the world level in 1994 and to about 70 percent in late 1995 (export taxes on resource goods were gradually lowered and finally abolished in 1996),[41] export restrictions and tariffs were reintroduced again shortly after the August 1998 currency crisis. As oil prices increased in 1999, so too did export tariffs. Since June 2000, crude oil export tariffs are set at EUR 2–7 per metric ton for every $2.50 increment in a world price of oil per barrel exceeding $12.50 per barrel. Because of the devaluation of the ruble in 1998 (and the faster increase in world fuel prices as compared to the growth of

---

[41] V. Popov, "Will Russia Achieve Fast Economic Growth?" *Communist Economies and Economic Transformation*, No. 4 (1998).

domestic fuel prices), domestic fuel prices once again in 1999–2000 were substantially below the world level. In early 2001 due to direct export restrictions (requirements to sell a certain percentage of oil in the domestic market) and export taxes, oil prices in Russia were less than 25 percent of the world level. In all countries where energy is cheap, the energy intensity of GDP is high: in FSU states electricity consumption per $1 PPP GDP is nearly two times higher than in EE countries, whereas in EE countries it is two times higher than in Western Europe (EBRD Transition Report 1998, p. 47). Moreover, energy intensity of GDP was relatively stable in Central European countries during transition, but increased by about 40 percent in 1989–95 in the Balkan and CIS states (EBRD Transition Report, 1999, p. 95).

If nonexport subsidies[42] and macroeconomic instability are bad, the appropriate political-economic question to ask is why they persist in transition economies. Why are Russia and other resource abundant CIS states still choosing to keep fuel, energy, and resource prices low and thus relying once again on import substitution, which seems to have lost in recent decades all support among economists and policy makers? Why do CIS countries have such a poor record of macroeconomic stability, with budget deficits, inflation, increased domestic and foreign indebtedness, and overvalued exchange rates leading to currency crises? It appears that at least in this respect, transition economies are quite similar to developing countries, where the political economy of subsidies and macro instability was thoroughly analyzed.

A number of arguments on why the decision-making process in a perfectly democratic environment may lead to suboptimal economic policy choices are found in the literature. If reforms lead to gains for the majority of the population in the long run, but only at a price of short-term losses for some groups, they can be blocked by the electorate and will never be carried out. Income inequalities give rise to the option of redistribution, which may be more attractive to the majority of the electorate than the option of promoting economic growth. Redistribution is harmful for growth, but for the poor majority losses resulting from the slowdown of economic growth may be counterweighted by gains from redistribution.[43]

---

[42] With the exception of China and Vietnam, there is no large-scale subsidization of export in transition economies. Subsidies are given primarily to households (i.e., consumers). This is the case in most postcommunist countries or noncompetitive industries (resource-rich CIS countries) with the goal of import substitution.

[43] Alesina and Rodrik, 1994, Op. cit.; T. Persson and G. Tabellini, "Is Inequality Harmful for Growth?" *American Economic Review* 84, No. 3 (June 1994), pp. 600–21.

Even when it is known that losses from economic reforms will affect only the minority, the uncertainty about the possible outcomes may lead a rational individual to vote against the reforms.[44] The uneven distribution of gains and losses and the uncertainty about the possible gains and losses appear to be not the only, but certainly the most potent theoretical justification for the "autonomous," if not authoritarian, leadership insulated from particularistic pressures.[45]

The political-economic foundations for suboptimal policies in transition economies seem to be no different than in other countries – at least here the postsocialist states appear to be far from unique. A decade ago, the research on the macroeconomics of populism in Latin America raised a similar question and suggested two answers: (1) sharp asset and income inequalities (as compared to Asian countries) and (2) sharp division between the primary products export sector controlled by the traditional oligarchy and employers and workers in industry and services.[46]

The heritage of the CPE put the transition economies into a situation somewhat similar to Latin American countries. Whatever the reasons for the wide-scale redistribution income in former socialist countries, in the very beginning of transition, after the deregulation of prices, they experienced a dramatic and quick increase in personal income inequalities and sectoral inequalities in the profitability of enterprises. Previously, under authoritarian regimes, the government was strong enough to impose substantial burden of transfers on the producers (the government revenues in most former socialist countries were way above 50 percent of GDP). Weak democratic governments, however, facing falling budget revenues, were not in a position to maintain large-scale open subsidization and had to choose between gradually eliminating the bulk of all subsidies and finding alternative ways of financing these subsidies (inflationary financing, building up domestic and foreign debt, maintaining the overvalued exchange rate, driving foreign borrowing up and/or foreign exchange reserves down).

In the first approximation, it seems like inflation results from the weakness of the governments in the region (CIS and southeastern Europe)

---

[44] Raquel Fernandez and Dani Rodrik, "Resistance to Reform: Status Quo Bias in the Presence of Individual Specific Uncertainty," *American Economic Review* 81 (5) (1991), pp. 1146–55.
[45] Dani Rodrik, "Understanding Economic Policy Reform," *Journal of Economic Literature* 34 (1995), pp. 9–41.
[46] Robert R. Kaufman and Barbara Stallings, "The Political Economy of Latin American Populism," in eds. R. Dornbush and S. Edwards *Macroeconomics of Populism in Latin America* (Chicago and London), 1991.

caused by the lack of consensus on the issue of financing the costs of economic reforms. The Chinese government was able to impose such a consensus "from above" using authoritarian methods, and in East European countries this consensus was built "from below" leading to the emergence of relatively strong democratic governments.

In contrast, the CIS and the southeastern Europe societies seem to have been more divided than that of Central European countries and Baltic states, where a greater consensus on how to proceed with economic reforms existed. Inflationary financing under these circumstances was a sort of a safety valve – a device allowing the financing of the reforms (with the inflation tax) without forcing the conflicting parties to come to explicit agreement. The alternative would have been open conflict between the confronting sides, which could have been associated with even greater costs than a highly inflationary environment. In this sense, the rate of inflation may be a pretty accurate measure of the degree of social consensus on financing the burden of reforms. Inflation plays the role of the "safety valve" that allows the government to function under the conditions of disagreement between major parties. As Russians put it, "inflation is the substitute for civil war" and "nobody yet died from inflation."

Once there is a need, whether mythical or real, to redistribute income in favor of the poorest social groups and weakest enterprises, coupled with the inability of the governments to raise enough taxes for this redistribution activity, the story unfolds pretty much in line with Latin American type macroeconomic populism[47] and leaves a strong sense of déjà vu. Constrained by the inability to raise tax receipts and by the simultaneous need to maintain redistribution in favor of particular social groups, the governments basically are left with only several options for indirect financing of subsidies.

The *first* one is to maintain control over particular prices. Price control for fuel, energy, and other resource commodities effectively takes rent away from the resource sector and redistributes it to consumers. This option is available to resource rich-countries, which may further explain why the resource endowment is found to have a positive effect on the shadow economy and corruption and a negative effect on growth.[48]

---

[47] Rudiger Dornbush and Sebastian Edwards, "The Economic Populism Paradigm," NBER Working Paper 2986, Cambridge, Mass., 1989; Jeffrey D. Sachs, "Social Conflict and Populist Policies in Latin America," NBER Working Paper 2897, Cambridge, Mass., 1989.
[48] J. Sachs and A. Warner, "Achieving Rapid Growth in the Transition Economies of Central Europe," Harvard Institute for International Development: January 1996; R. Auty,

The *second* alternative way to maintain subsidies under budget constraints is to resort to trivial inflationary financing of the government budget. The government in this case compensates for the shortfall of tax revenues by imposing the ruinous for growth inflation tax on everyone.

The *third* way is debt financing – either domestic or external borrowing. Debt financing makes sense when it buys some time for maintaining subsidies while conflicting parties are negotiating the way to get rid of them. If it continues for too long, however, it only makes things worse, as debt service payments impose an additional burden on the government budget.

Finally, the *fourth* way to continue redistribution with no funds in the budget is to maintain the overvalued exchange rate that favors consumers over producers and exporters over importers, leading to an increase in consumption at the expense of savings. Consumption increases in this case due to an increase in imports financed through external borrowing or foreign exchange reserves, and obviously provides only a temporary solution, leading to a balance-of-payments crisis in the longer term. It was shown for developing countries that overvaluation of the exchange rate is detrimental to economic growth.[49]

This is another reason why exchange rate-based stabilization and currency board arrangements are risky for transition economies.[50] By opening up the possibility for the appreciation of real exchange rate (and ensuring equilibrium only through a balance-of-payments crisis), these arrangements allow also for the continuation of populist policies and redistribution of income from producers to consumers.

Different countries in different periods resorted to one or more of the above-described mechanisms of implicit redistribution. In Russia, for instance, the government initially (1992–4) relied on controlling resource

---

"Resource Abundance and Economic Development: Improving the Performance of the Resource Rich Countries," RFA No. 44, Helsinki, UNU/WIDER.

[49] David Dollar, "Outward-Oriented Developing Economies Really Do Grow More Rapidly: Evidence from 95 LDCs, 1976–1985," *Economic Development and Cultural Change* 40, No. 3 (April 1992), pp. 523–44; William Easterly, "The Lost Decades: Explaining Developing Countries' Stagnation 1980–1998," World Bank, 1999; Victor Polterovich and V. Popov, "Accumulation of Foreign Exchange Reserves and Long Term Economic Growth," paper presented at 10th NES Anniversary conference, Moscow, December 2002 (<http://www.nes.ru/english/about/10th-Anniversary/papers-pdf/Popov-Polterovich.pdf> and <http://www.nes.ru/english/about/10th-Anniversary/papers-pdf/Popov-charts.pdf>).

[50] M. Montes and V. Popov, *The Asian Crisis Turns Global*, (Singapore: Institute of Southeast Asian Studies, 1999).

prices and inflationary financing. Since 1995, when exchange rate-based stabilization was carried out and the ruble reached 70 percent of its purchasing power parity value (i.e., Russian prices, including resource prices approached 70 percent of the U.S. prices, which was the apparent overvaluation of the ruble), the government has relied mostly on debt (domestic and foreign) financing and redistribution via overvalued exchange rate. Since the 1998 financial crisis, however, leading to the collapse of the overvalued rate and to the cessation of international and domestic debt financing, the Russian government relies largely on price controls (via export taxes and export restrictions) on major tradable goods (oil, gas, metals).

If transition economies showed anything new in the economics of subsidies and macrostabilization, it was the unusual (and previously unknown on such a scale) subsidization through the accumulation of nonpayments, barter transactions, and monetary substitutes. This may be termed the *fifth* way of indirect redistribution of income from competitive to noncompetitive industries – it occurs because the resource and energy sectors are net creditors, whereas most secondary manufacturing industries are net debtors in the arrears balance.[51] The energy and resource sectors are strongly encouraged, if not forced, to carry out such a transfer of funds by the government, which tries to avoid the shutdown of noncompetitive manufacturing plants.

There are plenty of explanations for the nonmonetary economy phenomenon,[52] and there is certainly much more to it than the mere transfer of resources to noncompetitive sectors. What needs to be explained is why these transfers from resource to nonresource industries take the odd form of arrears (instead of transparent direct subsidies or less transparent price subsidies). Nevertheless, whatever the origins of nonpayments and barter, CIS states should be "credited" for introducing this innovative form of hidden subsidization not observed in other countries on such a scale.

The impact of import substitution policies and macroeconomic instability on performance is negative and easily detectable. If inflation rates are included into basic regression explaining performance, they are statistically significant and improve the model.[53] The same goes for export

---

[51] C. Gaddy and B. Ickes, "Russia's Virtual Economy," *Foreign Affairs*, September–October 1998, pp. 53–67; R. Ericson and B. Ickes, "A Model of Russia's 'Virtual Economy,'" CEPR/WDI Annual Conference on Transition Economics, Moscow, July 2000.
[52] V. Popov, review of D. Woodruff's book "Money Unmade: Barter and the Fate of Russian Capitalism," *Journal of Policy Analysis and Management* (forthcoming).
[53] Popov, 2000. Op. cit.

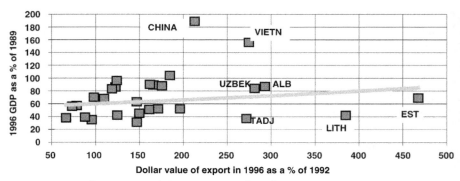

FIGURE 13. Export growth in 1992–96 and performance

growth rates – even after the inclusion of all other explanatory variables (initial conditions, institutional capacity, and inflation), the increase in exports during transition remains a highly significant explanatory variable.[54]

Indeed, in all fast-growing transitional economies the export sector was a main contributor to growth (see Fig. 13). Countries with an industrial policy designed to favor export-oriented industries (China and Vietnam) were more successful than those which did not adopt an explicit industrial policy (the Central European and Baltic countries), and far more successful than those (the CIS countries) that continued subsidizing noncompetitive industries. Two out of the three best-performing FSU economies – Uzbekistan and Estonia – registered the strongest growth of export in 1992–6 (see Fig. 13).

CONCLUSIONS

1. Economic performance (growth or decline) in transition economies did not depend on the speed of liberalization at the initial stages of transformation. The debate between shock therapists and gradualists that centered on the issue of the pace of liberalization overlooked the crucial importance of institutions for economic growth. The magnitude of the decline (transformational recession) was determined mostly by the initial conditions (distortions in industrial structure and trade patterns), by the weakening of the institutional capacity of the state, and by the better

[54] V. Popov, "Internationalisation of the Russian Economy: What Went Wrong," *EMERGO* 5, No. 2 (Spring 1998), pp. 53–84.

or worse macroeconomic and industrial policies. On all three counts, most FSU countries fell behind EE states and hence experienced poorer performance.

2. The weakening of state institutional capacity was especially pronounced in *illiberal democracies* – countries with poor traditions of the rule of law (CIS) undergoing rapid democratization. In this sense, early democratization incurred high economic and social costs and was detrimental to growth because it limited the ability of the poor-rule-of-law-states to ensure property rights, contracts, and reasonable business climate and order in general.

3. With respect to more traditional issues of the reform process (industrial policy and macroeconomic stabilization), postcommunist FSU countries do not appear to be unique – traditional theories of the political economy of reform seem to be perfectly applicable. The CIS model of economic transformation appears to be close to the Latin American one: a weak state, unable to either eliminate redistribution in favor of inefficient enterprises and sectors of the economy nor to carry out this redistribution openly, and thus resorts to hidden redistribution (inflation tax, debt financing, price controls, overvalued exchange rate, accumulation of nonpayments by noncompetitive industries).

4

Whither the Central State?
The Regional Sources of Russia's Stalled Reforms

Kathryn Stoner-Weiss

INTRODUCTION

This chapter argues that one important and often underemphasized reason for Russia's uneven economic recovery lies in the nature and evolution of political and economic decentralization. Following the collapse of the Soviet Union in December 1991, the Russian central state's ability to project its economic regulatory authority and reliably implement its policies in the provinces was seriously eroded. Indeed, the situation had become so desperate that among President Putin's first acts in office in May of 2000 were a reorganization of his presidential administration and the passage of a series of laws designed to reinforce federal authority beyond the Kremlin. In doing so, he attempted to address what has become one of Russia's most significant developmental challenges since the collapse of the Soviet Union – the central state's capability to govern in the periphery.

Beginning in 1990, a year prior to the ultimate demise of the Soviet Union, Russia's regions gained tremendous authority relative to their status under Soviet rule. Under the Soviet system, the country was so highly centralized that even trains as far as nine time zones away ran according to Moscow time; regional government officials were appointed and dismissed at the pleasure of the leadership of the Communist Party of the Soviet Union; and all prices and trade were controlled by central planners in Moscow. Within a few years of the collapse of the Soviet Union, however, Russia's eighty-nine regional governments (both legislatures and executives) were popularly elected; they became increasingly responsible for economic policies in their regions; they earned independent authority to tax; and some even developed their own foreign economic, credit, and trade policies. In short, decentralization (both political and economic) was far-reaching across Russia.

Yet despite the rapidity and extent of Russia's political and economic decentralization, markets have not thrived in the way that at least some of the comparative economic development literature predicted. Where some scholars (and many foreign policy advisors) argued that such decentralization could and should have led to market promotion and more successful economic reform,[1] ironically Russia's reform experience can most charitably be described as "stalled," "stunted," or "partial." In more than ten years of trying, the Russian state has proven itself unable to devise crucial dimensions of a market economy including, most notably, an effective system of adjudication of economic disputes and reliable protections of contracts and property rights. In sum, contrary to early expectations and the high aspirations of central state economic policy makers, Russia's experience with decentralization has proven to be market distorting rather than market promoting or "preserving."[2] This chapter endeavors to explain this outcome.

Russia's central state became a victim of what some have termed the dilemma of dual transitions. That is, when far-reaching market reform requires that the central state be strong and capable in certain important respects – most significantly the regulation of the economy – simultaneous political reforms divest the state of the ability to perform key market promoting functions.[3] In particular, I argue that instead of promoting market reform, Russia's sweeping political and economic decentralization has undercut the central state's ability to regulate nascent markets so that, at a minimum, property rights can be protected and contracts guaranteed.

I argue further that the Russian central state's growing inability to regulate the market in the periphery was a result of the early compromises that reformers were forced to make on privatization of large enterprises in particular. That is, the scope of economic reforms and the rapidity and nature of privatization in particular (such that insiders maintained effective

---

[1] Representative of this argument are the following: Barry Weingast, "The Economic Role of Political Institutions: Market-Preserving Federalism and Economic Development," *The Journal of Law, Economics and Organization* 11, No. 1 (April 1995), pp. 1–31; Gabriella Montinola, Yingyi Qian, and Barry Weingast, "Federalism, Chinese Style: The Political Basis for Economic Success in China," *World Politics* 48, No. 1 (October 1995), pp. 50–81.

[2] The term "market-preserving federalism" originated with Weingast et al.

[3] Xu Wang, "Mutual Empowerment of State and Society: Its Nature, Conditions, Mechanisms, and Limits," *Comparative Politics* vol. 32, no. 1 (January 1999), pp. 231–50.

control over their enterprises and became de jure as opposed to de facto owners) created political constraints on pushing macroeconomic reform further. The initial transfer from state ownership to private ownership simultaneous with political liberalization consolidated strong, narrow, and particularistic socioeconomic interests committed to preventing the central state from growing strong enough and constructing the right kinds of institutions to provide for basic regulation of markets. These groups benefited from stalled reform and had a vested interest in preventing further change as a result. Indeed, they preferred to co-opt regional government officials (and in some cases became the regional government) to lock in their early transitional gains rather than ensuring the construction of a strong, autonomous central state capable of regulating and curbing their rent seeking or market stunting activities.[4]

In sum, this chapter contributes to our understanding of the trajectory of Russia's transition and the nature of successful simultaneous political and economic transitions more generally. In particular, I note that decentralization is not a good in and of itself. Indeed, decentralization in the face of a central state lacking the authority to regulate, even minimally, economic policies at the subnational level can just as easily lead to stalled economic reform as to economic success. The Russian case illustrates the argument that there is no a priori reason to assume that faced with a weak or highly constrained central state incapable of regulating their actions, subnational governments will necessarily embrace further reform and capitalize on opportunities to compete for labor and capital. Instead, regional governments might as easily shun the market and even work to undermine further economic reform in their regions. A key ingredient then to successful market reform in postcommunist countries is not simply shrinking the central state's involvement in the economy, but rather ensuring that it maintains the capacity to regulate the national economy and exert some minimal level of control over other political and socioeconomic actors. The chapter ends by arguing that despite President Putin's

---

[4] See, for example, Joel S. Hellman, "Winners Take All: The Politics of Partial Reform in Post-Communist Transtions," *World Politics* 50, No. 2 (January 1998), 203–234; Raj M. Desai and Itzhak Goldberg, "The Vicious Circles of Control: Regional Governments and Insiders in Privatized Russian Enterprises," Policy Research Working Paper 2287, The World Bank, Washington, DC (September 2000); Joel S. Hellman, Geraint Jones, and Daniel Kaufmann, "Seize the State, Seize the Day: State Capture, Corruption and Influence in Transition," Policy Research Working Paper 2444, The World Bank (September 2000); and Kathryn Stoner-Weiss, "The Limited Reach of Russia's Party System: Under-Institutionalization in Dual Transitions," *Politics and Society* 29, No. 3 (September 2001), pp. 385–414.

concerted attempts to reassert the central state in the periphery, central weakness in governing the economy in the regions is likely to persist and serious macroeconomic reform to continue to stall as a result.

PART I: DECENTRALIZATION AND STALLED ECONOMIC REFORM

Russia's economic reform has made certain notable achievements over the last ten years, but has failed to progress in some key areas. This, in turn, has led to disappointing economic results. Recurring on the reform agenda are questions that have persisted since 1990, including the regulation of contracts, increased foreign investment, removal of internal trade barriers, increased tax collection, and the reliable protection of property rights.[5] Determining a single cause of the persistence of these key issues is difficult. An important and often overlooked factor, however, is the rapid decentralization of economic authority to provincial governments.

In the section that follows, I illustrate this with two kinds of evidence. First, drawing from a database of national news sources, I demonstrate the degree to which regional governments failed to comply with central state policy and the constitution – in particular on issues concerning economic regulation or having clear effects on regional economies – throughout the 1990s.

Second, because relative compliance to central state policy is an indirect measure of central state power to govern the economy in the periphery, a second, more direct, measure involves a closer examination of the interactions between central and regional policy actors. A crucial contributor to any state's ability to regulate its economy is its infrastructural power base – a bureaucracy that has some degree of autonomy from societal interests and that can also provide a reliable mechanism of organizational control and coherence.[6] I was able to delve more deeply into the infrastructure of everyday public administration in Russia through interviews with more than 800 public officials in seventy-two of Russia's eighty-nine regions. These interviews provide more detailed information regarding the concrete power relationships among public officials and between public officials and civil society in setting and implementing economic and social

---

[5] These problems were not only mentioned by Putin upon taking office in May of 2000, but were repeated again by Deputy Prime Minister Alexei Kudrin at the Davos Economic Forum on January 29, 2001. See Johnson's Russia List, January 29, 2001.
[6] Michael Mann in John Hall, ed., *States in History* (New York: Oxford University Press, 1986), p. 114, emphasis added.

policy at the regional level. To what degree do federal state agencies operate according to the principles and programs conceived by central officials in Moscow? Do supervisors alone influence the decisions of state officials? This unique dataset sheds light on these questions and provides an unusual look into the inner workings of Russian center-periphery relations – particularly in the area of economic policy.

The Compliance Problem

The Russian Federation is subdivided into a somewhat unwieldy three-tiered system of twenty-one republics (each bearing the name of a dominant non-Russian ethnic group), fifty-five oblasts and krais (predominantly ethnically Russian) including the special-status cities of Moscow and St. Petersburg (treated functionally as oblasts), and eleven autonomies (each of which are also predominantly non-Russian in ethnic makeup). In addition to those sections of the 1993 Constitution of the Russian Federation that outline the exclusive jurisdictional authority of the center and shared jurisdiction (Articles 71 and 72, respectively), forty-two of Russia's eighty-nine constituent units signed bilateral agreements and treaties with Moscow.[7] Each of these were separate deals with the federal government specifically tailored to the needs of each regional signatory such that they varied widely in terms of what was included. Some regions negotiated individual taxation packages with the center, while others gained additional rights over natural resource extraction and distribution. Although the treaty process was within Moscow's realm of influence, and was intended to provide some coherence and predictability to center-periphery relations, in fact central state policy coherence throughout the 1990s was under daily threat from almost all subnational units of the Federation – even from those regions that signed power-sharing treaties with the center.

Throughout the last decade of reform, the central state's varying ability to ensure that regional governments complied with its basic policies and the constitution proved to be a recalcitrant problem. But this problem went far beyond recurrent violent conflict in Chechnya, or the declarations of autonomy and sovereignty in some of the regions and republics of Russia in 1990 and 1991, to the more mundane tasks of everyday public

---

[7] Andrei Zagorodnikov, "Kakaia federatsiia nam nuzhna?" *Nezavisimaia gazeta*, October 9, 1998, p. 8.

administration. Noncompliance of regional governments to central state policies and laws provides a preliminary indicator of the state's capacity to govern – and govern the economy in particular – across territory. Reports (drawn from the national press) of regional noncompliance to federal policy and the constitution provide a thumbnail sketch of some of the most serious and persistent challenges that the central state faced to its authority in the periphery. They ran a gamut of regions and they remained relatively persistent across time from 1991 and the collapse of the Soviet Union, through to December 1999 and Boris Yeltsin's resignation as Russia's first elected president.[8] In particular, it is striking the degree to which the dominant forms of noncompliance have direct economic consequences both for regions and for the center.

Examples abounded of regions legislating in direct opposition to federal law and the constitution and of preempting federal authority. Although these examples range widely across regions of Russia, across time, and across policy areas, one consistent theme is the degree to which they directly affected the center's ability to regulate economic relationships in the periphery. For example, in 1996 the Ministry of Justice reported that of the 44,000 regional legal acts it reviewed, including gubernatorial orders, it found that "nearly half [that is, almost 22,000!] of them did not correspond with the Constitution of the Russian Federation."[9] Reportedly the regions of North Ossetiia, Voronezh, Samara, Arkhangelsk, Irkutsk, Tiumen, and Omsk passed legislation restructuring their judiciaries, a right exclusively reserved to the federal government by Art. 71 of the constitution. Other regions maintained illegal tariffs and taxes (Kareliia, Volgograd and Nizhnii Novgorod, Novosibirsk, Belgorod, and Moscow).[10] Still other regions introduced their own land codes in the absence of a federal land code. An estimated fifty-one of eighty-nine regions violated provisions of the law on local government such that some regional governors illegally appointed mayors of cities in their regions

---

[8] For an examination of the extent to which de facto policy autonomy has fallen to Russia's eighty-nine regions, see Kathryn Stoner-Weiss, "Central Weakness and Provincial Autonomy: Observations on the Devolution Process in Russia," *Post-Soviet Affairs* 15, No. 1 (January 1999) pp. 75–93.

[9] See, the *Izvestiia*, November 4, 1997 report as reproduced in the *Institute for East-West Studies, Russian Regional Report* 2, No. 38 (November 6, 1997).

[10] *Izvestiia*, November 4, 1997, in the *Institute for East-West Studies, Russian Regional Report* 2, No. 38 (November 6, 1997). See also Pavel Visotskii, "O konstitutsionnoi zakonnosti v Rossiskoi Federatsii," *Chelovek i pravo*, No. 13, 102 (November 1998), p. 2. The author is the First Deputy Head of the Department of Constitutional Law in the Ministry of Justice of the Russian Federation.

rather than holding elections for these posts.[11] Other regions claimed the right to ratify international treaties and even revise federal borders.[12]

In blatantly protectionist ways, regional governments slapped limits on labor mobility by maintaining restrictions on freedom of movement and choice of a place to live. Despite the fact that the Constitutional Court ruled that such restrictions were clear violations of the constitution, the residency permit system persisted in many regions of Russia (including Moscow oblast and the city of Moscow, Adigeia, Kabardino-Balkaria, Karachai-Cherkessia, Krasnodar, Stavropol, Voronezh, and Rostov oblasts).[13] In addition, the Mayor of Moscow, Yurii Luzhkov, steadfastly refused to implement the federal government's housing policy (again to control labor mobility).[14] Still other regions violated both the constitution and Russian law in maintaining immigration quotas and/or language requirements.[15]

Further, the Russian Ministry of Justice claimed that,

Almost all of the constitutions and charters [basic legal documents of republics and oblasts respectively] of the subjects of the Federation [89 subnational units] in sections dedicated to topics of jurisdiction between federal organs of state power and organs of state power of subjects of the Federation contain violations of the provisions in articles 71 and 72 of the Constitution of the Russian Federation.[16]

The most common kinds of violations of these two articles of the constitution again clearly affected economic policy at the regional level and the center's ability to influence and regulate markets. Many violations, for example, pertained to the ownership, use, and distribution of natural resources, with subjects of the federation claiming ownership despite the fact that the federal government had legal jurisdiction. Similarly, regions and republics frequently introduced unconstitutional laws regarding the

---

[11] ". . . While Administration Cracks Down on Other Regions," *Institute for East-West Studies, Russian Regional Report* 3, No. 5 (February 5, 1998). The specific reference is to the practice of Novosibirsk's governor, Vitalii Mukha.

[12] "Justice Ministry Warns Regions That They Are Not Complying with Federal Legislation," in *Institute for East-West Studies, Russian Regional Report* 2, No. 9 (March 6, 1997).

[13] Visotskii, p. 2.

[14] For more on both of these stories, see "Newly Elected Governors Grapple with Moscow, Regional Problems," *Institute for East-West Studies, Russian Regional Report* 3, No. 2 (January 15, 1998). For more on Luzhkov's refusal to implement federal housing policy, see also "Moscow Mayor Spars with Boris Nemtsov over Housing Reform," *Insititute for East-West Studies, Russian Regional Report* 2, No. 17 (May 15, 1997).

[15] Visotskii, p. 2.

[16] Ibid.

administration and distribution of federal property located on their territories. Others introduced laws establishing financial, credit, and hard-currency regulations – a right reserved exclusively for the federal government in Article 71. Finally, some regions even passed laws regarding the organization and activities of federal executive power (like branches of federal ministries) located on their territories and over whom they had no legal jurisdiction.[17]

According to analysis from the Ministry of Justice, the constitutions and charters of some regions (for example, Ingushetia, Kalmikia, Tatarstan, Bashkortostan, Tyva, Kabardino-Balkariia and Irkutsk oblast, and Khanti-Mansii autonomous okrug) claimed the supremacy of their laws over federal law. Others even foresaw the possibility of suspending federal law on the territory of the region if it contradicted the constitution or charter of the region (Sakha, Bashkortostan, Tyva, Komi, and Tatarstan).[18]

Figure 1 confirms that regional governments tended to violate federal law in areas that were specifically linked to the material well-being of their localities. For example, provincial violations of federal law in what I have termed economic areas (including violations of federal anti-monopoly regulations, banking and financial policy, tariff policies, federal budgetary policy, land and property policy, ownership of natural resources, price controls, privatization), trade (establishing illegal trade regimes with foreign countries or inhibiting free trade between their regions and others using forms other than tariffs), taxation (either by instituting illegal tax regimes or usurping federal tax authority), and misdirection of federal funds to regional projects together constitute half of all provincial violations of federal law and the constitution.[19]

---

[17] Ibid.
[18] Ibid.
[19] This dataset was compiled using the Lexis Nexus electronic database as well as Radio Free Europe/Radio Liberty Electronic Archives and the Eastview Publications electronic archives purchased by Firestone Library at Princeton University. The search of Russian national newspapers (that is, with news coverage and circulation across the country, rather than any particular region) generated approximately 500 articles cataloguing regional noncompliance to the constitution. With the assistance of two of my graduate students, Eric McGlinchey and Marc Berenson, I devised a list of policy areas by which to classify noncompliance into nine categories (economic, social, electoral requirements, the judiciary/legal, taxation, trade, citizenship, regional government structure, and misdirection of federal funds). Next, my team coded the articles gathered from the database so that each infraction was assigned a policy area. Many of the articles yielded more than one infraction per region, so the final number of observations was 846.

These data provide a thumbnail sketch of the extent of the center's noncompliance problem in the regions. I could not ascertain if the various newspapers typically emphasize

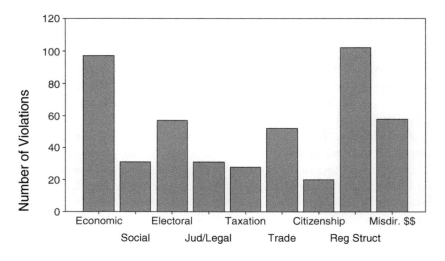

Violation Type

FIGURE 1. Regional Violations of Federal Law 1994-1999

Key to Violation Type

Economic = Includes violations of anti-monopoly regulations, pursuit of independent banking policies, pursuit of independent land, property or real estate laws, imposition of price controls, privatization violations.

Social = Includes civil/human rights abuses, violations of social welfare provisions, crackdown on regional media, violation of federal ban on death penalty, violations of language rights.

Electoral = Electoral Requirements for candidates and voters, local parliamentary immunity from prosecution, non-Russian language requirements for candidates, residency requirements for candidates, etc.

Judicial/Legal = Includes illegal judicial appointments, interference in the adjudication of law, usurpation of federal judicial or law enforcement authority, introduction of separate legal system (Sharia Law in Chechnia).

Taxation = Includes introducing regional taxes in areas where federal government has exclusive tax authority; other violations of federal tax law.

Trade = Includes pursuing international trade deals without the express consent of the federal government; maintaining trade restrictions on goods entering or exiting the region.

Citizenship = Includes residency registration requirements, regional laws indicating that regional citizenship is primary and citizenship in the Russian Federation is secondary for regional residents.

Regional Structure = Includes statements within laws of constitutions of regions indicating that the regional document supercedes federal law and the constitution; infringing on the rights of cities by appointing mayors; creating institutions that would administer regional policies in an area that is exclusively federal jurisdiction.

Misdirection of $$ = **Misdirection of federal funds** to regional projects including using federally transferred funds for a purpose other than that directed by the federal government; violations of federal budgetary policies.

With regard to variations in noncompliance patterns over time, Figure 2 indicates that regions became bolder in their dealings with the central state through the 1990s.[20] Although reported instances of noncompliance appeared to peak toward the end of the decade, there was a slow but steady increase in reported noncompliance throughout the time period for which we have data. It is important to note the other political and economic events with which the central state was dealing that might have influenced regional government behavior in becoming more or less compliant at particular points in time. First, noncompliant activity on the part of regional governments appears to have peaked when the national economy was in crisis. As the economy recovered somewhat, noncompliance slackened. This was the case in the year or so preceding the financial crisis in August 1998 and by 1999, when the economy began to show signs of recovery (the first year of positive GDP growth), noncompliance tapered to pre-crisis levels.

Second, it is notable also that noncompliant activity was consistently high from the third quarter of 1996 through the third quarter of 1999, following the first Chechen conflict and immediately prior to the second. During the three-year period of relative calm in Chechen-Russian Federation relations, regional governments stepped up their political/legal defiance of central authority, perhaps less fearful of (violent) retribution given the disastrous performance of the Russian military in Chechnya.

Following the spike in noncompliance in 1998 after the financial crisis, noncompliance remained high as regional governments sought to protect their localities from the fallout of the devaluation of the ruble in particular. This illegal behavior was relatively short-lived, however, and noncompliance declined steadily and then rather precipitously as the second Chechen conflict began in the fall of 1999. This big dip in noncompliant behavior then may have been a result both of the start of Russia's rebound in

---

one region more than another in their reporting or if some acts of compliance were simply easier to observe and were therefore overreported. In thinking about this problem, however, I have no sense of the ways in which biases would run or what weighting scheme would make sense in attempting to correct for this problem in the data. However, I am confident these data are the best currently available.

[20] We have some confidence that the temporal patterns we observe are not merely a result of fluctuations in the quality of newspaper coverage of the phenomenon through the 1990s in that Ministry of Justice reports issued regularly from about 1996 onward also indicate a steady increase in reported infractions. Thus, the patterns the Ministry reported seem to be parallel what our data show.

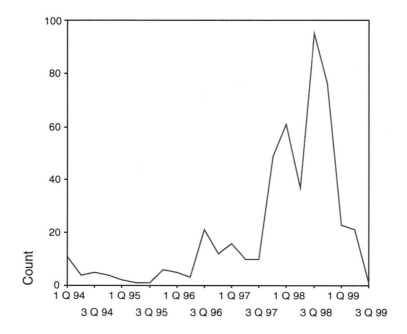

FIGURE 2. Regional Violations of Federal Law by Quarter, 1994–1999 (Count = Number of Violations, 1st Evt = First time noncompliant event appears in the newspapers)

economic growth and Putin's resumption of the Chechen conflict following several incidents of domestic terrorism. This second Chechen conflict was far more popular among the Russian electorate than the first conflict and it may be that regional governments made a strategic calculation, as they appear to have done during the first conflict between 1994 and 1996, that this was not a good time to aggressively pursue more legal and political challenges to central state authority.

Moreover, regional noncompliance to federal laws and policies was pervasive and persistent throughout the last decade of Russia's dual transition. Despite Putin's attempts beginning in 2000 to erase these violations (described in further detail in the second part of this chapter), reports of them persisted.[21]

---

[21] *East West Institute Russian Regional Report* (February 7, 2001) and Robert Orttung, "Putin's Governors General," Vol. 7, No. 20 (June 17, 2002) regarding Bashkortostan's constitutional changes resulting in even more noncompliant clauses than in 2000.

Central State Infrastructural Power in the Provinces

Despite the persistence of regional noncompliance to federal law and the constitution, it is possible that regional politicians passed offending legislation only to make a political point while their policies tended to basically abide by federal dictates nonetheless. If this were accurate, then simply citing examples of widespread legal noncompliance to federal power masks the reality of federal control over Russian public administration in the regions and regulatory control of the economy. One method of addressing this possibility is to actually ask public officials in the periphery about how policy was made and implemented concretely, and what influenced both of these processes – that is, to examine Russian central state infrastructural power in the periphery.

A more systematic assessment of the concrete power balance between the central state and the periphery, therefore, comes from extensive interviewing of 824 public officials in seventy-two Russian provinces.[22] Local teams of interviewers conducted face-to-face interviews between September 30 and November 30, 1999. In each of the seventy-two regions, we attempted to interview the same twelve officials, although as expected some refused to participate. Still, the response rate was strikingly high

---

[22] It is easier to list which of Russia's eighty-nine regions were not included in the interviewing process than those that were. Because of the dangers involved in going to the North Caucasus in the fall of 1999, neither Chechnia nor Ingushetia were included in the sample. In addition, it proved impossible to complete interviews in the city of Moscow, Moscow oblast, or Leningrad oblast. Because we were primarily interested in the relationship between republics and oblasts and krais and the center, none of the ten autonomous okrups or the one autonomous oblast were included. The survey was conducted in cooperation with Aleksandr Gasparishvili and Sergei Tumanov of the Opinion Research Center, Moscow State University. We employed the network of interviewers Gasparishvili and Tumanov constructed in the provinces during the 1990s. Teams of interviewers conducted person-to-person interviews of a list of respondents that we provided. On average, interviews lasted forty minutes.

I am particularly grateful to Professor Beth Mitchneck of the Department of Geography and Regional Development at the University of Arizona for generously sharing a questionnaire with me that she prepared for a survey of public officials she completed in seventy regions of Russia in 1997. Her questionnaire formed the foundation of many of the questions included in the questionnaire for my 1999 survey. We surveyed slightly different groups of public officials as Professor Mitchneck's survey included federal-regional-urban political and economic relationships and my own study was concerned more with the political and economic relationships between federal and regional level officials. For more on Mitchneck's results, see her "The Regional Governance Context in Russia: A General Framework," *Urban Geography*, 2001 and her "Regional Governance Regimes in Russia: The Cases of Yaroslavl' and Udmurtia," in Jeffrey Hahn, ed., *Regional Russia in Transition: Studies from Yaroslavl'* (Washington, DC: Woodrow Wilson Center Press, 2001).

(approximately 90 percent), providing a robust dataset with which to examine various aspects of Russian central state infrastructural power.

The twelve targeted officials included three elected officeholders: the regional or republican governor or president or his or her deputy (sixty-six respondents), the head of the regional or republican legislature or his or her deputy (sixty-eight respondents), and the mayor of the capital city of the region/republic or his or her deputy (sixty-eight respondents). In the interest of space and relevance, however, in this essay I use only the responses from the heads of executives (governors or republican presidents or their deputies).[23]

In addition, to try to gain a better picture of the types of linkages that existed among parts of the federal bureaucracy, we interviewed the head or deputy head of each of three federal funds: the Social Security Fund (sixty-eight respondents), the Medical Insurance Fund (sixty-eight respondents), and the Pension Fund (sixty-nine respondents). The logic here was to try to get a sense of the degree to which policy in the local branches of the federal funds was determined by the center versus regional political and socioeconomic forces. On paper, these regional branch funds were under the exclusive jurisdiction of their respective federal agencies in Moscow. Both the chair and deputy chair of regional branches of these funds were supposed to be appointed by and could be removed only by the government of the Russian Federation.[24] Thus, the officials working in these funds were federal, not regional, public officials.

The third group of respondents included the heads or deputy heads of six regional and republican departments (or ministries) of the administration (that is, on the executive side of regional government). These included the departments of the economy (sixty-nine respondents), health (seventy-one respondents), education (seventy-one respondents), social welfare (seventy-one respondents), trade (64 respondents), and agriculture (seventy-one respondents). These policy areas were chosen to provide

---

[23] In the larger project of which this essay is a small part, however, I am able to use more of the data from all respondents to make broader arguments regarding political and bureaucratic relationships within different components of the Russian state. See Kathryn Stoner-Weiss *Resisting the State: Reform and Retrenchment in Post-Soviet Russia* (New York: Cambridge University Press, forthcoming).

[24] A. P. Alekhin, A. A. Karmolitsii, and Iu. M. Kozlov, *Administrative Law of the Russian Federation* (Moscow: Zertsalo Press, 1998), p. 220. Note that a few regions (for example, Tatarstan) had negotiated special agreements with the federal government that enabled them to retain hiring and firing authority over these officials.

a mix of both economic and social policy areas.[25] Further, following former Soviet practice of *dvoinoe podchinenie*, most of these departments were officially dually subordinated to the regional government and respective federal ministries in Moscow. In designing this research program, it seemed reasonable to ask this group of actors which of the two levels of government actually influenced their work more in practice and to what degree nonstate actors played a role in their activities.

The questionnaire included both open-ended and closed questions to try to elicit as full and wide-ranging responses as possible. These interviews, in turn, were followed up by about thirty longer interviews in four focus regions to ensure the accuracy of the survey responses and to delve more deeply into the operations of Russian public administration. It is important to emphasize that in all of these interviews, public officials were not asked their *opinions* about Russian politics today. Rather, they were asked sets of questions regarding their own career paths, their own policy priorities in the near and longer terms, and quite specifically, how policy was made and implemented in the region in which they were employed (the key actors or sets of interests involved). As a result, the nine appointed officials (the heads of the three federal funds and the six heads of departments) were asked explicit questions about the influence their bureaucratic superiors in Moscow had over policy in their bailiwicks as well as the relative influence of local political and social actors. Significantly, the elected political officials (governors of oblasts or presidents of republics) generally supported their answers. The picture of the inner workings of the Russian state that emerged indicates the relatively strong influence of local versus central power in the concrete workings of government.[26]

---

[25] In an ideal world, we would have included all federal agencies at the provincial level in our sample, but this would have exceeded our means and the patience of the Russian Federal Security Service (FSB).

[26] All three groups of officials responded also to a series of questions about themselves and their career paths. Of the 824 officials included in our sample, 26.8 percent (or 221 respondents) were from nineteen of twenty-one republics; 73.2 percent (or 603) were from fifty-three of fifty-five oblasts and krais. In addition, 62.6 percent were the leaders of their respective institutions (that is, heads of departments or funds or top political officials like mayors or governors) while 37.4 percent were deputy leaders. The average age of respondents was 49.1 years, 78.8 percent were men and 21.2 percent women, and virtually all had completed secondary or postsecondary education. The mean number of years worked in their current positions was 7.78, indicating that most respondents had gained their current positions since the collapse of the Soviet Union in 1991. Only

How Is Policy Made and What Influences Implementation?

FEDERAL FUNDS. A detailed assessment of the central state's infrastructural power comes from interviews completed with 205 branch representatives of three of Russia's federal funds. These are among the largest federal agencies in Russia and are responsible for collection of social assistance payments, provision of national health services, and pension collection across the country. Moreover, the tasks they are supposed to perform affect the lives of almost the entire Russian population. The quality of their operations, therefore, matters a great deal to average Russians.

The series of questions asked of the federal funds was designed to probe the degree to which regional political, social, and economic forces influenced the activities of these federal branch officials as compared to the influence of their superiors and administrative directives emanating from Moscow.

Table 1 presents a mixed picture regarding the functioning of organizational hierarchies. Respondents were asked to indicate on a scale of 1 to 5 (where 1 is not at all and 5 is a great deal) the degree to which various groups and organizations influenced their fund's activities. The higher the mean score reported in the table, therefore, the more influence a particular group or organization has. On the one hand central state officials, as we might expect, are clearly highly influential in the activities of the federal funds. Table 1 shows that both the normative acts of the federal fund and the leadership of the heads of federal funds strongly influenced their activities (with means of all respondents from the funds shown in the last column of the table as 4.63 and 4.61, respectively).

A large number of respondents, however, indicated that the regional governor or president of their republic was also strongly influential (mean

---

2.7 percent (or twenty-two respondents) reported that they had previously worked for the Communist Party of the Soviet Union (CPSU).

Although some of the foregoing is superficially encouraging – suggesting that perhaps few officials in high office in the post-Soviet state are holdovers from the old regime – more detail on their work histories makes this picture slightly fuzzier. Almost a quarter of them worked previously in the organs of executive power at the local level (either in the city or regional government) during the period preceding the collapse of the Soviet Union, an additional 28 percent worked in enterprises, and an additional 5.7 percent worked in organs of regional or local legislatures. In addition, 70.5 percent of this group of respondents reported that they held high ranks in their former positions – either the primary leader or deputy leader. In sum, at least half of the respondents had ample experience in the old system, and more than two-thirds of this group held some sort of high leadership position under the old regime, if not necessarily within the CPSU.

Whither the Central State?

TABLE 1. *Influences on Fund Activities.*

(Q. To what degree do the following organizations and groups influence the activity of your department, administration, or fund?)

Respondents were asked to indicate their response on a five-point scale: not at all = 1, a little = 2, moderately = 3, a good deal = 4, very strongly = 5. Means were calculated such that the higher the mean, the greater the degree of reported influence. Means are reported in regular type; standard deviations appear in parentheses.

Degree of Influence:	Federal Officials in Republics N = 56	Federal Officials in Oblasts N = 148	Mean of All (Excluding No Response) N = 204
Normative acts of federal funds	4.71 (0.62)	4.61 (0.94)	4.63 (.86)
Leadership of federal funds	4.65 (0.65)	4.59 (0.85)	4.61 (0.80)
Heads of executives of regions (presidents in republics and governors in oblasts)	4.55 (.90)	4.57 (1.36)	4.56 (1.33)
Presidential representative	2.63 (1.37)	2.92 (1.52)	2.85 (1.39)

of 4.56 for all respondents again shown in the last column of the table). The difference between the paired means of the head of executive and the normative acts of the federal fund as well as between the head of executive and the heads of the federal funds was statistically significant at the .01 level. There was also little variation but no statistically significant difference between the reported degree of influence of heads of executives between respondents in the ethnically non-Russian republics included in the sample versus the oblasts (with means of 4.55 and 4.57, respectively). In sum, this is a surprisingly high degree of influence given that the elected heads of regional executives (presidents of republics and governors of oblasts) are not supposed to have any direct influence over federal officials in their regions.

Adding further complexity to the picture of the extent to which federal state infrastructural power influences the actions of federal officials stationed in the provinces is the weak influence of the federal government's main agent in the periphery – the presidential representative.[27] Only 13 percent of respondents from federal funds indicated that the

---

[27] As the survey was conducted in the fall of 1999, these references to the presidential representative refer to that office prior to Putin's May 2000 reform.

presidential representative had a very strong influence over their activities, with over 20 percent indicating he had no influence whatsoever. The mean score, therefore, for the influence of the presidential representative was the lowest of all organizations named – 2.85, although this office was slightly more influential in oblasts than in republics. (The difference between the paired means of the presidential representative and the regional head of executive for all regions was significant at the .01 level.)

The presidential representative is a good example of a failed attempt on the part of the central government to reign in the provinces. On paper, the job of the presidential representative was to serve as the eyes and ears of the federal executive in the provinces as well as to coordinate the actions of branches of federal agencies at the regional level. But based on the extent to which he reportedly influenced the activities of federal fund officials, clearly this mechanism of institutional coordination and oversight was failing. Indeed, judging from these responses, contrary to expectations when the post was created in 1991 (and revamped in 1998 and then again in 2000 and discussed in more detail in section two of this chapter), the presidential representative clearly provided no significant counterweight to the influence of regional governors on federal officials based in the provinces.

Aside from asking about the degree to which various agencies and organizations influenced their regular activities, federal fund officials also were asked to name those organizations, groups, and leaders that were most effective in helping to implement the programs and responsibilities of their agencies. Significantly, the respondents from the funds reported that the sources of funding for their respective agencies were largely federal. Despite this, however, the tremendous influence of heads of regional executives in the work of the federal funds – again without any official capacity in this regard and with little overt fiscal influence – is striking.

Table 2 demonstrates that in terms of actually accomplishing concrete tasks on the ground, heads of executives (regional governors of oblasts and presidents of republics) and different departments of the oblast executive prove slightly more helpful – mentioned 30.12 percent and 11.02 percent of the time, respectively – than do the leadership of the federal funds and federal organs of power (ministries) – 27.1 percent and 8.09 percent, respectively. Other local forces, like local organs of self-government (that is, city- and county-level government), the mass media, unions, and regional business circles – also play notable roles in the functioning of the federal

TABLE 2. *Organizations Identified as Most Effective in Implementation of the Policy Priorites of Three Federal Funds.*

(Q. Name please three organizations, groups, or leaders from the following list with whom you work most effectively in implementing the priorities of your fund. (N = 205))

Organization, Group, or Leader	Total Number of Mentions	Percent of Total Number of Mentions (N = 205)
Local business circles	16	2.75%
Unions	30	5.16%
Political parties and movements	0	0.00%
Other social organizations	1	0.17%
Means of mass information	26	4.48%
Church	2	0.34%
Leadership of the federal fund	161	27.71%
Head of executive power of the oblast	175	30.12%
Presidential representative in the region	9	1.55%
Different oblast departments	64	11.02%
Federal organs of power	47	8.09%
Local organs of self-government	46	7.92%
None of the above	3	0.52%
Total number of responses	581	100.00%

funds. Societal organizations and political parties play little or no role in the work of the funds.

Moreover, although superiors in Moscow clearly played an important role in the functioning of these three federal agencies (as we would expect), regional governments sometimes proved as or even more important. Follow-up interviews conducted in four focus regions to ensure the accuracy of the survey (and to fill in some of the rich detail of these relationships) support this perspective. For example, in Orenburg oblast the head of the regional branch of the federal pension fund reported quite cheerfully that although her salary was technically paid by the federal fund in Moscow and the building in which her offices were housed belonged to the federal fund, the governor of the region himself had recently promised her a new apartment in a more desirable building. She noted that not only could the regional administration provide important perks to federal fund employees (like housing), but also that she could not fulfill the mandate of her office without the support of the governor of her region. His relationships with regional enterprises were absolutely crucial in extracting pension fund revenues. "By necessity," she explained, "we are part of a united team. Regions with effective federal funds work this way."[28]

The closeness and dependency of the funds on regional political actors is somewhat surprising given that, strictly speaking, the local funds are branches of federal agencies. Thus, regional and local officials lacking official jurisdictional authority were assuming significant jurisdictional responsibilities over federal agents posted in the provinces. This may explain why regional officials appeared to have the authority to grab money intended for the payment of pensions at the regional level. Effectively, they held as much or greater sway in the lives of federal branch officials than did distant federal bureaucrats in Moscow.[29] Certainly, administrative superiors in Moscow held considerable influence over the activities and priorities of their agents based in the provinces, but regional interests were as or more influential in practice. Federal agencies showed preliminary signs of capture by provincial politicians, and this may be one cause of some of the policy compliance problems the center faced in the periphery in the last ten years.

DEPARTMENTS OF REGIONAL AND REPUBLICAN ADMINISTRATIONS. Where federal agencies held notable sway over the activities of fund branch officials, the influence of the central state over appointed officials within the regional executive (or administration, as it is often called) is far less. As noted earlier, on paper the departments and committees of the regional administration are dually subordinated to federal and regional agencies. This is an administrative holdover from the Soviet period. In practice, in the post-Soviet era the picture is quite different, providing further evidence of the wavering infrastructural authority of the post-Soviet central state de facto in the provinces. The 417 representatives (included in our sample) of regional and republican departments of executive power were asked a series of questions designed to probe the various influences on their decision-making processes: what factors influenced the general activities of their departments; and with what groups, individuals, and institutions they worked most effectively in implementing their policies.

---

[28] Author's interview with the head of the Orenburg branch of the Pension Fund of the Russian Federation, May 11, 2000.

[29] An interview completed on June 20, 2000 in the Republic of Bashkortostan with the head of the Bashkortostan Medical Insurance Fund confirmed that when federal fund directives from Moscow contradicted republican government policy or law, "the government comes first. The Moscow Fund could write for an explanation or tell me they don't like something. They can criticize me, but order me they cannot."

TABLE 3. *Factors Influencing Activities of Departments.*

(Q. To what degree do the following factors influence the activity of your department?
    Respondents were asked to indicate their response on a five-point scale: not at all =1, a little = 2, moderately = 3, a good deal = 4, very strongly = 5. Means were calculated such that the higher the mean, the greater the degree of reported influence.)

Degree of Influence:	Economic Departments N = 200	Social Policy Departments N = 210	Means of All Excluding No Response N = 410
Regional Influences:			
Agreement between oblast/repub. exec. and leg. powers	4.27 (1.03)	4.39 (.87)	4.33 (.96)
Other departments of the regional administration	3.57 (1.03)	3.64 (1.06)	3.61 (1.03)
Ag't between oblast administration and city	4.05 (1.05)	4.41 (.80)	4.25 (.96)
Governor/president of region	4.86 (.41)	4.90 (.34)	4.88 (.38)
Decisions of oblast legislature	4.30 (.85)	4.25 (.86)	4.27 (.35)
Federal Influences:			
Federal law	4.18 (1.00)	4.19 (.91)	4.18 (.95)
Presidential decrees	3.81 (1.24)	3.85 (1.13)	3.83 (1.18)
Presidential representative	2.68 (1.30)	2.72 (1.28)	2.70 (1.29)
Federal ministries	3.43 (1.15)	3.70 (1.04)	3.57 (1.10)
Federal financing	3.39 (1.65)	3.90 (1.37)	3.65 (1.53)

Table 3 provides some insight into the relative strengths of federal versus regional factors influencing departmental activities. If we divide the table into two sections – the first section for regional influences and the second for federal – it is striking how much more influential regional institutions are over federal policy instruments in the activities of regional departments of the administration.

Governors of oblasts and krais and presidents of republics were by far the most significant influence on the activities of the departments of the administration (mean score of 4.88, shown in the last column of the table). It is not surprising that the heads of regional administrations had the most influence over agents of their administrations, but it is notable how much more influential they were compared to federal ministries in particular (3.57) considering the official fiction of dual subordination.

(The differences between these two paired means is significant at the .01 level.)

Also notable in Table 3 is the smaller degree of influence of federal law (4.18) as compared to regional law (4.27). (The difference between this set of paired means is significant at the .01 level.) Further, federal financing appeared to be a relatively important factor in the activities of departments of regional administrations (with a mean score of 3.65), but it was less important than any single regional factor, but one (the influence on one department within the administration on another). (Again, differences between the mean of responses regarding the influence of federal financing were paired with each of the means depicting regional influences, and differences were significant at the .01 level.)

Finally, if we compare responses across policy type (economic versus social), a few interesting similarities and differences emerge in regional versus federal influences on departmental activities. Respondents from departments that were more strongly focused on economic policy (the departments of agriculture, trade, and the economy) as opposed to social policy (social welfare, education and health departments) appear to be slightly more influenced in some respects by regional than federal factors. For example, the decisions of the oblast legislature mattered slightly more to the activities of regional departments with economic foci (4.30) than they did for departments more closely tied to social policy (4.25), although clearly oblast legislation was important to both sets of departments. Further, the decisions of federal ministries to which these departments also reported were slightly less important to the activities of regional departments concerned with economic policy than those concerned with social policy (means of 3.43 and 3.70, respectively, with the difference between the paired means statistically significant at .01). Federal financing was also more important for departments working in the social policy realm than in the economic policy realm (with means of 3.90 and 3.39, respectively). Although the difference between this pair of means is small, it is statistically significant at the .05 level.

Differences between factors influencing these two policy types, however, were not great and the same general pattern is discernible for both. For example, for both sets of departments (economic and social), heads of the regional executive (governor or republican president) were by far the most influential factors in the activities of the departments surveyed, with means of 4.86 and 4.90, respectively (the difference between this pair of means was not statistically significant). Finally, in both instances very few regional factors were less influential than any single federal factor. Indeed,

TABLE 4. *With whom do you work most effectively in implementing the priorities of your department? (Total n = 417)*

Respondents were asked to indicate up to three organizations. As a result, the total number of responses exceeds the 417 respondents in this part of the survey.)

	Total Number of Mentions	Percent of Total Number of Mentions
Local/regional business circles	138	11.9%
Entrepreneurs from other regions	21	1.8%
Unions	26	2.2%
Political parties and movements	2	0.2%
Other social organizations	13	1.1%
Media	68	5.9%
Church	2	0.2%
Oblast/republican legislative organs	184	15.9%
Leadership of oblast administration	351	30.3%
Local organs of self-government	206	17.8%
Federal organs of power	149	12.8%
TOTAL	1,160	100.0%

only in the cases of the influences of other departments of the regional administration for both economic and social policy departments (means of 3.57 and 3.64, respectively), and only in the case of the influence of agreement between the regional administration and the city for economic departments (mean of 4.05), were means of regional influences smaller than the mean of any single federal factor.

The group of departmental representatives also indicated what societal groups and institutions they worked with more or less effectively in implementing the policy priorities of their departments. (Results are reported in Table 4.) Respondents were asked to name three organizations or institutions (in no particular order), and were also invited to add to the list we provided. Assistance in implementing policy was understood as ranging from providing funds or other material assistance to providing publicity or organizational and technical resources.

Significantly here too, regional heads of executives were by far the most important force in policy implementation – with 30.3 percent of mentions. Regional legislatures and city governments were also important to the policy implementation process with 15.9 percent and 17.8 percent of mentions, respectively. Federal organs of power (including federal ministries and commitees) placed fourth with 12.8 percent. Following very closely, however, were regional business circles. This category includes heads of regional enterprises and may also be taken in at least a few cases to mean regional criminal groups. It is striking that this group was only slightly smaller (11.9 percent) than were federal organs of power in terms of influence on regional departmental administrators.

Moreover, the evidence in this section indicates that relative to regional administrative and political bodies, federal infrastructural power was lower and this may be the root of the regional noncompliance problem. Federal authorities and organizations have less influence in determining policy priorities at the regional level than did regional state forces. Federal authorities and organizations clearly had considerably less influence over the activities of departments of regional administrations than did regional political forces (both legislative and executive in particular). Given the striking degree of influence regional governors in particular had over federal agencies (the funds) and over agencies that were ostensibly dually subordinated to federal and regional officials (the departments of regional administrations), it is important to examine in greater detail the influences upon the governors themselves.

POLITICAL OFFICIALS (GOVERNORS OF OBLASTS, PRESIDENTS OF REPUBLICS). The group of political officials in the regions responded to a virtually identical set of questions as the group of appointed regional officials working in the various departments of regional administrations.

Table 5 provides comparative detail regarding federal versus regional influences on the general activities of regional heads of executives. As with Table 3, regional factors were almost universally more influential than federal factors. Federal financing and federal law were clearly important to the activities of the administrations in the provinces (with means of 4.13 and 4.25, respectively), but neither of them were more influential than agreement between branches of government at the regional level (mean of 4.61) or the decisions of the regional legislature alone (4.31), although financing was slightly more influential than agreement between the oblast administration and the administration of the capital city of the province (4.23). (Differences between paired means were significant at the .01 level.) Federal ministries proved slightly less important an influence over the general activities of the administration than did regional departments (means of 3.23 and 3.35, respectively, with a statistically significant difference of .05 between paired means). Presidential decrees proved less influential (mean score of 3.75) than federal laws (4.13) and the decisions of regional legislatures in particular (4.31), with differences

TABLE 5. *Factors Influencing the Activities of Regional Administrations (Executives)*

Q. To what degree do the following factors influence the activities of your administration?

Respondents were asked to indicate their response on a five-point scale: not at All = 1, a little = 2, moderately = 3, a good deal = 4, very strongly = 5. Means were calculated such that the higher the mean, the greater the degree of reported influence. *Note that in a few regions there was no presidential representative at the time of the interviews. Responses were deleted from these regions.)

Degree of Influence:	Means of All Excluding No Response (N = 72)
Regional Influences	
Agreement between oblast/republican executive and legislative branches	4.61 (.72)
Departments of the regional administration	3.34 (1.08)
Agreement between oblast/republican administration and capital city	4.23 (.99)
Decisions of oblast/republican legislature	4.31 (0.81)
Federal Influences	
Federal law	4.13 (0.89)
Presidential decrees	3.75 (1.08)
Presidential representative*	2.60 (1.33)
Federal ministries	3.23 (1.00)
Federal financing	4.25 (1.01)

between these two pairs of means significant at the .01 level. As with the responses in Table 3 from representatives from regional departments of the administration, regional heads of administration report that presidential representatives have little influence on the activities of their governments (mean score of 2.60).

The fact that decisions of the regional legislature were reported by both heads of administrations (Table 5) and representatives from departments of the administration (Table 3) to be more influential on their decision processes and activities than were federal laws may provide some basis for the resiliency of noncompliance in the 1990s. Moreover, the evidence in Tables 3 and 5 in particular suggests that if federal law were to conflict with regional law, regional law would likely triumph in practice. This provides some of the administrative underpinnings of chronic regional noncompliance with federal law.

TABLE 6. *Groups, Organizations with Which Heads of Executives Work Most Effectively in Implementing the Priorities of Their Administrations.*

(Q. With whom do you work most effectively in implementing the priorities of your administration? Total N = 207. Respondents were permitted to mention up to three groups or organizations.)

	Number of Mentions	Percent of Total Number of mentions
Local/regional business circles	135	26.7%
Entrepreneurs from other regions	25	5.0%
Unions	17	3.4%
Political parties and movements	15	3.0%
Other social organizations	9	1.8%
Media	54	10.7%
Church	3	0.6%
Oblast legislative organs	75	14.9%
Federal organs of power	92	18.2%
Local organs of self-government (city governments)	54	10.7%
TOTAL	505	100.0%

Finally, in addition to federal versus regional organs of government, heads of regional executives reported with which societal forces they worked most effectively in implementing the priorities of their administrations. This is reported in Table 6.

Somewhat unexpectedly, regional business circles were mentioned by far the most frequently – garnering 26.7 percent of mentions. In fact, although federal organs of power were of use at the policy implementation stage (garnering 18.2 percent of mentions), the federal level was mentioned markedly less than regional business interests. Other social forces that in more developed democracies we might expect would influence policy implementation – such as churches, unions, or other voluntary social organizations – were mentioned infrequently (between 0.6 percent and 3.4 percent of total mentions), although the media proved surprisingly effective with 10.7 percent of total mentions.

In sum, these results provide a complex picture of the relationships between central and regional components of the Russian state. The survey of public officials provides some empirical underpinnings to the pervasive regional noncompliance to federal authority – particularly concerning regulation of the national market – that has persisted in Russian regions throughout the last decade. Regional governments effectively usurped policy-making authority (and economic policy authority in particular) more than the center "delegated" it. Russia has not witnessed a gradual and natural creation of a nascent federal system as much as a rapid, damaging decentralization that has left the central state unable to effectively regulate policy in the periphery. Federalism is generally taken to require the autonomy of at least two levels of government, each sovereign in their specified spheres of policy.[30] Yet in Russia the central state became so disempowered in the regions that it is fair to argue that the system of center-periphery relations at the end of the 1990s did not meet this baseline requirement of federalism. As a result, Russian decentralization did not help to promote competition among regions for investment and labor or to reduce trade barriers – key ingredients for growing markets – as these require not only the devolution of economic policy-making authority to regional governments, but also a central state strong enough (even if limited in the scope of its responsibilities) to regulate basic market functions across the country.

It is also fair to argue that the Russian central state did not merely tolerate mild or limited transgressions of its policies and regulations to avoid a major upheaval of the political and social system or alternately, because tolerating such transgressions was a "go along to get along" strategy to make the system function. That is, unlike the U.S. experience with prohibition laws or school segregation, for example, where the federal government tolerated violations of its laws to prevent serious social disruptions, in the Russian case the range of transgressions was so great, it is hard to see how or why the central state or society at large would benefit from "going along." Further, there is firm evidence that the center sought to prevent these transgressions – from appeals to the Constitutional Court, to a careful cataloging of noncompliance by the Ministry of Justice, to regulations demanding that regional officials respect the autonomy of federal officials working in their provinces, to demands that violations of federal law and the constitution be retracted and corrected.

Clearly such transgressions hindered the capacity of the central state to ensure the delivery of public goods and to encourage further development of market mechanisms and economic growth. Throughout the 1990s pensions were usually paid late if at all, labor mobility remained low, domestic and foreign investment remained sluggish, and the economy rapidly and deeply declined.

[30] William Riker, *Federalism: Origins, Operation, Significance* (Boston: Little, Brown, 1964), p. 3.

Instead, noncompliance to federal authority, undergirded by the co-optation of central bureaucrats in the provinces, represented a real erosion of central state authority. The Russian central state throughout the 1990s effectively lost its ability to maintain a common market and establish a single economic expanse. Russia, therefore, still has not reaped the rewards of models of decentralized development, as these require constraints on not just the central state, but also an institutional and political framework capable of ensuring constraints on regional governments as well. In the absence of a central state strong enough to ensure capital and labor mobility, the elimination of internal trade barriers, and the protection of property rights and contracts, Russia's decentralization process has been more market stalling than market promoting. The next section endeavors to explain how and why this happened.

PART II: W(H)ITHER THE CENTRAL STATE?: THE ROOTS OF REGIONAL RESISTANCE

Russia's economic misfortunes are sometimes contrasted to China's relative successes. Although a thorough comparison of Russian and Chinese reform paths is obviously beyond the scope of this essay, it is useful to underscore that one clear difference is the comparative degree to which the Chinese central state retained its authority to govern the economy vis-à-vis regional governments. When China initiated the decentralization of its economy, it did not simultaneously initiate decentralizing political reform. Indeed, the central government in China retained the power of promotion and dismissal of regional officials through the resiliency of the Communist Party where Russian reformers under Boris Yeltsin allowed competitive elections for regional government across Russia by 1995. Further (and relatedly), Chinese central officials effectively delegated their authority where, in contrast, Russian central officials largely had their economic policy-making authority wrested from them by newly elected regional actors. The Chinese center has retained its ability to regulate the economy and control the pace and scope of market development. The Russian central state clearly has not.

Undeniably, the decision of Russian reformers to undertake simultaneous democratic and market reform was far bolder than the decision of Deng Xiaoping to embrace markets alone. Indeed, the relative successes of the first ten years of Russia's reforms were primarily in the political rather than the economic realm. Despite how badly things were going

Whither the Central State?

economically for Russia, in the first decade of reform at least, elections were held, free speech was permitted, and political pluralism persevered. (Under President Putin, the latter two political gains have come under serious threat, however). But Russia's path was intrinsically more challenging than China's as a result. Introducing political liberalization simultaneously with sweeping economic change meant that the latter occurred in a far more unpredictable political context. Russia faced the daunting task of rebuilding its entire economy while operating under a novel set of political constraints.

As a result, new interests like regional political actors and powerful economic groups entered the central state's political arena as they tried to limit its incursion into their economic affairs. The formation of these groups really began even prior to the collapse of the Soviet Union when Mikhail Gorbachev introduced his Law on Cooperatives (1988) and Law on State Enterprises (1987). These laws enabled enterprise directors to steer resources out of the control of state planning agencies. State enterprises were henceforward allowed access to new domestic and foreign markets as well as being permitted to create daughter companies in the form of cooperatives through which they could spin off profits from the sale of excess productive output. Not only did they become adept at the practice of hiding revenues from central planners or reselling excess enterprise production for a personal profit, but under Gorbachev's reforms (particularly the allowance for the establishment of cooperatives), opportunities for enterprise directors to reap more personal wealth from state property were also greatly increased.[31] The Law on Cooperatives in particular allowed wily enterprise directors to set up cooperatives that were sometimes no more than joint ventures or lease agreements that generated private profits from state-owned assets. Enterprise directors clearly had doubts about the center's ability to punish their activities beyond the plan. This in turn provided motivation to collude with regional authorities through horizontal networks to extract inputs and dispose of outputs beyond the plan rather than working through the traditional vertical hierarchies of Soviet central planning agencies. A wave of "spontaneous" privatizations was initiated in the late 1980s whereby enterprise management took de facto control of their factories.

---

[31] Similar arguments can be found in Vitali Naishul, "Institutional Development in the USSR," *Cato Journal* 11 (Winter 1992) as well as in Michael McFaul, "State Power, Institutional Change, and the Politics of Privatization in Russia," *World Politics* 47, No. 2 (January 1995), pp. 210–43.

Following the collapse of the Soviet Union in December 1991, Boris Yeltsin's team of economic reformers launched a program of rapid privatization in 1992 to create a new class of private owners and to destroy the powerful formerly Soviet ministries charged with controlling the planned economy. This on the face of it was positive if the goal was to provide the foundation of a market economy – private ownership. But the speed and scope of the privatization process and the compromises made to achieve privatization (including allowing a strikingly high degree of insider ownership in light of the amount of insider privatization that had already taken place) created a pocket of private interests capable of capturing parts of the state for personal gain. The economic transition, therefore, consolidated the power of a segment of society with a vested interest in keeping the state weak in exactly those areas that a competitive market requires that the state be strong. These interests remain untamed and directly challenge the degree to which the state can regulate markets and implement policy beyond the Kremlin. There was (and remains) often strong resistance to central state policies and regulation at the local level and few institutional solutions to overcome this resistance. The impetus to contradict and failure to comply with central policies as well as the co-opting of federal bureaucrats then came not from elected public officials alone, but from the small circles of business interests by whom they were captured, to whom they became accountable and with whom their futures are closely intertwined.

These early beneficiaries from the transition had little interest in promoting central state regulation of their activities. In order to protect their early financial and property gains (and prevent further losses in the form of bankruptcies, for example), they have effectively carved up and co-opted parts of the state – particularly at the regional level – for personal financial advantage. As a result, regional governments in Russia tended to pass legislation that contradicted the federal constitution predominantly in ways that affected economic conditions in their regions, thereby undermining the central state's ability to even minimally regulate their activities.

The underlying cause of a region establishing a citizenship requirement for voters or language requirements for elected officials in contradiction to the federal constitution was to limit and control who was entitled to select regional leaders, who those regional leaders would be, and what policies they would pursue. (These are categorized as "regional structure" in Figure 1.) Regional violations of federal housing and privatization policies were also designed to ensure that regional interests controlled valuable regional assets. Restructuring of judiciaries was yet another strategy to control mechanisms by which ownership disputes might be resolved, ensuring once again that regional interests were protected and advantaged. (These violations are categorized as "judicial/legal" in Figure 1.) The imposition of illegal tariffs and taxes on goods entering many regions ensured that local goods and services were privileged over those from outside the region. Restrictions on freedom of movement through the residence permit system that persisted in many regions (and categorized as "citizenship" in Figure 1) was a strategy for limiting labor mobility in local production facilities, maintaining the prevailing economic balance of power and preventing further change. Finally, declarations of regional ownership of natural resources were further mechanisms by which regional governments, under the influence of regional economic interests, aimed to ensure they benefited the most from what lies under their soil.

To provide more detail regarding how exactly regional economic interests became entangled in regional government, it will be useful to review evidence from other recent studies as well as to recall some of the compromises made during the early phases of privatization in Russia. Analyses by the World Bank support the argument and evidence here that both regional governments and enterprise insiders had vested interests in maintaining the status quo and therefore in working to keep the central state from upsetting this regional balance of forces.[32]

The interdependence and collusion between regional enterprises and governments can be traced back to the Soviet era, but was further extended through the 1992 privatization program that institutionalized the de facto ownership that many managers had established over their factories in the late 1980s. All three variants of the 1992 mass privatization program under Yeltsin (and under which 15,000 firms were privatized) enabled

---

[32] In particular, see Raj M. Desai and Itzhak Goldberg, "The Vicious Circles of Control: Regional Governments and Insiders in Privatized Russian Enterprises," Policy Research Working Paper 2287 (Washington, DC: The World Bank, Europe and Central Asia Region Private and Financial Sectors Development Unit, February 2000); Joel S. Hellman, Geraint Jones, Daniel Kaufmann, "Seize the State, Seize the Day: State Capture, Corruption and Influence in Transition," Policy Research Working Paper 2444 (Washington, DC: The World Bank, World Bank Institute Governance, Regulation and Finance Division and Europe and Central Asia Region, Public Sector Group, and European Bank of Reconstruction and Development Office of the Chief Economist, September 2000); Joel S. Hellman, Geraint Jones, Daniel Kaufmann, Mark Schankerman, "Measuring Governance, Corruption and State Capture: How Firms and Bureaucrats Shape the Business Environment in Transition Economies," (Washington, DC: The World Bank, World Bank Institute Governance, Regulation and Finance Division and European Bank for Reconstruction and Development Chief Economist's Office, April 2000).

insiders – managers and workers alike – to purchase up to 51 percent of shares outright. The fact that privatization vouchers were also tradable under the program allowed insiders to buy additional vouchers. This ended up being about 65 percent on average.[33] Thus, the early compromises built into the 1992 privatization program enabled insiders to maintain effective control over their enterprises. This in turn initiated a property rights regime that proved both difficult to change and a drag on investment and productivity.

The 1992 privatization program made this huge concession to managers of large Soviet-era enterprises in order to effectively buy and ensure their participation in the privatization program.[34] This compromise was also a way to provide some assurance to newly elected regional governments that regional outsiders would not immediately be empowered to substantially interfere with the regional economy for which they were now accountable through elections. Nonetheless, the hope was that gradually outsiders would invest in these firms and that ownership and management would become separated. Almost a decade later, however, there was general agreement that managers and employees continued to hold 50 to 60 percent of shares in privatized enterprises.[35]

Managers' de facto control often exceeded their actual direct ownership of shares of their companies as many employee shares did not come with voting rights. Managers also routinely employed tactics (like threatening layoffs or firings, withholding wages, etc.) to prevent employees from selling their shares to outsiders. Moreover, "despite other positive signs in the Russian economy, the enterprise sector remained in a low investment, low productivity trap."[36] Wage, supply, and tax arrears persisted and interenterprise barter payments reached half of all industrial sales by mid-1999.[37] Insiders received particularized benefits while the general state of productivity and investment declined. Although the original argument for rapid privatization was to prevent asset stripping by

---

[33] Desai and Goldberg, p. 4.
[34] Andrei Shleifer and Daniel Treisman, *Without a Map: Political Tactics and Economic Reform in Russia* (Cambridge: MIT Press, 2000), pp. 27–34. Note that I am not making any normative argument or judgment regarding the wisdom of these concessions. I am merely pointing out their political effect on regional government relationships with enterprises.
[35] Desai and Goldberg, p. 5.
[36] Ibid. p. 7.
[37] Ibid. Their source for this economic data is Russian Economic Baromerter and Russian Economic Trends. World Bank, "Dismantling Russia's Nonpayments System: Creating Conditions for Growth," 1999.

industrial managers in state-owned enterprises, the measure backfired. World Bank analysis indicates that,

> instead of increasing a firm's value through reinvestment, enterprise manager-owners have typically extracted income streams from these firms at the expense of minority shareholders. The managers have diverted cash flows to offshore accounts and shell corporations, concentrated losses among subsidiaries held by outsiders . . . and delay[ed] payments of dividends.[38]

Other studies by the World Bank characterize the dynamic between enterprises and the state in some postcommunist countries – including Russia – as indicative of a "capture economy."[39] This denotes both the influence a firm may have on the formation of laws as well as administrative corruption, which may entail not only conflict of interest of government officials but also private payments by firms to public officials to "distort the prescribed implementation of official rules and policies."[40]

Analyses employing the 1999 Business Environment and Enterprise Performance Survey (BEEPS) of over 3,000 firms in twenty countries in Eastern Europe and the former Soviet Union indicate that both older and newer firms engaged in attempts to influence and often capture the state. This behavior on the part of firms was to ensure the perpetuation of the property regime described previously that favors them (by limiting competition and entry into their markets, receiving a favorable tax regime, thereby preserving their rent seeking opportunities and otherwise protecting them from central state regulation and oversight), but that provided negative externalities to the economy as a whole.

It would be a mistake, however, to assume that regional governments were merely victims of state capture rather than frequently willing participants in an interdependent or more collusive relationship. For their part, regional governments sought to maintain involvement in and sometimes control over the operations of regional enterprises particularly important to the regional economy – even if the latter were formally privatized. The intent was to prevent large-scale changes within enterprises that might threaten the local workforce with unemployment and "to preserve the rent-seeking opportunities for vested interests."[41] Moreover, a system of

---

[38] Desai and Goldberg, p. 9.
[39] Hellman, Jones, and Kaufmann. The BEEPS data indicate that Russia is a comparatively "high capture" economy.
[40] Hellman, Jones, and Kaufmann, p. 2.
[41] Desai and Goldberg, p. 10.

TABLE 7. *The Influences of Societal Groups and Organizations on the Activities of Regional Political Officials (governors or deputy governors of oblasts and presidents of republics.)*

(Q.To what degree do the following organizations and groups influence the activity of your administration?

Respondents were asked to indicate their response on a five-point scale: not at all = 1, a little = 2, moderately = 3, a good deal = 4, very strongly = 5. Means were calculated such that the higher the mean, the greater the degree of reported influence.)

Degree of Influence:	Means of All Excluding No Response (N = 66)
Local and regional business circles	3.71 (1.0)
Unions	2.58 (1.0)
Political parties	2.12 (1.10)
Social organizations	1.88 (.97)
Media	3.34 (0.94)
Church	1.98 (1.15)

interdependence grew up between regional business and government that favored the economic status quo:

In certain regions . . . the nexus of interdependence between government officials and enterprise management typically grant[ed] management quasi-governmental powers, including influence over executing and law-enforcing apparatus in a given locality, . . .[42]

Evidence of the influence of regional business circles, versus other social forces, on regional politics and politicians comes also from the survey responses of public officials reported in Table 7. Top political officials in the regions were asked to indicate to what degree social, political, and economic groups and organizations influenced the activities of their administrations. Local and regional business circles were reportedly more influential than any other social or political group or institution, with a mean of 3.71 (differences between this mean paired with each of the others in the table below were statistically significant at the .01 level). This stands in particularly stark contrast to the influence of social organizations (for example, political lobby groups like Soldiers' Mothers) with a mean of 1.88, unions (mean of 2.58), and political parties (mean of 2.12).

[42] Ibid.

A relatively small contingent of respondents in our survey of officials (11.9 percent) reported that at the same time they worked for the regional government, they also worked outside of the regional government and legislative structures. Of those, 46.9 percent reported that their private sector position was in an enterprise within the region and that they held a leadership position in the enterprise. In the absence of strong conflict of interest laws, this provides some evidence of the penetration of regional government by powerful business interests. It also demonstrates that although there has obviously been some direct incursion into regional government by regional economic interests, these groups have obtained a remarkable degree of influence without actually having to assume administrative positions themselves.

The penetration of regional economic interests goes far beyond these tentative forays into the bureaucracy itself to more determined and far-reaching penetration of legislatures and executives of many regions. From detailed analysis of regional electoral data, we know that regional legislatures were frequently filled with deputies elected to represent powerful local economic interests throughout the 1990s. In 1997, the Central Electoral Commission reported that, "In practically all legislative organs of the subjects of the Federation it is possible to meet leaders of strong enterprises and commercial structures of the region. In the Republic of Sakha (Yakutia) it is the leaders of diamond and gold enterprises, in the Republics of Komi and Tatarstan and Tiumen and Sakhalin oblasts it is oil companies. In Cheliabinsk oblast it is metallurgical factories, and in Murmansk oblast, it is the Kol'skii Nuclear Power Station." As the Central Electoral Commission itself noted, this resulted in the "strengthening of the influence of economic lobbyists on the economic policies of subjects of the Russian Federation. Aside from this is the threat of confrontation of the regional elite with the federal center in constructing the interests of the regions."[43]

In addition, regression analysis from our survey of regional government executives combined with the data on regional noncompliance to federal law and the constitution provides a reliable indicator of the extent to which business interests may influence regional executives' policy decisions and policy independence from the center. For example, there is strong evidence that the twenty-eight regions (of the sixty-six included in the dataset) with the most resilient records of noncompliance to federal

[43] *Vybopry*, p. 637.

policy (that is, having greater than the mean number of violations per region) are regions where the heads of executives (or their deputies) reported significant influence of regional business interests on the activities of their administrations. The coefficient for business group influence on the governor is 5.48 and significant at .05, indicating that in regions where the reported influence on the governor by business groups was high, the region committed more than five additional noncompliant acts.[44]

There is reason to believe, therefore, that the underlying cause of the central state's growing inability to govern in the Russian periphery throughout the 1990s was a result of the influence exercised by regional business interests on policy makers and bureaucrats. This has important implications for the past and future policy instruments and institutional mechanisms that the central state might use to enhance its capacity to govern the economy in the Russian periphery.

The Failures of Past and Present Mechanisms of Enhancing Central State Capacity

Some analysts of Russia might argue that in the past, the central state maintained some control over regions through strategic dispensation of budgetary transfers. Daniel Treisman, for example, claims that regions and republics who "most adroitly manipulated the weapons of early sovereignty declarations ... managed to extract substantially more [from Moscow] than those that were more docile."[45] By effectively buying off the most aggressive and noncompliant regions, Treisman maintains, Moscow was able to stem a secessionist tide in the early 1990s. That is, despite sovereignty declarations by a number of republics of the Federation,

---

[44] The percentage of the population that was not ethnically Russian also appeared to be important in explaining the behavior of the most noncompliant regions in this dataset, but with a relatively small coefficient of −.301, it was not as important as the influence of business groups on the leading political figure in the region, the governor. A region's status as a net donor to the federal budget (as opposed to status as net recipient) had a large, positive coefficient as my theory would predict (5.74), but was not quite significant at an acceptable level. The same is true for a region's volume of industrial production. More detailed models exploring these relationships can be found in Chapter 5, "Retrenchment over Reform: Obstacles to Central Authority in the Periphery," of Kathryn Stoner-Weiss, *Resisting the State: Reform and Retrenchment in Post-Soviet Russia* (New York: Cambridge University Press, forthcoming).

[45] Daniel Treisman, "The Politics of Intergovernmental Transfers in Post-Soviet Russia," *British Journal of Political Science* 26 (1996), p. 327. See also Daniel Treisman, *After the Deluge: Regional Crises and Political Consolidation in Russia* (Ann Arbor: University of Michigan Press, 1999).

only Chechnya actually attempted to secede, while others gained budgetary concessions from Moscow in return for their remaining in the Federation.

The picture of the central state that this sort of argument depicts, however, is a more or less coherent unit able to act adroitly and resolutely, albeit in a limited way. But faced with the array of examples herein of regional governments defying the central government and the skewed hierarchy of relationships governing the actions of federal and regional officials in the provinces indicated by our survey, it is difficult to accept this conceptualization as completely accurate. Further, Tables 3 and 5 quite clearly indicate that although fiscal transfers and other forms of financial contributions from the center matter, they had less influence on regional government executives as a group and on regional departments of the executive than some key regional political and economic forces in particular (for example, agreement between the regional executive and legislature and the governor or president of the region alone). At best, it is more likely that the center's strategic distribution of budgetary funds *may* have helped to curb early regional secessionism – perhaps the most extreme form of noncompliance to the central state. But this practice does not appear to have been successful in stemming the steady tide of smaller, regular infractions against federal law and central policy that occurred later. This kind of "legal separatism" and noncompliance was clearly pervasive throughout the 1990s and even seemed to increase toward the end of the decade.[46] So even if control over fiscal flows was an important instrument in curbing regional secessionism in the past and those taps can be turned off gradually in the future, experience demonstrates that this is an imprecise and clumsy instrument for curbing less dramatic, but equally damaging, regional challenges to the central state's ability to govern key aspects of the economy.

Undeniably, however, during his eight and a half years as Russia's president, Boris Yeltsin chose to force compliance to the constitution and federal law in certain key instances in some regions throughout the 1990s.[47]

---

[46] The term "legal separatism" comes from former First Deputy Prime Minister, Anatolii Chubais. See "Center Continues to Rail Against 'Legal Separatism,'" *Institute for East-West Studies, Russian Regional Report* 1, No. 10 (November 6, 1996).

[47] For example, Yeltsin issued a decree to compel Udmurtiia's parliament to follow a Constitutional Court ruling and end its practice of appointing mayors in the republic. See "Newly Elected Governors Grapple with Moscow, Regional Problems," *Institute for East-West Studies, Russian Regional Report* 3, No. 2 (January 15, 1998). Throughout the spring of 2000, Putin issued a number of similar decrees to errant regions and republics.

But these tended to be interventions on big issues of symbolic importance to the federal government. More recently, President Putin managed to win some concessions from a few regions in reversing their most severe constitutional transgressions.[48] Even more significantly perhaps, Putin introduced what he hoped would be an institutional remedy to the weakness of the central state in the periphery. He created a new layer of his presidential administration, the thrice-reformed office of presidential representative. In May 2000, Putin installed new federal representatives (governors general) in each of seven newly created "super districts" (each encompassing approximately twelve to fifteen oblasts, krais, republics, or autonomies). As with the two previous iterations of this office under Yeltsin, the new representatives of the federal executive had poorly defined responsibilities. It is unclear, for example, whether they were supposed to oversee the actions of regional governments in general or merely federal bureaucrats in the regions.[49] Further, both heads of regional administrations and federal bureaucrats, like the heads of the regional branches of federal funds, quickly became resentful of what they perceived as ineffective interference in their activities.[50] In a study of the results of this reform in the southern federal district, Natalia Zubarevich reported that the governor general there had done little to stop gubernatorial patronage of local companies. She concluded, "the presidential envoy's battle with corruption is selective, of little impact . . . and achieves its purposes only when the envoy's interests coincide with the interests of another level of government [either city or oblast level]."[51] Referring to the activities of the president's envoy in his region, the governor of Leningrad oblast asserted that by the summer of 2002, "results are not visible" and that "We need to create the appropriate conditions for business, not set up gosplans [referring to

---

[48] Too much can be made of his relative successes in this regard thus far, however. Many "corrected" laws themselves have been found to be further infringements of the constitution or federal law. See *East West Institute's Russian Regional Report* 6, No. 5 (February 7, 2001).

[49] See Soobshenie Press-Sluzhbii Prezidenta Rossiiskoi Federatsii, 2000-05-13-002 Ukaz "O polnomochnom presdstavitele Prezidenta Rossiiskoi Federatsii v federal'nom okruge." (Decree on the authority of the representative of the president of the Russian Federation, May 13, 2000). See also the interview with Sergei Samoilov, Head of the Presidential Administration of the Russian Federation in the *East West Institute's Russian Regional Report*, August 4, 2000.

[50] Robert Orttung, "Leningrad Governor Critical of Federal Reforms," Russian Regional Report, August 2, 2002 and Robert Orttung, "Putin's Governors General," *East West Institute's Russian Regional Report* 7, No. 20 (June 17, 2002).

[51] Natalia Zuberevich, "Kazantsev Has Little Impact in the Southern Federal District," *East West Institute's Russian Regional Report* 7, No. 29, (November 25, 2002).

the huge former Soviet economic planning agency]."[52] Indeed, this institutional solution to the center's problems in the regions appears to have merely created an additional layer of the Russian state – a strategy that has already proven ineffective in enhancing governing capacity in post-Soviet Russia.[53] Finally, just as some regions were more assertive than others vis-à-vis their authority with the federal government through the 1990s, according to a 2002 report compiled by a group of western analysts of Putin's federal representatives, "weak governors tend to heed and meet with federal representatives, while powerful ones keep their distance."[54] In sum, Putin's creation of these seven federal districts headed by representatives accountable directly to him did little to interrupt previous patterns of center-periphery relations in Russia.

Beyond this reform, however, Putin achieved the adoption of two important laws in the State Duma. One reestablished the way in which Russia's upper house of parliament, the Federation Council, is formed such that regional governors and heads of regional legislatures no longer automatically gained seats. Instead, two representatives from each region would be approved by each regional legislature (and executive). Although at first glance this appeared to significantly weaken the influence of the governors on central policy by effectively removing them from their privileged place in federal politics, it was not obvious that the goal of strengthening the central state vis-à-vis the provinces was achieved. Because the two new representatives are appointed and dismissed at the pleasure of regional legislatures and executives, it is unclear exactly how much regional power and gubernatorial influence in particular would be diminished in the operations of the Federation Council.

---

[52] As quoted in Orttung, August 2, 2002.
[53] Indeed, the Russian state apparatus actually grew by the end of the 1990s relative to its size in the first few years following the collapse of the Soviet Union. The Russian State Committee on Statistics reported in 1999 that despite central state efforts to cut the size of the Russian bureaucracy, it grew steadily in terms of the number of officials employed in federal agencies and regional administrations. Whereas in 1994, for example, there were a reported 1,004,000 officials employed at all layers of the state, that number had increased each year to reach 1,133,000 by the end of 1999. Not surprisingly, therefore, state spending on its apparatus also increased steadily since 1994 (the first year for which figures were available) from 1.73 percent of all state spending in 1994 to 2.4 percent in 1998. These numbers are reported in Vitaly Golovachev, "Russian Bureaucrats Reproducing Like Rabbits," *Trud*, June 14, 2000. Data on state spending comes from the federal law on the budget for each of the corresponding years. These laws are published in *Sobrianie aktov gosudarstvennog zakonodatelstva Rossisskogo Federatsii* (Moscow: Government of the Russian Federation, 1994, 1995, 1996, 1997, and 1998).
[54] Orttung, "Putin's Governors General."

Potentially more potent, Putin's second legislative initiative enabled the president to dismiss regional governors and legislators who, according to the Russian courts, passed laws or decrees in violation of federal law or the constitution. Although this was an ostensibly hefty political weapon to hurl at recalcitrant regional authorities, it has not greatly enhanced central state capacity to govern the economy in the periphery. By 2002, the regional lobby in the State Duma amended this law such that it became virtually impossible to use in practice.[55] Finally, the evidence and arguments throughout this essay indicate that even if Putin were successful in using his new legislative tool occasionally to remove an errant governor or dismiss a rebellious legislature, at present there is no comparable mechanism by which to challenge the election of a new governor or legislator similarly entrenched in local elite business circles whose interests so often conflicted with central policies throughout the last decade.

A notable example of the practical political weakness of this seemingly powerful tool occurred in early 2001 in Putin's dealings with the governor of Primorskii Krai, Evgenii Nazdratenko. Putin did not resort to using his new legislative powers to oust Nazdratenko. On the contrary, this particularly corrupt and long-standing enemy of the central state resigned as governor. He was then, inexplicably, appointed the director of the federal government's fishing ministry regulating a notoriously corrupt industry that remained deeply involved with his former regional administration. In the gubernatorial elections that followed his resignation, a noted businessman and head of a regional bank in Primorskii Krai defeated the Kremlin's preferred candidate easily.[56]

Far from being able to summarily rid himself of the leaders of regional resistance in Russia, which the evidence here has indicated tended to be republics in particular, but those with the most economic resources to lose, Putin has suffered several legal and political defeats that have left the regional leadership structures of the 1990s largely intact. In July 2002, the Constitutional Court ruled that all terms served by regional governors prior to the passage of the October 1999 federal law on the organization of regional government do not count toward the two-term limit established by the 1999 law. This meant that many regional leaders would be able

---

[55] Ibid.
[56] See "Nazdratenko-Backed Candidate Leads after First Round, Kremlin Routed," *East West Institute's Russian Regional Report* 6, No. 20 (May 30, 2001) and Paul Goble, "Darkin Wins in Far East, None of the Above Finishes Second," *Radio Free Europe/Radio Liberty NEWSLINE* 5, No. 115, Part I (June 18, 2001).

to run for third and fourth consecutive terms such that in 2002 there were fifty-three governors of eighty-nine regions who could potentially rule their provinces for another four to eight years, bringing their total rules to as long as twelve to twenty years.[57] The relative political silence concerning the Court's decision was widely interpreted as a retreat on the part of Putin's administration in its effort initiated only two years earlier s to curb the authority of regional political actors.[58]

Further, despite strong presidential administration involvement in regional elections between October 2000 and January 2002, the incumbency rate for regional governors and presidents was a startling 65.4 percent.[59] There was high participation by business elites in regional elections – either trying to run candidates of their own or backing incumbent candidates in exchange for preferential tax and budgetary treatment.[60] Despite the purported spread of "Unity" (now "Unified Russia") among regional politicians, the "gubernatorial regimes" of the 1990s remain in power – with Unity's backing or without it.

It is also unclear as to the concrete effect on Russian federal relations of the dissolution of many of the bilateral treaties that helped to confuse the already complicated system of federalism. Notably, however, the fourteen treaties that Putin left in place are the ones that the federal government signed with the more notorious and persistent noncompliant regions. Signing these agreements did little to stem the tide of noncompliance, and as a result they did little to clear up the muddy waters of jurisdictional transparency or equity. Beyond this, however, the treaties were so widely variable that some regions like Tatarstan and Sverdlovsk negotiated considerable economic and tax privileges for themselves while others amounted to little more than expressions of friendship and solidarity between the regional signatory and the federal government. It is unclear what effect, if any, dissolving these documents would actually have on Russian federal relations and the practical authority of the central state in particular.

---

[57] Vladimir Ryzhkov, "A New Era of Stagnation," *Moscow Times*, July 25, 2002 in Johnson's Russia List, #6371, July 26, 2002.
[58] See, for example, Sergei Markedonov, "Chechnya in the Context of Russian Federalism," *Russian Regional Report* 8, No. 8 (May 21, 2003).
[59] Rostislav Turoskii, "Itogi i uroki gubernatorskikh vyborov," in Boris I. Makarenko, ed., *Politika v regionakh: gubernatorii I gruppy vlianiia* (Moscow: Center for Political Technology, 2002), p. 11.
[60] Rostislav Turovskii, "Gubernatory I oligarkhi: istoriya otnoshenii," in Makarenko, ed., pp. 76–107.

Forced resolution of noncompliance may have been the biggest success of Putin's efforts to regain control at the regional level, but the longevity of this is questionable if we look at past patterns from the 1990s. We know, for example, from the patterns identified in section one of this chapter that noncompliance declined when the economy began to improve in 1999 and was higher when the economy was relatively bad (1998 and the financial crisis). Buoyed by an increase in domestic production in the wake of the 1998 ruble devaluation (when imports became too expensive for the average Russian consumer, causing a revival in domestic production) as well as an increase in world oil prices, the Russian economy began to grow in 1999 for the first time since the Soviet collapse. At the same time, reports of regional noncompliance to federal law have decreased markedly. But if past is predictor, and economic growth were to decline (indeed, the rate of growth has declined steadily since 1999 when it reached an apparent peak of 9 percent of GNP but fell to 5 percent in 2000, 3.5 percent in 2001, about 4.0 percent in 2002) and 6.0 percent in 2003,[61] regional resistance in the form of noncompliance to federal law and the constitution may well increase again.[62]

Like Heracles of Greek mythology battling the many-headed Hydra that was capable of sprouting two new heads as soon as one was severed, Putin may strike down one aspect of the central state's problem in the periphery by removing an unruly governor in one province or another, only to be faced with a new regional leader with the same powerful ties similarly opposed to central interests.

Moreover, Putin's remedies are the wrong kind of institutional cures for what ails the Russian economy and central state regulatory capabilities in the periphery. For it is not just errant political officials, but a certain segment of regional socioeconomic interests and their capture of regional politics, that have done the most damage to the creation of a unified economic space in Russia capable of sustaining and promoting further market reform and sustained growth. To reiterate, these interests often operate at cross-purposes with the central state and are at the root of regional government noncompliance to central authority as well as the co-opting of federal bureaucrats and regional governments. In the absence of institutions that incorporate these interests and laws that restrain their

---

[61] These figures come from Johnson's Russia List, November 11, 2002.
[62] Indeed, reports have surfaced in the summer of 2002 of the resurgence of 1990s phenomena like barter and increased wage arrears to doctors and teachers in seventeen regions of Russia, despite federal insistence that these practices end.

powers in the provinces, the result now – and in the foreseeable future – is a pervasive inability for the central state to govern the Russian economy in any coherent or predictable way. For this reason, renewed efforts at large-scale economic reform are likely to stall once central policy makers attempt to promote them beyond the walls of the Kremlin. Indeed, it is striking that President Putin delayed much needed microeconomic reform in his first term in office despite a compliant Duma.

CONCLUSIONS: RUSSIAN CENTRAL STATE CAPACITY AND THE FUTURE OF POLITICAL AND ECONOMIC CHANGE

If the Soviet system was a classic example of state hyperinstitutionalization and the primacy of politics over economics, then the first wave of post-Soviet reformers appeared intent on establishing the renewed Russian state as one in which free market economics would reign over politics and the state. Their concern regarding the impact that the "grabbing hand" of the state would have on Russia's emerging market economy proved overdrawn compared to the deleterious effects of the grabbing hands of the beneficiaries of the early stages of the reform program.[63] The very process of economic reform and its early missteps and compromises unleashed the forces that would work against the establishment of a cohesive state capable of minimal regulation of the market. Indeed, the Russian case highlights the tension between the necessities of decreasing the role of the state in postcommunist economies while at the same time ensuring that the new states that replace them are infrastructurally capable of regulating the economy sufficiently to produce well-functioning markets. Even the minimal state pictured by Russia's early neoliberal reformers should not have become an infrastructurally weak state. On the contrary, for the successful transition from planned to market economy, the state had to be capable of providing sufficient legal protections for the equal protection of property rights and the separation of private from public interest.

Paradoxically, however, more than ten years after the initiation of its dual economic and political transition, the post-Soviet state is neither minimalist nor infrastructurally capable of providing many of the conditions a fully functioning market economy demands. The empirical evidence and arguments here indicate the dilemma of dual transitions such that

[63] Hellman, Jones, and Kaufmann.

economic change and the simultaneous reorganization and reconstitution of state institutions are not always complementary processes. On the contrary, economic interests that emerge out of the shift from public to private property rights regimes may work to weaken or stall the establishment of a state capable of regulating their new economic activities. Thus the process of economic transition itself sometimes works to undermine further political and macroeconomic change initiated by the state.

We see evidence of this in the Russian central state's persistent inability over the last decade to effectively and reliably transmit its authority across territory, particularly in the area of economic policy. Its authority in this regard was challenged not by regional government actors alone, but by regional economic actors made politically powerful through the early processes of economic change – particularly the reform of property rights. These groups benefited from a central state that was incapable of regulating their activities and circumscribing their power through regulation. As a result, they worked to penetrate, co-opt, and control branches of federal bureaucracies based in the regions, regional bureaucracies, and, most importantly, regional politicians including governors and legislators.

This dynamic presents a serious challenge to the future of Russia's political and economic reform effort. Regardless of the amount of financial aid it receives from international organizations, the quality of its fiscal or social policies, or even the budgetary and political threats issued by the president, if the central state remains stymied in its efforts to extend its authority to govern across territory, then positive changes will continue to come slowly, if at all, to the lives of average Russians.

5

Parties, Citizens, and the Prospects for Democratic Consolidation in Russia

Timothy J. Colton

Scarcely anywhere has the semi-democratized political system of the new Russia appeared to stand in stiffer contrast to its predecessor, the prototypical communist dictatorship, than in the area of partisan activity. The Soviet regime banned overt opposition and insisted that all legitimate social interests find expression through one hierarchical pseudo-party. Having long since reduced elections, the hub of a traditional party's operations, to single-candidate charades, "the" party – the Communist Party of the Soviet Union (CPSU) – functioned essentially as ideological policeman, personnel department, and master coordinator and fixer for a disjointed state bureaucracy.[1] *Perestroika* unleashed a quantum change in the late 1980s. Mikhail Gorbachev's sudden inauguration of electoral competition telescoped the universalization of the franchise, the work of generations in the West, into a few frenzied months. The same emancipating impulse led him to cripple the CPSU administrative apparatus and to ease curbs on public association, assembly, and communication. Politicized groups of all manner and description rapidly formed and took the stage. Elimination of the CPSU's legal monopoly in 1990 enabled almost any faction with an articulate spokesman and a photocopying machine to pose as a political

---

[1] The classic study remains Jerry F. Hough, *The Soviet Prefects: The Local Party Organs in Industrial Decision Making* (Cambridge, Mass.: Harvard University Press, 1969). See also Merle Fainsod, *Smolensk under Soviet Rule* (Cambridge, Mass.: Harvard University Press, 1958); T. H. Rigby, *Communist Party Membership in the U.S.S.R., 1917–1967* (Princeton: Princeton University Press, 1968); Peter Rutland, *The Politics of Economic Stagnation in the Soviet Union: The Role of Local Party Organs in Economic Management* (Cambridge: Cambridge University Press, 1993); and Timothy J. Colton, *Moscow: Governing the Socialist Metropolis* (Cambridge, Mass.: Harvard University Press, 1995).

party or movement. Two years after the Russian Federation emerged from the wreckage of the USSR in 1991, the Yeltsin constitution of 1993 enshrined the rights to organize parties and to vote freely for them. Aided by low barriers to entry, proportional-representation (PR) voting rules, and budget-subsidized campaigns, parties and party-like entities proliferated in Russia. Thirteen of them nominated slates of candidates for the State Duma in 1993, forty-three did so in 1995, twenty-six in 1999, and 23 in 2003; 8 of them crossed the 5 percent threshold for seating in the Duma under PR in 1993, 4 in 1995 and 2003, and 6 in 1999.[2] The campaigns the more competent parties and quasi-parties wage have grown more professional and more sophisticated with every passing election.[3]

For many political theorists and analysts of comparative politics, parties and democracy go together like the proverbial horse and carriage. "The development of parties," Maurice Duverger wrote magisterially, "seems bound up with that of democracy."[4] Scott P. Mainwaring notes that, despite challenges to them, in place after place parties "have continued to be the main agents of representation and are virtually the only actors with access to elected positions in democratic politics."[5] If the Russians, their inherited undemocratic baggage and all, can construct a harlequin party system from scratch, perhaps anyone can.

To declare victory, however, would be premature. It is anything but clear why party building in Russia went so swimmingly in the 1990s and indeed what success means in the circumstances. In raw numbers, democratic theory would pronounce 43 or twenty-three parties superior to one but would not recommend either number over, say, nine or three.

---

[2] Half of the 450 Duma deputies are elected by PR from national lists and half in single-member districts where independents along with party nominees may run. Legislation on the books for the parliamentary elections of 1993, 1995, and 1999 assigned nomination rights to any organization registered with the Ministry of Justice whose bylaws authorized it to take part in political activity. A new law adopted in 2001, at the initiative of President Vladimir Putin, limits entry to duly constituted political parties (now defined more tightly than in the past and with requirements for membership and local organization) and electoral blocs containing at least one party. Some Russian liberals criticized the law as oppressive and even unconstitutional.

[3] See Timothy J. Colton and Michael McFaul, *Popular Choice and Managed Democracy: The Russian Elections of 1999 and 2000* (Washington, D.C.: Brookings Institution Press, 2003). The sophistication extends to negative and at times vitriolic techniques as well as to more uplifting campaigning.

[4] Maurice Duverger, *Political Parties*, 3rd ed., trans. Barbara and Robert North (London: Methuen, 1964), p. xxiii.

[5] Scott P. Mainwaring, *Rethinking Party Systems in the Third Wave of Democratization: The Case of Brazil* (Stanford: Stanford University Press, 1999), p. 11.

Parties, Citizens, and the Prospects for Democratic Consolidation 175

When one evaluates the fledgling parties or any political phenomenon, one should be cognizant of the warnings that on the post-Soviet scene most appearances are illusory and that ostensibly democratic practices are often pretenses masking undemocratic realities.[6] Duverger in his day cautioned that the advent of self-proclaimed parties does not guarantee that they will actually serve the ends of representation and accountability. It all hinged, he wrote, on social and political context and on the quality of the links forged between politicos and citizens. In industrial societies, "the rise of parties and especially of working-class parties has alone made possible any real and active cooperation by the whole people in political affairs." In developing nations, however, Duverger observed that parties as often as not were hollow shells whose bosses mimicked the genuine article for sinister purposes: "Here parties are formal in character: rival factions struggle for power, using the voters as a soft dough to be kneaded as they will; corruption develops and the privileged classes take advantage of the situation to prolong their control."[7]

The present essay bears down on one selected aspect of party development, namely, the resonance parties have achieved in Russia's recently enfranchised electorate. What, I ask, have rank-and-file citizens made of the political parties, long outlawed, that sprout in their midst? Of special interest in comparative perspective are partisan sentiments. Have the Russians taken steps to normalize their electoral politics by attaching themselves to parties? If so, why? And what are the implications for our understanding of democratization? In addressing these matters, I rely chiefly on survey data gleaned during the 1999–2000 national election cycle, as power passed from Boris Yeltsin, the founder of the system, to his less liberal and more statist heir, Vladimir Putin.

RUSSIANS AND THEIR PARTY SYSTEM

Behavioral signs in the mass and elite arenas suggest that, cheerfully or grudgingly, most Russians accept multiparty politics. Popular majorities have turned out to vote in parliamentary elections orchestrated primarily

---

[6] This is the unifying theme of Lilia Shevtsova, *Yeltsin's Russia: Myths and Reality* (Washington, D.C.: Carnegie Endowment for International Peace, 1998). Indictments of the corruption of Russian politics and economics fold into attacks on U.S. policy in Stephen F. Cohen, *Failed Crusade: America and the Tragedy of Post-Communist Russia* (New York: W. W. Norton, 2000), and Peter Reddaway and Dmitri Glinski, *The Tragedy of Russia's Reforms: Market Bolshevism Against Democracy* (Washington, D.C.: U.S. Institute of Peace Press, 2001).
[7] Duverger, *Political Parties*, p. 425.

by the political parties. The participation rate was 54 percent of age-eligible citizens in the PR portion of the trailblazing election of 1993, 64 percent in 1995, 62 percent in 1999, and 56 percent in 2003. The continual hatching of new parties demonstrates that astute suppliers have been bullish about market demand for their product.

That is not to say we have to search far to find cause for skepticism and concern. Russian electoral turnout has fallen shy of the average for all democracies by ten or fifteen percentage points. Among voters, the heavy support for the top party for most of the 1990's, the neo-communist KPRF (Communist Party of the Russian Federation), might be construed as a slap at political and partisan pluralism as much as an embrace of it. The parties themselves project a dismal image. Media commentators and intellectuals seldom have a kind word to say, portraying them time and again as squabbling collections of mediocrities. It is as true nowadays as when the epithet was coined in the early 1990s that Russia is flush in *divannyye partii*, "sofa parties" isolated from the grassroots and whose activists would fit comfortably into one Moscow living room. The leadership rolls of the parties and quasi-parties are short on statesmen and long on publicity hounds and pranksters.[8] For many parties, the corollaries of numerical proliferation have been minuscule size and fleeting life spans. "The erratic and changing supply of parties," Richard Rose rightly complains, "has often worked against the possibility of holding elected leaders accountable" in Russia.[9] The parties are most vulnerable to being impeached as a sideshow to the serious business of governing the country. Their influence in federal institutions is confined to the legislature, the junior branch according to the constitution of 1993. This secondary status is to some degree by design.[10] Even in parliament, party caucuses share the pulpit with independents in the lower house, the Duma – 30 percent of the deputies returned in single-member Duma districts in the 2003

---

[8] The high-water mark for silly parties was the Duma election of December 1995. Entrants included the Beer Lovers' Party (which drew almost a half-million votes), a coalition headed by the guru of a religious cult, four electoral blocs named after individual politicians, and a municipal workers' trade union.
[9] Richard Rose, "How Floating Parties Frustrate Democratic Accountability: A Supply-Side View of Russia's Elections," in Archie Brown, ed., *Contemporary Russian Politics: A Reader* (Oxford: Oxford University Press, 2001), p. 215.
[10] See Michael McFaul, "Explaining Party Emergence and Non-Emergence in Post-Soviet Russia: Institutions, Agents, and Chance," *Comparative Political Studies*, vol. 34 (December 2001), pp. 1159–87. In the 1999 pre-election wave of the survey of the Russian electorate utilized in this paper, 37 percent of respondents agreed with the statement, "It does not matter who is elected to the State Duma, because practically all important decisions in Russia do not depend on them." Forty percent disagreed, and the rest were undecided or could not respond.

election, down from 53 percent in 1999, won their seats without party labels – and have been absent in the upper house, the Federation Council. In the dominant executive branch, Russia's first and second presidents, Yeltsin and Putin, were elected and re-elected as nominees of nonpartisan umbrella groups and refused to sponsor or join parties. Neither the Council of Ministers nor the bureaucracy beneath it has a partisan basis. The parties, moreover, have barely begun to penetrate regional and local politics on Russia's vast periphery.[11]

It therefore comes as no surprise that when Russians are invited to appraise their political parties in surveys, derogatory opinions are quick to spill out. Table 1 passes on some results from waves 1 and 2 of a three-wave panel survey of a large probability sample of the electorate done in the weeks before and after the 1999 Duma election (see the Appendix for technical details). Wave 2 incorporated the full battery of election-survey questions of the Comparative Study of Electoral Systems (CSES), several of which plumb the individual's outlook on political parties. Some other party-related questions were put to respondents separately.

As the first and second sections of Table 1 convey, most Russians as of the dawn of the Putin era did not reckon the political parties collectively to be dependable or empathetic. About twice as many voiced complete or qualified distrust as any amount of trust – the dreariest scores elicited among the eight state and nonstate institutions about which the question was broached.[12] By about an equal margin, citizens doubted that parties "care what ordinary people think" (counting positions 1 and 2 on the five-point scale as signifying that parties care and positions 4 and 5 as signifying that they do not).[13]

---

[11] See on this last point Kathryn Stoner-Weiss, "The Limited Reach of Russia's Party System: Under-Institutionalization in Dual Transitions," *Politics and Society*, vol. 29 (September 2001), pp. 385–414, who finds that more than 80 percent of deputies elected to regional councils from 1993 to 1998 were independents; and Henry E. Hale, *Crashing Parties: Electoral Markets, Party Substitutes, and Stalled Democratization in Russia* (book ms., 2003), who reports that from 1995 to 2000 the mean share of a region's legislators elected as partisans was 12 percent and that provincial governors ran for reelection as party nominees a mere 3 percent of the time. A legal change, effective in July 2003, changes some of these facts. It requires that as in the State Duma half of all deputies to regional assemblies be elected on party lists.

[12] The most widely trusted institutions in our survey were the Russian Army (trusted to some degree by 77 percent of respondents) and the Russian Orthodox Church (70 percent). The mass media were in next-to-last place (trusted by 30 percent).

[13] A cognate question couched in terms of the responsiveness of Duma deputies drew a less barbed reaction. Thirty-four percent of respondents indicated agreement with the proposition that members of the Duma "know what ordinary people think" and 39 percent indicated disagreement.

TABLE 1. *Citizen Assessments of Russian Political Parties, 1999–2000*

Survey question and responses	Percent
Trust in political parties[a]	
Fully trust	1
Trust	27
Mistrust	45
Completely mistrust	8
Don't know	19
Parties and ordinary people[b]	
(1) Political parties in Russia care what ordinary people think	12
(2)	12
(3)	24
(4)	16
(5) Political parties in Russia don't care what ordinary people think	32
Don't know	4
Benefits of multiparty competition[c]	
Fully agree	4
Agree	36
Indifferent	17
Disagree	24
Fully disagree	6
Don't know	12
The need for parties in Russia[d]	
(1) Political parties are necessary to make our political system work	32
(2)	21
(3)	20
(4)	8
(5) Political parties are not needed in Russia	10
Don't know	10
Attitude toward number of parties Russia currently has[e]	
Too few	1
About the right number	6
Too many	88
Don't know	6

Survey question and responses	Percent
Ideal number of parties for Russia [f]	
0	2
1	25
2–5	57
>5	16

[a] From postelection interview (N = 1,846 weighted cases). Question reads, "Let us talk a little about how much you trust or mistrust various political institutions and organizations. Tell me if you fully trust, trust, mistrust, or completely mistrust . . . the political parties."

[b] From postelection interview (N = 1,846 weighted cases). Question reads, "Some people say that political parties in Russia care what ordinary people think. Others say that political parties in Russia don't care what ordinary people think. Using the scale on this card, where 1 means that political parties care about what ordinary people think and 5 means that they don't care what ordinary people think, where would you place yourself?"

[c] From postelection interview (N = 1,846 weighted cases). Statement reads, "Competition among various political parties makes our system stronger."

[d] From postelection interview (N = 1,846 weighted cases). Question reads, "Some people say that political parties are necessary to make our political system work in Russia. Others think that political parties are not needed in Russia. Using the scale on this card, where 1 means that political parties are necessary to make our political system work and 5 means that political parties are not needed in Russia, where would you place yourself?"

[e] From preelection interview (N = 1,919 weighted cases). Question reads, "In your opinion, are there too few political parties in Russia, about the right number, or too many parties?"

[f] From preelection interview, among respondents who gave a number (N = 1,483 weighted cases). Question reads, "How many parties, in your opinion, should Russia have?" Answers giving a numerical range coded at the midpoint of the range.

The remaining parts of Table 1 send a more upbeat message. The third and fourth questions summarized touch on the systemic utility of parties. Individuals who felt that multipartism strengthens the Russian political system outnumbered opponents of this notion by 40 percent to 30 percent. The CSES question about whether parties are "necessary to make our political system work" invoked yet more positive feedback, with a shade over half agreeing the parties are necessary and fewer than 20 percent disagreeing.

The array of responses on the last two questions encapsulated in Table 1, giving a verdict on the number of parties active in Russian politics, underscores the complexity of opinion while pointing on balance in a mildly hopeful direction. Frustration with the unwieldiness of the party system is palpable. Eighty-eight percent of those surveyed in 1999–2000, 13 percentage points more than the ratio when the question was asked in 1996,[14] deemed the country to have too many parties. This antagonism would be deadliest to democratic norms of government if it bestirred Russians to sacrifice political competition altogether. Fortunately, only a minority have taken their anger to this extreme. The bottom panel of Table 1 gives answers to an open-ended question about the number of parties Russia ideally ought to have. A sprinkling of individuals in our 1999–2000 survey sample would have liked none at all. One citizen out of four espoused the nakedly authoritarian solution, a one-party system. Of these individuals, 53 percent were more than fifty years old and 36 percent voted for the KPRF list in December 1999.[15] But the most striking conclusions telegraphed by the data are that about three-quarters of Russians were in favor of, not against, a multiplicity of parties, and that overwhelmingly they wanted them to be moderate in quantity. The mean number of parties they thought optimal for Russia – 4.0 – bespeaks greater tolerance of multipartism than Philip E. Converse and Roy Pierce picked up in their landmark study of representation in early Fifth Republic France.[16] More apposite, maybe, proponents of no parties or of one leviathan party were slightly harder to come by in Russia a decade after the collapse of communism than they were in Portugal in 1984, ten years after the overthrow of the right-wing Estado Novo dictatorship.[17]

---

[14] The question was asked, along with a question about the number of parties Russia should have, in the last wave of a similar panel study of which I was an organizer in 1995–6. See Timothy J. Colton, *Transitional Citizens: Voters and What Influences Them in the New Russia* (Cambridge, Mass.: Harvard University Press, 2000), p. 106.

[15] The proportion voting for the KPRF is among persons who participated in the election and answered the number-of-parties question (N = 1,172 weighted cases). Forty-seven percent of KPRF supporters with a preference for the number of parties were in favor of the single-party option.

[16] The mean number of parties preferred in France was 2.5 in 1967. It had been 2.9 in 1959. Philip E. Converse and Roy Pierce, *Political Representation in France* (Cambridge, Mass.: Harvard University Press, 1986), p. 56. As in France, the number of parties preferred is associated in Russia with attitudes toward the utility of parties and of interparty competition. For example, the mean rose from 2.4 among citizens who strongly disagree with the statement that partisan competition "makes our system stronger" to 5.5 among citizens who strongly agree with the statement.

[17] Portuguese figures from Thomas C. Bruneau and Alex Macleod, *Politics in Contemporary Portugal: Parties and the Consolidation of Democracy* (Boulder, Col.: Lynne Rienner, 1986), p. 33. In a closed-ended question, Bruneau and Macleod found 7 percent of the entire Portuguese electorate to prefer no parties, 20 percent to prefer one party, 13 percent two parties, 40 percent three or more parties, and 20 percent to be unable to answer the

The apparent trend over time is as encouraging as the central tendency of opinion. Specifications of the number of parties Russians thought their homeland deserved were higher at the end of the 1990s than they had been in the mid-1990s. Survey informants had favored a mean of 2.8 parties in the system in 1996 and had more trouble answering the question then.[18] The 25 percent of informants approving a one-party system in 1999 was a drop from 33 percent in 1996. Among respondents coveting more than one party, the mean total of parties favored swelled from 3.9 in 1996 to 5.0 in 1999.

As with so many political beliefs in Russia, preferences vis-à-vis party diversity differ sharply by generation. Purposive political socialization in Soviet days, and the dearth in authoritarian conditions of firsthand exposure to diversity, have left the elderly and middle-aged more impatient with multiple parties than younger persons who were reared in more lenient times. The age gradient is the keynote of Figure 1. In both the 1999 and the 1996 sampling of the electorate, the youngest group saw merit, on average, in approximately double the number of parties that the oldest group wanted. But notice that the drift toward assent in multiparty competition from one canvassing of opinion to the next gripped young and old alike. It testifies to a process of social learning that has affected the populace across the board.

PARTISANSHIP: DOES THE SHOE FIT?

Political scientists working on parties and the mass public in the entrenched liberal democracies have been preoccupied with the affinities citizens feel for specific parties, not with diffuse orientations toward party systems. This is because they most commonly canvass parties with the aim of explicating voting choice and electoral cleavages. An individual in the voting booth selects from among a menu of voting options. The party

---

question. In Russia in 1999, those proportions were 1, 19, 12, 45, and 23 percent. In a survey done in 1985 in four southern European countries with experience of authoritarian government, levels of support for a no-party or single-party system were 16 percent of all respondents in Portugal, 14 percent in Spain, 10 percent in Greece, and 7 percent in Italy. Leonard Morlino, *Democracy between Consolidation and Crisis: Parties, Groups, and Citizens in Southern Europe* (Oxford: Oxford University Press, 1998), calculated from tables on pp. 137, 144.

[18] The response rate to the question about the desired number of parties was 62 percent in 1996 but 77 percent in 1999. The question wording was identical.

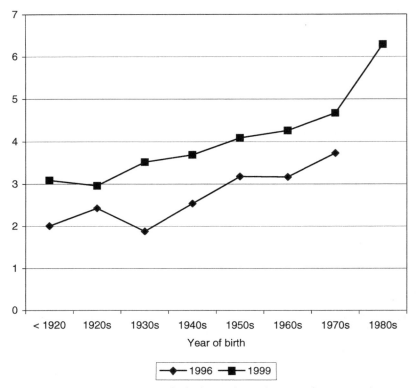

FIGURE 1. Citizen Opinions of Ideal Number of Parties for Russia by Year of Birth, 1996 and 1999

system conventionally frames those options, but is not in its own right up for grabs in elections.

A fulcrum of electoral research in the United States and Western Europe for fifty years has been the concept of "party identification." The locus classicus of the theory, *The American Voter*, claimed in 1960 that most U.S. citizens possess a "psychological identification" with a party – a tie it rephrased variously as an "affective attachment," "affective orientation," "allegiance," "loyalty," or "commitment" to the party. For those harboring it, "the strength and direction of party identification are facts of central importance in accounting for attitude and behavior," shaping them either directly or indirectly through a "perceptual screen."[19]

---

[19] Angus Campbell, Philip E. Converse, Warren E. Miller, and Donald E. Stokes, *The American Voter* (New York: John Wiley and Sons, 1960), pp. 121, 133.

In the eyes of *The American Voter*, partisanship was implanted through adolescent and early adult socialization: most people adopted the identity of their parents, unless paternal and maternal identities diverged. Locating the historical wellspring of such self-images was not the book's mission. It did deal all the same cursorily with change in Americans' party attachments, typifying them as "firm but not immovable" and saying any wholesale overturning of party identifications would be a rarity: "Our surveys force us to the conclusion that only an event of extraordinary intensity can arouse any significant part of the electorate to the point that its established political loyalties are shaken."[20] The authors gave as examples the U.S. Civil War, about which they had no attitudinal data, and the New Deal, about which they had decades-old recall data from their interviews in the 1950s.

The concept of partisan identification, judiciously employed, is in principle germane to the study of new or partially built democracies. In part this is because information about identification can unlock voting decisions – which are not the focus of this essay – and in part because partisanship may serve as a glue for the entire polity. As Leonard Morlino discovered in Greece, Italy, Portugal, and Spain, partisanship in a transitional milieu can be an "anchor of consolidation" of the nascent democratic order.[21] In democracies that have consolidated, write Susan J. Pharr and Robert D. Putnam, attachments to political parties are "one of the most widely studied of political attitudes." They alert citizens to the activities of policy makers and "make the political marketplace orderly," allowing individuals to be "committed to [a] party's goals and the principle of representative democracy that parties signify."[22] In an important new study, Donald Green, Bradley Palmquist, and Eric Schickler tether partisanship to citizens' identifications with social groups and maintain again that it helps propel individuals into political competition: "Their interest and level of emotional engagement increase as they embrace the team as their own. Although not irresistible, the desire to see one's team prevail powerfully influences the probability of casting a vote for the candidate of one's party." Party attachments, they add, "dampen the electoral tides that would otherwise produce much larger electoral victories for the

---

[20] Ibid., pp. 148, 151.
[21] Morlino, *Democracy between Consolidation and Crisis*, pp. 169–70.
[22] Susan J. Pharr and Robert D. Putnam, "Introduction," in Pharr and Putnam, eds., *Disaffected Democracies: What's Troubling the Trilateral Countries?* (Princeton: Princeton University Press, 2000), p. 17.

party favored by short-term forces," hence "contributing to the stability of electoral outcomes over time" and lessening the danger of political polarization.[23]

To be sure, cogent objections can be and have been raised to the uncritical transfer of the received wisdom about party identification in the West into the transitional polities of the ex-Soviet bloc. Some of the misgivings aired in the small literature on the subject revolve around on the practical obstacles to any profound psychic commitment cohering in the abbreviated time scale of postcommunist politics, a point initially made by Stephen White, Richard Rose, and Ian McAllister in *How Russia Votes*, the first full-length monograph on voting in Russia.[24] If one takes as the benchmark the tenacious mind-set profiled in *The American Voter*, it is fanciful to imagine that present-day Russians will pass muster. Solidarity with parties a few years or even months old cannot have been ingrained as it has been with a decades-old American or British party.

No less pertinent to attachments to any public cause are the longevity and harshness of the dictatorship that Russia's semi-democracy replaced. The USSR's Marxist-Leninist regime persevered for seventy-odd years, for almost all of which political organization outside the official structures was taboo, punishable by severe sanctions. The longest-lived authoritarian order in twentieth-century Western Europe, the right-wing regime in Portugal, lasted about 60 percent as long (forty-one years, from 1933 to 1974). The military juntas that exited in Latin America in the 1970s and 1980s had mostly held power for ten to fifteen years, and in much of the region authoritarian and liberal governments had alternated for generations. Modern noncommunist authoritarians have been less methodical than communists in repressing opposition groups, often permitting them to survive in the political underground and to communicate with exiles and foreign sympathizers. In Spain, for example, the PCE (communist party) and PSOE (the main socialist party), which between them bagged nearly 40 percent of the seats in the 1977 parliamentary election, "had

---

[23] Donald Green, Bradley Palmquist, and Eric Schickler, *Partisan Hearts and Minds: Political Parties and the Social Identities of Voters* (New Haven: Yale University Press, 2002), p. 206.

[24] See Stephen White, Richard Rose, and Ian McAllister, *How Russia Votes* (Chatham, N.J.: Chatham House, 1997), p. 137, which refers to an "absence of party identification" in Russia. The point is restated more categorically in Richard Rose, Neil Munro, and Stephen White, "How Strong Is Vladimir Putin's Support?," *Post-Soviet Affairs*, vol. 16 (October–December 2000), p. 297: "The very concept of party identification is tautological in Russia, for it originated as a summary way of describing an individual's commitment to a party built up over decades of socialization experiences."

existed as antisystem movements throughout the Franquist regime and thus entered the transition to democracy with previously established ideologies, organizational hierarchies, public images, significant levels of affiliation, and historical traditions."[25] In the Soviet Union, the first infant parties made their debut only months before the implosion of the old order.

Revulsion at Soviet habits could further interfere with post-Soviet political attachments. Although the CPSU was never an orthodox political party, it called itself a party, had a party program, recruited and disciplined a mass membership, and collected monthly dues. William Miller, Stephen White, and Paul Heywood allege that bitter memories of the CPSU's hegemony and of the rituals and obligations it imposed had the effect of poisoning the well for democratic as well as autocratic parties in the successor states, leaving voters "peculiarly allergic to the idea of committing themselves to any party."[26]

Yet another villain could be the sheer clutter of the partisan landscape in the Russian Federation and, of a piece, the character of the parties that inhabit it. A hardy handful of these organizations have persisted from year to year and election to election. More typically, however, Russian parties are invented out of whole cloth, alter name tags and legal denominations periodically, split and merge at will, and come to a sorry end, vanishing without a trace.[27] Eighteen of the twenty-six parties and quasi-parties to campaign for the Duma in 1999, and three of the six to secure PR seats, were in the running for the first time. Converse and Pierce

---

[25] Richard Gunther, Giacomo Sani, and Goldie Shabad, *Spain after Franco: The Making of a Competitive Party System* (Berkeley: University of California Press, 1986), p. 42. Both parties were founded long before General Franco's regime took power – the PCE in 1920 and the PSOE in 1879.

[26] William L. Miller, Stephen White, and Paul Heywood, "Twenty-Five Days to Go: Measuring and Interpreting the Trends in Public Opinion During the 1993 Russian Election Campaign," *Public Opinion Quarterly*, vol. 60 (Spring 1996), p. 124. Miller, White, and Heywood did find, nevertheless, that about 20 percent of Russians had a party attachment in 1993, and cite related surveys around the same time showing levels of partisan identification of 38 percent in the Czech Republic, 33 percent in Slovakia, 28 percent in Hungary, and 14 percent in Ukraine. See also William L. Miller, Stephen White, and Paul Heywood, *Values and Political Change in Postcommunist Europe* (London: Macmillan, 1998), p. 411.

[27] Loopholes in Russian electoral law have encouraged last-minute reorganizations. Under the rules in effect in 1999, parties or political movements wishing to campaign for the Duma had to have registered one year before election day, but they and other political organizations were permitted to join in electoral blocs any time until the commencement of the campaign.

comment in their study of France in the 1950s and 1960s that incessant partisan flux left identifiers in the lurch when their favorites folded. The politically orphaned could always fasten on another party, but, "Identifications initiated afresh tend to intensify themselves only at slower and slower rates, the older the individual is at the time of initial adoption." In addition, the fractionation of the French party system sapped inhibitions against defection: "if one political system packs ten times as many parties into a given political space as another, then one would expect cross-party changes in such a system to be somewhat easier."[28] Both those points assuredly could pertain in Russia right now.[29]

A final brake on the spread of party ties could be a variation on the malaise that afflicts political parties in most of the western democracies. The disrepute in which, we have seen, Russians hold their party system overall may well rub off on individual parties. Just as bad, Russians' esteem of the parties may suffer from their alienation from the political system in general. In the older democracies, the growth in political anomie and distrust has run in parallel to a decrease in rates of party identification, leading some scholars to speak of a "decline of parties" as part and parcel of a waning of attachments to democratic institutions.[30] In Russia, similar feelings could perversely nip identification in the bud – keep it from solidifying in the first place, before it has had a chance to erode.

Do these impediments fatally stack the deck against partisanship in Russia? Not necessarily, provided we relax purist assumptions that partisanship must always be static and must always be transmitted by lengthy socialization. Even in the ultra-stable United States, subsequent research disclosed identities to be more migratory than *The American*

---

[28] Converse and Pierce, *Political Representation in France*, pp. 83, 89. Similar points are made in Mainwaring, *Rethinking Party Systems in the Third Wave of Democratization*, pp. 28–35.

[29] Elite and mass volatility as an impediment to party identification in postcommunist Eastern Europe are stressed in Hubert Tworzecki, *Learning to Choose: Electoral Politics in East-Central Europe* (Stanford: Stanford University Press, 2002), chap. 4.

[30] For discussion, see Peter Mair, ed., *The West European Party System* (Oxford: Oxford University Press, 1990); Russell J. Dalton, "Political Support in Advanced Industrial Democracies," in Pippa Norris, ed., *Critical Citizens: Global Support for Democratic Governance* (Oxford: Oxford University Press, 1999), pp. 65–6; Larry M. Bartels, "Partisanship and Voting Behavior, 1952–96," *American Journal of Political Science*, vol. 44 (January 2000), pp. 35–50; and Russell J. Dalton, "Political Cleavages, Issues, and Electoral Change," in Lawrence LeDuc, Richard Niemi, and Pippa Norris, eds., *Comparing Democracies 2: New Challenges in the Study of Elections and Voting* (London: Sage, 2002), pp. 189–209.

Voter presented them to be.[31] If occurrences of "extraordinary intensity" can rattle extant partisan loyalties, as that book inferred from the historical record, it is realistic to suppose they could midwife partisanship when regimes are in transit, even in a society seemingly so inhospitable to partisan activity. John H. Aldrich in *Why Parties?* intriguingly refers to the "brand names" modern parties display and the set responses they evoke.[32] The citizen may be not so different from the shopper in the supermarket aisle or the car buyer on the dealer's lot, swayed on some purchases by an inchoate, partly emotive fondness for one trademark or look over another. Loyalties that abide over many years or decades would stand to influence decisions more definitively, but a relatively short-lived taste, whatever its derivation, may also have an impact, and it may eventually evolve into a deep-seated attachment.[33]

Upon close scrutiny, the other a priori arguments against the possibility that partisanship will spring up in contemporary Russia are also less than ironclad. The CPSU-fomented allergy to parties, for instance, needs to be empirically verified; if a factor, it might reasonably be expected to fade with the passage of time. The formal and passive participation of the communist past, for its part, might have produced an internal predisposition toward partisan involvement, not against it, as historians have shown was the experience of many Italians brought up under interwar fascism.[34] It is also of note that one fragment of the defunct Soviet system did last more or less intact – the *Communist Party of the Russian Federation* (KPRF) for which tens of millions of citizens have cast their ballots

---

[31] See, for example, Morris P. Fiorina, *Retrospective Voting in American National Elections* (New Haven: Yale University Press, 1981), and Richard G. Niemi and M. Kent Jennings, "Issues and Inheritance in the Formation of Party Identification," *American Journal of Political Science*, vol. 35 (November 1991), pp. 970–88. For an alternative view, portraying partisanship as on the whole stable, see Green, Palmquist, and Schickler, *Partisan Hearts and Minds*.

[32] John H. Aldrich, *Why Parties? The Origin and Transformation of Party Politics in America* (Chicago: University of Chicago Press, 1995), pp. 289–90. See also James M. Snyder and Michael M. Ting, "An Informational Rationale for Political Parties," *American Journal of Political Science*, vol. 46 (January 2002), pp. 90–110.

[33] To push the point, we lack a plain rule for judging that the allegiance to a political or a supermarket brand has cemented once and for all. How long does an attachment to a favorite soft drink or automotive brand – or to a political party – have to persist to be considered long-term? Is there a category intermediate between short-term and long-term loyalties? These are questions without hard-and-fast answers.

[34] See Morlino, *Democracy between Consolidation and Crisis*, pp. 208–9, citing research by Gino Germani and Ruggero Zangrandi. Morlino contrasts Italy with the "demobilizational" tradition of Franco's Spain.

since it was incorporated as the legatee of the CPSU in 1993, and which is a possible partisan magnet for leftist Russians. Furthermore, the pervasive distrust of the party system and of the larger political order would not rule out a Russian, any more than a Swede or a Canadian, simultaneously being turned off by the system and trusting one chosen party in it.[35] The post-Soviet political culture differs in particulars from the mood of civic disengagement that has seeped into so many advanced industrial democracies. In the established democracies, in any event, the erosion of partisanship has been from near-saturation levels, and in most countries it has left solid majorities still professing party sympathies.[36] Nor need the irritating profusion of parties absolutely preclude party feeling. The splintering of France's party system in the 1950s and 1960s did not suffice to stop partisanship for various groups from finding a wide and expanding popular base there, as Converse and Pierce realized from their research, and like findings have been reported for the turbulent politics of Canada and Italy in the 1990s.[37] This could also be true of Russia in the 1990s and beyond.

GETTING THE MEASURE OF RUSSIAN PARTISANSHIP

In previous work, I have avoided applying the venerable idiom "party identification," with its undertones of inbreeding and endurance, to the ex-USSR, sticking with the looser phrase "transitional partisanship." Arguing about labels now may be more a semantic than a substantive exercise. Like full-fledged partisan identification, I see the core of transitional partisanship as an autonomous, visceral sense of kinship with a political party. As compared with identification as normally visualized in the West, in democratizing Russia partisanship crystallizes in the short to medium term, not basically in the course of a protracted political education, and is assailable by other short-run forces and so quite volatile.

Scholars have for some years been on the watch for partisan feeling in the post-Soviet nations. In addition to Stephen White and his British

[35] See Sören Holmberg, "Down and Down We Go: Political Trust in Sweden," in Norris, *Critical Citizens*, p. 108.
[36] See Dalton, "Political Support in Advanced Industrial Democracies," p. 66, and Richard Gunther and José Ramón Montero, *The Anchors of Partisanship: A Comparative Analysis of Voting Behavior in Four Southern European Democracies*, Estudio/Working Paper 2000/150 (Madrid: Centro de Estudios Avanzados en Ciencias Sociales, Instituto Juan March de Estudios e Investigaciones, March 2000), pp. 11–13.
[37] Converse and Pierce, *Political Representation in France*; Green, Palmquist, and Schickler, *Partisan Hearts and Minds*, chap. 7.

collaborators, Geoffrey Evans and Stephen Whitefield discuss polls conducted in 1993–4 in Russia and seven nearby countries. Thirteen percent of their Russian respondents interviewed in mid-1993 gave answers imparting "party identification" or "party attachment," the puniest share of any of the countries; Lithuania led with 50 percent.[38] Arthur H. Miller and a research group from the University of Iowa, quarrying more recent data, come to a more buoyant assessment. They found that about half of Russians, 60 percent of Lithuanians, and 30 percent of Ukrainians had a party identification in the spring of 1995. By 1997 partisanship had risen to an average of 61 percent (61 percent in Russia, 70 percent in Lithuania, and 27 percent in Ukraine).[39]

Indices of party identification are notoriously sensitive to question wording in the West and are sure to be so in a post-Soviet society. Difficulties, some unavoidable, crop up with the questions attempted to date. Surveys in Russia will commonly inquire if a citizen is a "supporter" of any party and show the respondent a card listing the eligible parties. There is a category problem with "party," as functional equivalents to parties in the former Soviet Union often come in different legal guise (such as a political "movement," "association," or "bloc"). The availability of the show card may inflate the affirmative responses. Formulating the question in terms of support is also debatable, as it may confuse affective attachment with voting intention, past voting practice, or utilitarian rating of a party's program. Surveys in western democracies routinely build qualifiers such as "generally speaking" or "usually" into party-identification questions. This has not been done in most post-Soviet research,[40] and it would have struck respondents as strange in the pioneering years of multiparty politics.

The CSES ID module, which to the best of my knowledge was not fielded in Russia until 1999, is probably more suitable today than before. It opens with the query, "Do you usually think of yourself as close to any particular political party?," asks what that party is, and then asks

---

[38] Geoffrey Evans and Stephen Whitefield, "The Politics and Economics of Democratic Commitment: Support for Democracy in Transition Societies," *British Journal of Political Science*, vol. 25 (October 1995), pp. 499–500.

[39] Arthur H. Miller, Gwyn Erb, William M. Reisinger, and Vicki L. Hesli, "Emerging Party Systems in Post-Soviet Societies: Fact or Fiction?" *Journal of Politics*, vol. 62 (May 2000), pp. 455–90; Arthur H. Miller and Thomas F. Klobucar, "The Development of Party Identification in Post-Soviet Societies," *American Journal of Political Science*, vol. 44 (October 2000), pp. 667–85.

[40] An exception is Miller, White, and Heywood, whose lead question was worded, "Generally speaking, do you think of yourself as a supporter of any political party?"

those who gave negative responses if there is a party "to which you feel yourself a little closer than to the others." An intensity item rounds out the series.[41] The best thing about these questions is that they lend themselves to comparison with the dozens of other countries covered in the CSES project. To be fruitful in Russia, they need to be opened up to quasi-party organizations, and recondite problems of translation have to be dealt with.[42]

I report here on work in Russia in which I have participated as a principal investigator. The set of partisanship questions utilized is, I think, a modest improvement on the alternatives, but its forté is its availability for longitudinal comparisons. Research partners and I administered the identical questions five times over five years: in the first and last waves of a three-wave election study in 1995–6; in a poll done on a consulting basis in early 1998; and again twice in the aforementioned panel set up to study the parliamentary and presidential elections of 1999–2000 (see the Appendix). The sample frame and the Russian research group have been constant in all five surveys. In each interview, the respondent is asked whether there is "any one among the present parties, movements, and associations about which you would say, 'This is my party, my movement, my association.'" The possessive "my" renders in the Russian vernacular the exclusivity and warmth at the heart of partisanship without injecting a false permanency into it. Persons who answer "Yes" to the opening question are asked, unprompted, to name the organization and to say whether it "reflects your interests, views, and concerns" completely or partially. Remaining respondents are then asked if any party or party surrogate "reflects your interests, views, and concerns more than the others" and if so to name it.[43]

The sequence of questions can be used to devise a binary measure of the presence of partisanship and an ordinal scale of its intensity. Postcommunist "strong partisans," as I call them, have a party of "their" own, recall its name, and say it fully embodies their concerns. "Moderate partisans"

---

[41] Arthur Miller and his coauthors use a question sequence quite close to this one: "Is there one particular party that expresses your views better than any of the other parties?" If yes, "Which one?" followed by an intensity question.

[42] After much debate, my Moscow colleagues and I came up in 1999 with Russian phraseology that describes the party or quasi-party as being close to the citizen, not the other way around, and that omits the qualifier "usually." No other version seems to be literate in the language.

[43] As a check on comprehension, the first of the four surveys, in late 1995, also asked respondents to name several of the leaders of the party with which they identified. Most had no trouble doing so.

Parties, Citizens, and the Prospects for Democratic Consolidation 191

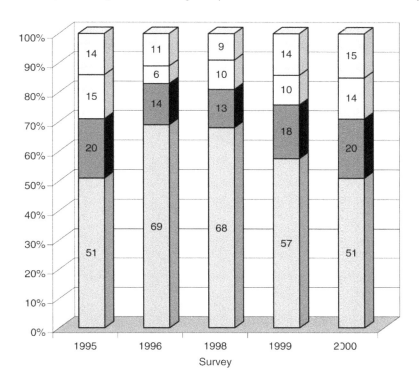

FIGURE 2. Partisanship in the Russian Electorate, 1995–2000

are the same but say their favored party fulfills their needs only partially. "Weak partisans" name a party that gratifies them more than the others. Nonpartisans offer straight negative responses or cannot answer.[44]

The distribution of partisanship in the voting-age population, as metered by the four-point strength scale, is tracked over the years 1995 to 2000 in Figure 2. The segment of the whole who come across as partisans – strong, moderate, or weak – ranges from a low of around one in three voting-age Russians in the summer of 1996 to a high of around one in two in the autumn of 1995 and the spring of 2000.

Figure 3 classifies the partisans by party of preference in our 1999 pre-election snapshot of the electorate. Eighty-five percent of them signaled

[44] Respondents who claimed to be partisans but could not name the party, or who named more than one party, were coded as nonpartisans.

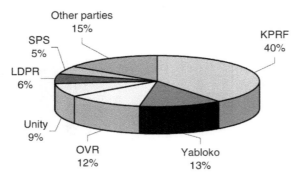

FIGURE 3. Distribution of Partisans, 1999

an affinity for one of the half-dozen parties that were to hurdle the 5 percent barrier in that December's PR vote for the Duma. Leading the parade, as happened in every one of the polls, was the KPRF, which had the sympathy of 40 percent of those we designate as partisans in 1999. Noncommunist parties and near-parties accounted for 60 percent of the partisan pool: the liberal Yabloko party, formed by Grigorii Yavlinskii and several confederates in 1993, with 13 percent of all partisans; the centrist OVR (Fatherland-All Russia) bloc, assembled by Yurii Luzhkov and Yevgenii Primakov in 1998 and 1999, at 12 percent; the pro-Kremlin Unity bloc organized on the eve of the 1999 campaign and endorsed by then Prime Minister Putin, with 9 percent; Vladimir Zhirinovskii's nationalist and populist LDPR (Liberal-Democratic Party of Russia), dating from 1990, with 6 percent; and the SPS (Union of Rightist Forces), an alliance cobbled together in 1999 from a miscellany of liberal groups, with 5 percent. Fifteen percent of partisans all told were disciples of a smattering of smaller parties and movements that fell short of 5 percent in the popular vote.[45]

The data, in short, do confirm the existence, though hardly the ubiquity, of some variety of partisan sentiment. Spurned collectively, the parties, or some of them, would seem nonetheless to have struck a chord singly with a multitude of Russian citizens. The 43 percent who were

---

[45] The distribution of partisans among parties had altered some by the time of our survey interviews with these same eligible voters following the presidential election of March 2000. In that encounter, the shares of three of the parties (the KPRF, Unity, and SPS) had increased and those of the rest of the parties had decreased. The KPRF had its own candidate in the presidential election, Gennadii Zyuganov, while Unity and most of the SPS leadership endorsed Vladimir Putin.

Parties, Citizens, and the Prospects for Democratic Consolidation 193

confessed partisans in the winter of 1999–2000 would disappoint by the standards of most of the core western democracies but land somewhere in the wide spectrum prevalent in Latin America in the 1990s.[46] It would come in about five percentage points below Spain's and Portugal's rate in the mid-1980s, a decade after the restoration of democratic rule, and about twenty-five points below Greece at the time.[47] These are not stellar results, but neither are they abysmal.

There is no obvious reason why aggregate levels of partisanship in the Russian electorate, as calibrated by our survey instrument, waver as they do. Short-term fluctuation in partisanship totals is not unknown in other nations.[48] Sampling or measurement error may bear some of the blame, although the panel format of four of the five Russian polls, the large samples, and the continuities in sample frame, research team, and questionnaire should have kept such errors to a minimum.[49] For what it is worth, the CSES questions, which I do not go into here, yield appreciably higher estimates of the incidence of partisanship.[50] Writing several years ago out of the 1995–6 data, I speculated that the ebb visible at that time was owing to the presidential election of 1996 being a less partisan affair than the Duma election of the winter before. The flow in the opposite direction in between the analogous elections of 1999 and 2000 refutes that diagnosis. In many countries, revealed partisan identification dips

---

[46] Party identifiers in Latin America have been found to number from a little over 30 percent of the adult population in Brazil and Venezuela to 67 percent in Uruguay. Mainwaring, *Rethinking Party Systems in the Third Wave of Democratization*, p. 31. In four of the eight Latin American countries for which this information was available, the share was less than 40 percent.
[47] Morlino, *Democracy between Consolidation and Crisis*, p. 169.
[48] In Italy, for example (ibid.), survey researchers found the overall level of partisanship to be 76 percent in 1958, 52 percent in 1985, and 63 percent in 1989.
[49] Green, Palmquist, and Schickler show in *Partisan Hearts and Minds* that interviewer and respondent error and random perturbation may produce greater inconsistency in responses to survey questions than there is in underlying attitudes. They are writing about individuals, however, and my comments concern the aggregate size of the partisan pool.
[50] Responses to the CSES questions would have made 65 percent of our respondents partisan identifiers in the second-wave survey done in the winter of 1999–2000 and 55 percent in the second-wave survey in the spring of 2000. The first figure is twenty-two percentage points higher than that rendered by the "my party" questions at the time and the second is six points higher. But the first run with the CSES questions was in a postelection poll, which makes for an inexact comparison with the preelection poll in which the "my party" questions were given. In the spring of 2000, when the gap in results between the CSES and the "my party" questions proved to be narrower, the questions were asked in the same postelection interview.

some between elections, and preelection surveys frequently unearth lower levels than postelection surveys. These generalizations might rationalize the depleted Russian figure in 1998 and maybe the abatement from late 1995 to mid-1996, but shoot a blank for 1999–2000. Election-by-election comparisons within the two genres do not resolve the mystery, either. Those meeting the partisanship criteria slipped from 49 percent of adults before the 1995 Duma election to 43 percent before the 1999 Duma election, whereas they climbed from 31 percent after the 1996 presidential election to 49 percent after the 2000 presidential election.

There are no grounds for taking the last comparison – 2000 versus 1996 – to be authoritative, comforting although it might be to see a secular increase in transitional partisanship. No such party-friendly or democracy-friendly trend can be discovered in the survey data. Partisanship in Russia is not unambiguously on the move from low levels to high levels or vice versa. Having broken through in the early to mid-1990s, when specialists began to detect it in public opinion polls, it then seemed to stall. Were later research to divulge that pause to be permanent or, worse, were the partisan stratum to shrink drastically, it would be time to ponder gloomy conclusions. Given the ground-zero embarkation point of a decade ago – no normal parties, no partisanship – for now we should emphasize the strides made and be agnostic about what comes next.

SOURCES OF PARTISANSHIP

The plain fact that a sizable subset of the population has evinced partisan attitudes in post-Soviet Russia counters blanket assertions about the logical or practical impossibility of their arising there. But it fails to pinpoint what it is in the transitional setting that facilitates the inception of partisanship. On that topic, research on the postcommunist countries and the mammoth comparative literature on parties and voting, which by and large treats partisanship as a prime mover and not a resultant of other factors, are almost mute.

Having exploited the polling data as a barometer of partisanship in the aggregate, I shall now use it to gain leverage on some sources of partisanship at the individual level. This can be done by examining variation in partisanship at the individual level and relating it statistically to hypothesized determinants. My spotlight shifts, in other words, from *how many* Russians have partisan awareness to *who* in Russia does and what we can infer about partisanship *dynamics* from that information.

Parties, Citizens, and the Prospects for Democratic Consolidation 195

The variation in the attitudinal outcome most urgently in need of elucidation is the division between transitional partisans and nonpartisans. Partisans have affiliated themselves with a party; nonpartisans are unattached. But the situation is less cut-and-dried than this, for on crucial points the enthusiasts of one party – the Communist Party of the Russian Federation – are a tribe apart. Communists comprised the better part of one-half of all partisans in 1999. Theirs is the sole big party to have campaigned without letup against the political and social status quo of the Yeltsin decade and, since 1999, of the post-Yeltsin dispensation under Putin. Only the KPRF, tracing its ancestry to the defunct CPSU, moors itself in the values, heroic myths, and rhetorical style of Lenin, Stalin, and the Soviet regime. Although noncommunist partisans are heterogeneous in not a few respects, for getting at the genesis of partisanship in the 1990's it is useful to lump them together and to separate them analytically from the clientele of the KPRF.

Potential Causes

I test for three generic kinds of explanation of individual-level partisanship. They echo themes and theoretical lineages prominent in the scholarship on political parties and behavior and were anticipated in our discussion of attitudes toward the party system and aggregate levels of partisanship in Russia.

One strategy hunts out clues to the puzzle in the *social characteristics* of citizens. The premise is that underlying sociological realities predispose certain individuals to invest psychically in a political party or movement.[51] This may be because membership in a social group equips someone with political aptitudes or skills, exposes them to favorable environmental influences, instigates people to connect parties to interests or identities they share with peers in the group – or makes some elusive difference we do not yet know how to spell out.

I single out several social indicators for attention:

- *Age*. We have already seen that acquiescence in multiparty competition has varied by generation, with younger Russians being more acceptant of it than their elders. Conceivably, this pattern will slosh over into partisanship. It could be that the tendency to take on board any kind of

---

[51] The sense of the argument here is close to what Europeanists have called "social partisanship." See Gunther and Montero, *The Anchors of Partisanship*, pp. 15–27, and again Green, Palmquist, and Schickler, *Partisan Hearts and Minds*.

partisanship goes down with advancing age. Conversely, the chances of coming to be a partisan expressly of the stodgy and backward-looking KPRF could be indifferent to age or could even go up with age.
- *Education.* Formal schooling is as discerning a marker as any of social status and modernity. Assuming that high status and a modern mentality stimulate participatory behavior, and counting partisanship as an oblique form of participation, it should follow that better-educated Russians will be more likely than the poorly educated to be partisans. With the KPRF, the tie might be fainter because that party sells itself as the champion of society's have-nots and might raise the hackles of the well educated.
- *Community size.* Similar reasoning would prescribe a relationship between partisan proclivities and urbanization, a central dimension of modernization. The larger the community of residence, the more apt a Russian living in it should be to identify with a political party. Again, the KPRF may buck the logic of this claim, as it tirelessly woos the denizens of villages and small towns, and we know from the published returns that it has done well in national elections there.
- *Sex.* Men all but monopolize senior governmental and party positions in Russia and tend to vote more regularly than women and to be better informed about politics. This would imply that males will more often pick up partisan allegiances.
- *Past CPSU membership.* About one-tenth of Russian adults belonged to the Communist Party of the Soviet Union at its membership peak in the late 1980s. One could well envision the values and personal connections accrued in the onetime ruling party tilting ex-members toward affiliation the KPRF and against affiliation with other groups.
- *Winner in reforms.* Individuals who prospered as Russia's economy staggered through liberal reforms in the 1990s might be more receptive to its new political order, and partisanship of one hue or another could ensue naturally from that. Presumably, economic winners would instinctively align themselves with pro-reform parties, while economic losers, unless they withdraw from politics completely, would identify with the adversaries of the reform course in the KPRF.[52]

---

[52] These suppositions are somewhat reminiscent of the view of partisan identification in the United States as a "running tally" of citizen evaluations of political and especially economic trends. See especially Fiorina, *Retrospective Voting in American National Elections.* Fiorina was writing about fluctuation in partisanship in established party-dominated polities, not about the initiation of partisan affinities.

A second approach would root partisanship in the sphere of *political engagement*. Irrespective of their biographies and of social traits that may handicap them or give them a head start, some individuals are better informed about and more caught up in political activity than others. A transitional political system is mercurial, and the parties and other players that populate it are unusually numerous and unusually precarious. Against this messy backdrop, we may conjecture that the politically engaged will be more amenable to becoming partisans by virtue of having the willingness to commit and the knowledge to sort through the bewildering and conflicting information about players and issues that is endemic to a country undergoing regime change. In a stable democracy, "a standing decision to identify with one or another party" may furnish a decision guide to "voters who have difficulty handling the cacophony of varying political claims and arguments."[53] In a proto-democracy or semi-democracy, where the cacophony is more deafening by an order of magnitude, the biggest hindrance is how to amass the acumen to arrive at that standing decision. The most inquisitive and the best briefed may have an inbuilt edge.[54]

Concretely, I propose to check out the influence on partisanship of a triad of measures of political engagement:

- *Interest in politics.* Interest in public affairs among the members of our 1999–2000 survey sample ran the gamut from keen absorption in political issues to nonchalance, with a clustering toward the interested end. The indicator I will resort to is a count of the frequency with which citizens follow politics. About 40 percent of respondents said they followed politics all the time, about as many did so sometimes, and the rest followed politics rarely or not at all.
- *Viewing TV news.* Russians, like the citizens of all industrial societies, get the lion's share of their political news from the mass media, and the supreme medium is television.[55] In the winter of 1999–2000, roughly

---

[53] W. Phillips Shively, "The Nature of Party Identification: A Review of Recent Developments," in John C. Pierce and John L. Sullivan, eds., *The Electorate Reconsidered* (Beverly Hills: Sage, 1980), p. 227.
[54] Partisanship may also reinforce political engagement. The statistical analysis attempted here will test for association only, not for direction of the causal arrow.
[55] Ninety-six percent of our survey respondents watched television, for an average of three-and-a-half hours a day, and 89 percent said television their "basic source of information about political events," versus 8 percent for radio and 3 percent for newspapers. See Colton and McFaul, *Popular Choice and Managed Democracy*, appendix C.

every second person watched the television news daily, every fourth watched almost daily, and every fourth watched less often or never.
- *Talking politics.* Aside from the electronic media, most Russians tap into private, face-to-face networks of communication about politics. These circuits cycle and recycle information and advocacy surrounding public personalities, organizations, and controversies. As an indicator, I will use a straightforward index of reported frequency of contact. About one-quarter of survey respondents told interviewers during the Duma campaign of 1999 that they had conversed about politics with family members or friends every day during the preceding week; about one-fifth had such conversations almost every day, an equal fraction several times, and about 40 percent had talked politics once or never during the week.

If political engagement does foster partisanship in a transitional polity, these variables ought to have independent but reinforcing consequences. The more a Russian takes a personal interest in politics, tunes in to the television news, and/or talks politics, the higher the chances should be of him or her adopting partisan attitudes. We can predict the effect to be greater on affiliation with parties other than the KPRF, a familiar icon of a bygone age.

Our last bundle of explanations come under the rubric of *political opinions*.[56] We have encountered two of the opinions considered in the review of Russian attitudes toward the party system; two others are about ideology:

- *Parties and ordinary people.* Cynicism about the political parties and how they relate to ordinary people is rampant in post-Soviet Russia (see Table 1). One would suspect that citizens who most devoutly believe the parties to be untrustworthy and remote from popular interests will be less susceptible to partisan appeals than persons who take a sunnier view of the parties' motives.

[56] In attempts elsewhere to model determinants of voting behavior in Russia (see Colton, *Transitional Citizenship*, and Colton and McFaul, *Popular Choice and Managed Democracy*), I have conceptualized issue opinions as having the same causal standing in relation to voting decisions as partisanship. In approaching determinants of partisanship here, I deviate slightly from that imputed causal sequence, and two of the opinions used (about the party system) are not ones we would normally think of as impacting on the vote. Statistical estimates of the effect of partisanship on electoral choice will control for issue preferences whether they are considered to be casually prior to or equivalent to partisanship.

- *Ideal number of parties.* Although almost all Russian voters look askance at the welter of obscure and ineffectual parties, opinions about remedy extend from outright suppression of competition (one party or none) to living with ten or more parties. One would predict that tolerance of a larger number of parties will abet partisanship in favor of the noncommunist parties that burgeoned in the 1990s; a propensity for a smaller number of parties should be congruent with partisanship for the KPRF.
- *Democratic political regime.* Alternatively, partisanship may be nurtured by personal opinions related to political issues grander than those relating to the party system as such. The grandest has to do with the nature of Russia's political regime. Asked to select from a four-way list the kind of political system most appropriate for their country, about one-quarter of survey respondents in 1999–2000 opted for the unreformed Soviet regime and about as many for either the current political system or a western democracy. The most popular setup, to the liking of more than 40 percent, was a reformed version of the Soviet system – "the Soviet system, but in a different, more democratic form" – a fictive arrangement that in the minds of many apparently would graft political pluralism onto a strong and paternalistic state. About 10 percent of respondents were not able to answer the question.
- *Left-right scale.* A final opinion that may mold partisanship is a measure of ideological consciousness. Sixty-eight percent of survey subjects were able to place themselves on an eleven-point left-right scale. The terminology of left and right has increasingly acquired in Russia the meaning it has in the European Union countries, with "left" standing for a preference for governmental intervention on economic and social questions and "right" for a laissez-faire stance.[57] Individuals of leftist and rightist orientation have incentives to latch onto political parties that present views corresponding to their own – notably the KPRF for left-wingers and more liberal parties for right-wingers.

---

[57] Using data from 1995–6, I argued to the contrary in "Ideology and Russian Mass Politics: Uses of the Left-Right Continuum," in Matthew Wyman, Stephen White, and Sarah Oates, eds., *Elections and Voters in Post-Communist Russia* (Cheltenham, UK: Edward Elgar, 1998), pp. 161–83. I have come around on this question, largely because the left-right discourse in Russia has become more coherent and more citizens are now able to place themselves on a left-right scale. See also Geoffrey Evans and Stephen Whitefield, "The Evolution of Left and Right in Post-Soviet Russia," *Europe-Asia Studies*, vol. 50 (September 1998), pp. 1023–42.

Estimates of Association

Table 2 sets down the results of a multilayered statistical analysis of Russians' partisanship in 1999–2000. It enlists as independent variables all the indicators just catalogued. The dependent variable is a three-way categorical measure with values for KPRF partisanship, affiliation with any other party, and nonpartisanship. Associations with the explanatory variables have been estimated by multinomial logit, a maximum likelihood procedure well suited to the analysis of a dependent variable consisting of discrete, nonordered categories.[58] The parameters recited in the table are not the logit regression coefficients, which are of no substantive interest, but estimated first differences in the predicted probability of the outcome occurring, computed from a statistical simulation.[59] Each first difference stands for the change in the predicted probability that a citizen will adhere to the given attitude accompanying a change in the value of the explanatory variable from its minimum to its maximum value, holding the specified control variables constant at their medians. For each estimation, the control variables include all other variables in the same causal category plus all variables in categories postulated to be causally prior to the explanatory variable highlighted, if any. I posit that the sociological variables are causally antecedent to all other variables and the political-engagement variables are causally antecedent to the political-opinion variables. The controls in the analysis guard against omitted-variable bias and filter out the confounding effect of other variables placed at earlier or equivalent stages of the causal flow. For each variable in the model, Table 2 records only the reduced-form effects with the proper controls locked in. The other parameters are suppressed for the sake of economy of presentation.

This statistical tool proves to be powerful and discriminating. It brings out manifold associations and does full justice to the intricacy of the attitudinal result. The presence of a statistically valid parameter in Table 2, positively or negatively signed, signifies the presence of a nonrandom relationship in the population between the outcome and the causal factor

---

[58] Good descriptions of the algorithm may be found in G. S. Maddala, *Limited-Dependent and Qualitative Variables in Econometrics* (Cambridge: Cambridge University Press, 1986), chap. 2, and J. Scott Long, *Regression Models for Categorical and Limited Dependent Variables* (Thousand Oaks, California: Sage, 1997), chap. 6.

[59] The regressions and simulations were done with Michael Tomz, Jason Wittenberg, and Gary King, CLARIFY: Software for Interpreting Statistical Results, Version 2.1 (Cambridge, Mass.: Harvard University, January 5, 2003 – at <www.king.harvard.edu>). CLARIFY is used in conjunction with the STATA package.

TABLE 2. *Total Effects of Social Characteristics, Political Engagement, and Political Opinions on Partisanship (Differences in Predicted Probabilities)*[a]

Explanatory variables	Partisan of KPRF	Partisan of other party	Nonpartisan
Social characteristics (controlling for other social characteristics)			
Year of birth[b]	−.20**	.07	.14*
Education[c]	.01	.22**	−.23**
Community size[d]	−.11**	−.02	.13**
Man[e]	.04**	.04*	−.09**
Past CPSU membership[e]	.13**	−.01	−.12**
Winner in reforms[f]	−.10**	.12**	−.02
Political engagement (controlling for social characteristics and other indicators of political engagement)			
Interest in politics[g]	.07**	.16**	−.24**
Viewing TV news[h]	−.03	.15**	−.12**
Talking politics[h]	.05**	.13**	−.19**
Political opinions (controlling for social characteristics, indicators of political engagement, and other political opinions)			
Parties and ordinary people[i]	.03*	.09**	−.12**
Ideal number of parties[j]	−.07**	.11*	−.04
Democratic political regime[k]	−.13**	.14**	−.01
Left-right scale[l]	−.19**	.19**	−.00

** *p* # .01
* *p* # .05

[a] Sample N = 1,916 for the analysis with the social characteristics on y and 1,839 for the analysis including political engagement and political opinions.
[b] Eight-point index with values for 1919 or earlier, 1920s, 1930s, 1940s, 1950s, 1960s, 1970s, 1980s.
[c] Six-point index with values for none or elementary education, incomplete secondary, secondary, secondary specialized, incomplete higher, higher.
[d] Five-point measure by quintile within the survey sample.
[e] Binary measure.
[f] Question reads, "In general, did you win or lose as a result of the reforms carried out in the country in the 1990s?" Generates a five-point index with values for lost, mostly lost, won some and lost some (volunteered response), mostly won, and won.
[g] Question reads, "Some people constantly follow what goes on in politics, while others are not interested in it. What can you say about yourself? Do you follow political events all the time, sometimes, very rarely, or do you not follow them at all?"
[h] Five-point index with values for frequency over the past seven days of zero, once, several times, almost every day, and every day.
[i] Question wording given in Table 1, note b. Values coded in reverse order from question wording. Missing values coded at the sample mean.
[j] Question wording given in Table 1, note f. Missing values coded at the sample mean. Values of more than ten coded at fifteen.
[k] Question reads, "What kind of political system, in your opinion, would be most appropriate for Russia?" Responses were "the Soviet system we had in our country before *perestroika*," "the Soviet system, but in a different, more democratic form," "the political system that exists today," and "democracy of the western type." Missing values coded at the sample mean.
[l] Question reads, "In politics people sometimes talk of left and right. Imagine a scale from 0 to 10 where 0 means the left and 10 means the right. Where would you place yourself on this scale?" Missing values coded at the sample mean.

we have laid out in hypothesis form. Many such associations have been uncovered. Most yet not all of them are in the predicted direction.

As can be seen in the top panel of the table, partisanship in transitional Russia is structured to some degree by citizens' social characteristics. The associations are asymmetrical, as is consonant with the multiple tradeoffs possible under the model.[60] Ceteris paribus, older persons, residents of smaller communities, and former members of the CPSU are markedly less liable than others to be nonpartisan and are more liable to be KPRF partisans. The young, urbanites, and individuals who never belonged to the CPSU are more likely than their compatriots to be nonpartisans and less likely to identify with the KPRF. Males have better odds than women of becoming partisans of both the KPRF and the other parties. For education and profit from the reforms of the 1990s, the calculus is rather different: the more highly educated are less likely to be nonpartisan and more likely to be non-KPRF partisans; reform winners are more likely than average to be non-KPRF partisans and less likely to be KPRF partisans.

The steepest social effects on partisanship are those generated by education. The one sociodemographic variable for which the associations contradict expectations is community size. When modernity is gauged by a high level of formal education, it cuts against nonpartisanship (and for noncommunist partisanship); when gauged by residence in a big city, it favors nonpartisanship (and disfavors KPRF partisanship). The most fascinating of the correlations with the sociological variables is that with age. If this association speaks to a societal "allergy" to partisanship at all, it is with a curious twist. It is the young in Russia, those having had the least contact with Soviet socialization, who have had the greatest antipathy to partisanship; the elderly are more likely to be politically partisan, but have been drawn in numbers only to the KPRF, the keeper of the socialist flame.

The middle panel of Table 2 bears out all three of our hypotheses about the catalytic effects of political interest and communication. As expected, Russians who are absorbed in politics, watch television newscasts faithfully, and talk politics with family and friends are less likely than the politically apathetic to eschew partisanship. More eager to partake in public life and having access to more abundant and more well-sifted information, the politically involved better navigate the topsy-turvy map of

---

[60] The differences in predicted probabilities are constrained to sum to zero, and the predicted probabilities from which they are derived sum to one. The model does not stipulate more than that.

transitional politics and stand a better chance of striking up a connection with a party. Interest in political issues, which governs motivation, has a stronger impact than the two variables measuring access to information. In each instance, noncommunist partisanship is the cardinal beneficiary of political engagement. For affiliation with the old-line KPRF, the effects are more meager than for the other parties, about whom fresh information is more of a necessity, and on the point of TV news viewing there is no significant relationship with KPRF partisanship. In a nutshell, being wired into the post-Soviet political environment makes the most difference to kinship with the parties that stand for post-Soviet ways.

In the lower panel of Table 2, we also find compelling evidence that political opinions color the partisan outcome. Judgments about the party system per se are a large part of the story. For both of the party-related opinions tested for, partisan feelings in favor of post-Soviet parties benefit from positive assessments of the party system. The perception that Russian parties empathize with ordinary people tips the scales against nonpartisanship and toward non-KPRF partisanship, having a tiny positive effect on the odds of alignment with the KPRF. The measure of the total number of parties favored discriminates between supporters of the KPRF, who tend to prefer fewer parties, and supporters of other parties, who are prepared to countenance more; there is no unmediated effect on the chances of being nonpartisan. As for preference for a more democratic political regime, it militates against identification with the KPRF and for identification with other parties. And location on the left-right continuum has the most potent effects of any of the opinion variables. Extraneous though it may be to disagreements about the parties and their defects, ideology impels many Russians to make connections with the partisan realm. Like attitude toward the number of parties, it cleaves KPRF partisans from the devotees of other parties, having no bearing on the nonpartisan category.

CONCLUSION

Few things would be as auspicious for democratic consolidation in Russia as the construction of an orderly party system and, underpinning it, a robust set of subjective identities yoking citizens to the major parties. This essay, concentrating on popular attitudes, has flushed out some glimmerings of a benign outcome. Most Russians distrust their parties in ensemble, accuse them of being impervious to their concerns, and recoil at the overcrowding of the partisan forum with inept, fly-by-night outfits. Even so, sentiments we can recognize as partisan, albeit tentative and murky ones, have been afoot in the electorate, confuting some of the more pessimistic premonitions about Russian parties. According to soundings in 1999–2000, in the vicinity of 40 to 50 percent of Russians exhibited a brand-name loyalty to a political party. A worrisome snag for the analyst is that there is no unimpeachable trend in these numbers. No one can say for sure whether stagnation, a second wind for partisanship, or decay will set the tone in the decade ahead.

For now, we are left to mull over what we know about the props of transitional partisanship and their ramifications. The provisional partisan attachments we see are not set in a vacuum. They are responsive to Russia's social structure, modes of political engagement, and opinions about the parties and about broader public issues. As those background factors change over time, so too can we expect changes in manifestations of partisanship. Generational succession and the gradual departure of former cardholders in the CPSU will tend to thin the ranks of KPRF partisans, and today's younger cohorts have until now been more aloof than their seniors from the partisan game. But relief may yet come from the current spurt in higher-education enrollments and the ripening of the post-1998 economic recovery ripening into a sustained boom, which is creating more winners and hence more potential converts to centrist and right-wing parties.[61] On the political-engagement and political-opinion fronts, the key to an upturn will be progress at the elite level in making party politics more exciting, less frivolous, and more plugged into decision making with real stakes. Party leaders who had more of a say in the country's government and were held to account for the heated words and cheap slogans they fling in the State Duma might inspire more confidence that they care about their constituents. Several recent revisions to the electoral rules – tighter registration requirements for federal parties, a switch to a mixed PR-district system for choosing regional assemblies, and the decision to lift the threshold for PR seating in the Duma to 7 percent (as of the 2007 parliamentary election) – may converge on a streamlining of the party system that would provoke hurrahs all around and make party politics more legible to rank-and-file citizens.

Russia's new strongman, Vladimir Putin, and his design for making Russia a "managed democracy" presided over by a strengthened state are

---

[61] The flip side of the coin is that growth may in theory reinforce social stratification and spur economic losers to affiliate with the KPRF. But no such effect was noticeable in the electoral cycle of 2003–04, in which the KPRF lost about half of its vote base.

far from unrelated to party issues.[62] As part of the package, he supported the rule changes intended to prune the number of parties and, unlike Yeltsin, lent his personal authority to the latest incarnation of the "party of power," the United Russia party (formerly the Unity bloc). Aided by Putin's reputation and one-sidedly favorable coverage in the media, United Russia swept to victory in the Duma election of December 2003, taking some 38 percent of the popular vote for the PR lists and two-thirds of the 450 Duma seats. In March 2004 Putin won re-election to a second term with more than 70 percent of the popular vote. Hanging in menacing fashion over the whole electoral game is the possibility that Putin will go much further – that the creeping authoritarianism inculcated by him, his Kremlin allies, and associates in the Russian security services will undo the democratic freedoms granted in the 1980s and 1990s. Were political competition to be curtailed from above, the development of mass partisan consciousness below and of party organization in the middle would be distorted and, in the worst case, made irrelevant by the consignment of parties to a decorative role. In such a scenario, Duverger's bleak vision of voters as "soft dough" to be kneaded without limit by the powers-that-be would prove if anything to be an understatement of the truth.

As the saga unfolds, it will behoove hands-on students of Russian and post-Soviet politics to address their research results to comparativists as much as to area scholars. By the same token, specialists on mass politics or on other parts of the world – North America included – should assimilate the good Russia-centered work that will materialize. Many of Russia's travails today have cropped up in scores of other countries. But much of the legacy its party builders, like its state builders, confront either is unique or synthesizes stock elements in uniquely perplexing ways. Learning from how they cope with or crack under the strain will be instructive to us all.

APPENDIX: SURVEY DATA

This chapter mostly relies on data collected in the first two waves of a three-wave panel survey of the Russian electorate executed before and after the State Duma election of December 19, 1999. My co-PI on the project was Michael McFaul of Stanford University and the Carnegie Endowment for International Peace. Our partners in Russia were the research group

---

[62] See Colton and McFaul, *Popular Choice and Managed Democracy*, chaps. 1 and 8.

at the Institute of Sociology of the Russian Academy of Sciences led by Polina Kozyreva and Mikhail Kosolapov. The research was funded by the National Science Foundation and the National Council for Eurasian and East European Research. In wave 1 of the survey, 1,919 persons were interviewed between November 13 and December 13, 1999. Of them, 1,842 were reinterviewed in a wave 2, between December 25, 1999, and January 25, 2000, and a wave 3 was to follow after the presidential election of March 26, 2000. Respondents were selected in a multistage area-probability sample of the voting-age population, with sampling units in thirty-three provinces of the Russian Federation.[63]

Occasional reference is made to data from an analogous election survey done in the same sample frame in 1995–6. The investigators were William Zimmerman and myself, collaborating with the same Russian colleagues. That sample was larger – 2,841 respondents in wave 1 in November–December 1995, dwindling to 2,456 in wave 3 in the summer of 1996. I make passing reference in the text and in Figure 1 to proprietary data from a survey done in 1998 on a consulting basis. Commissioned by John Marttila Communications of Boston, the poll was fielded in January–February of that year by Kozyreva and Kosolapov. The sample frame was the same as for the other surveys and the number interviewed was 1,541.

All univariate and bivariate statistics given in the article are weighted by household size, to correct the bias toward members of small households generated by the sampling method used in the survey. The multivariate analysis is carried out with the unweighted data.

---

[63] Sampling procedures were similar to those given in Colton, *Transitional Citizens*, pp. 236–8. One province was substituted for another in Siberia.

6

Comparative Democratization: Lessons From Russia and the Postcommunist World

Valerie Bunce

RECENT DEMOCRATIZATION[1]

Our understanding of recent democratization, both in theoretical and empirical terms, has been strongly influenced by the experiences of Latin America and southern Europe.[2] This is largely because the global wave of democratization began in these two regions. At the same time, scholars with expertise in these areas had an analytical advantage: they had long wrestled with issues of regime change, in whatever direction. Indeed, when a group of specialists in these two regions first convened at the Social Science Research Council to think together about democratization, the countries they studied were for the most part not yet moving from authoritarian to democratic rule.

The contributions of the transitions school, as members of this group came to be known, have been considerable. However, a question remains. Do the approaches, the concepts, and the arguments that have developed in the course of analyzing democratization in the "south" still stand, once we broaden our geographical and, therefore, historical and variable horizons? Does the addition of new cases, in short, lead us to rethink the origins, the practices, and the sustainability of new democracies?

The purpose of this chapter is to provide an answer to this question, by adding the postcommunist experience to the equation. In particular,

---

[1] I would like to thank Nancy Bermeo, George Breslauer, Michael McFaul, Phil Roeder, and Kathryn Stoner-Weiss for their comments on an earlier draft of this essay.
[2] The most influential work was the four-volume series edited by Guillermo O'Donnell, Philippe C. Schmitter, and Laurence Whitehead, *Transitions from Authoritarian Rule* (Baltimore: Johns Hopkins University Press, 1986).

I will conduct a conversation between two bodies of research: analyses of Latin America and southern Europe, which have collectively constituted the reigning wisdom in the field of democratization studies, and analyses of postcommunist politics in general and Russian politics in particular. Three relationships, all central to the comparative study of democratization, will be revisited – in particular, between the state and democratization, between the strategies of transition and subsequent political trajectories, and, finally, between the quality and the sustainability of democracy. Before we begin this dialogue, however, a prior question needs to be addressed; that is, why Russia is treated as a "first among equals" – to invoke a nostalgic phrase from communist era scholarship.

RUSSIAN TYPICALITY

The Russian case is of particular interest for two reasons. One is that the Russian experience is unusually rich in the puzzles it presents and the insights it produces. This is in large measure because of its muddied profile as "neither stable nor in revolution, neither a consolidating democracy nor a repressive authoritarianism, neither a market economy nor a command economy."[3] The ambiguities of Russian developments testify to the density of the transformational agenda; that is, the simultaneous construction of democracy, the nation, the state, and capitalism.

The other reason to focus on Russia is more controversial. Russia represents in many important respects the modal postsocialist case. At first glance, this would seem to be curious proposition, given the common presumption that Russia is unique – an argument that has found recent support in some unlikely quarters, including a number of economists who have been wrestling with the perverse outcomes of Russian reforms.[4] It is undoubtedly true that Russia has some distinctive characteristics, including, for example, the sheer physical span of the country and its former role as the "other" superpower. However, that should not obscure the important ways in which Russia represents the central tendency in what

---

[3] George Breslauer, "Evaluating Yel'tsin as a Leader," *Post-Soviet Affairs* 16, no. 1 (2000), 3.
[4] John Thornhill, "Russia's Unique Economy May Have Led to 1998 Crisis." *Financial Times*, February 22, 2000, 3. Also see Brian Pinto, Vladimir Drebentsov, and Alexander Morozov, "Non-Payments Cycle in Russia Suffocates Economic Growth – Proposal of World Bank Economists," *Transition: Newsletter about Reforming Economies*, World Bank/William Davidson Institution, 10, no. 6 (December 1999), 1–5; Joseph Stiglitz (former chief economist of the World Bank), "What I Learned at the World Economic Crisis," *The New Republic*, April 17, 2000.

is, to be sure, an unusually diverse region. Let us turn first to the economic and social sides of the equation. Russia is located at the regional average (in rough terms) with respect to its level of economic development and its progress on economic reforms (as indicated, for instance, by private sector share of the economy). On the social side, we see in Russia as in much of the region declining population, rising crime rates, and levels of literacy and urbanization that are above those found in countries at comparable levels of economic development. At the same time, the national diversity of the Russian Federation (with Russians comprising 82 percent of the population) represents the central tendency in the region – thanks in large measure to the dissolution along republican and therefore also national lines of the Soviet, Yugoslav, and Czechoslovak federations.

Russia's political profile is also typical in many respects. Like the vast majority of its neighbors, Russia is a new state, having returned in December 1991 to the approximate boundaries of its distant predecessor, the Russian empire of the mid-seventeenth century. At the same time, Russia has no democratic tradition and is considered, therefore, both an improbable and a fragile democracy. However, it has also been, despite its many flaws, a durable one.[5] In all these respects, Russia represents the dominant tendency in the postcommunist region.

Russia is also highly representative in its political details. Russia has a presidential system of government (only seven of the postcommunist regimes are parliamentary); Russia has held multiple competitive elections, as have nineteen other regimes in the region; Russian labor has been on the whole fragmented and weak[6]; and the Russian party system, while managing to structure the electorate in the sense of producing relatively stable ideological cleavages and voter commitments over time, has been nonetheless very slow to crystallize and lacks ideological definition.[7]

---

[5] See Michael McFaul, "Lessons from Russia's Protracted Transition from Communist Rule," *Political Science Quarterly* 114, no. 1 (1999), 103–30 and Steven L. Solnick, "Russia's 'Transition': Is Democracy Delayed Democracy Denied?" *Social Research* 66, no. 3 (Fall 1999), 789–824.

[6] See, in particular, Paul Christensen, *Class/Power/Politics: Labor, Management and the State under Gorbachev and Yeltsin* (Dekalb: Northern Illinois University Press, 1999); Stephen Crowley, *Hot Coal/Cold Steel: Russian and Ukrainian Workers from the End of the Soviet Union to the Postcommunist Transition* (Ann Arbor: University of Michigan Press, 1997). For similar arguments from the vantage point of east-central Europe, see David Ost, "Illusory Corporatism in Eastern Europe: Neoliberalism, Tripartism, and Postcommunist Class Identities," *Politics and Society* 28, no. 4 (December 2000), 503–30.

[7] Michael McFaul and Nikolai Petrov, "The 1999 Duma Elections in Comparative Perspective," in Michael McFaul, Nikolai Petrov, Andrei Ryabov, and Elizabeth Reisch, *Primer on Russia's 1999 Duma Elections* (Moscow: Carnegie Moscow Center, 1999), 3–10; Regina

Perhaps the most surprising aspect of Russian politics – and one that is, again, the central tendency in postsocialism and just as surprising when viewed from that larger vantage point – is the *absence* of both significant political and economic polarization among citizens and the limited role as well of extremist parties commanding widespread popular support.[8]

THREATS TO DEMOCRACY

Specialists in Latin America and southern Europe have argued in virtual unison that the biggest threat to democracy is the military. This observation has strong empirical support. For example, one can point to the long history of military interventions in Latin American politics, most of which terminated democratic politics, although some of which oversaw a return to democracy. There is, in addition, the attempted military coup d'état in Spain in 1982, which constituted by all accounts the most serious threat to democracy in the post-Franco era. A final indicator is the political power and legitimacy accorded the military in many contemporary Latin American constitutions, their democratic claims notwithstanding.[9]

Smyth, "Power as Patronage: Russian Parties and Russian Democracy," Policy Memo Series 106, Program on New Approaches to Russian Security, the Davis Center, Harvard University, February 2000; Ted Brader and Joshua Tucker, "The Emergence of Mass Partisanship in Russia," *American Journal of Political Science* 45 (January 2001), 69–83. On parties in east-central Europe, see Anna Grzymala-Busse, *Redeeming the Communist Past: The Regeneration of Communist Parties in East Central Europe* (Cambridge: Cambridge University Press, 2002); Herbert Kitschelt, Zdenka Mansfeldova, Radoslaw Markowski, and Gabor Toka, *Post-Communist Party Systems: Competition, Representation, and Inter-Party Cooperation* (Cambridge: Cambridge University Press, 1999); and Hubert Tworzecki, *Learning to Choose: Electoral Politics in East-Central Europe* (Stanford: Stanford University Press, 2002).

[8] See Richard Ahl, "Society and Transition in Russia," *Communist and Post-Communist Studies* 32 (1999), 175–93; David Mason and Svetlana Sidorenko-Stephenson, "Changing Public Perceptions and the Crisis of Confidence in the State: The Yeltsin Legacy," in Gordon B. Smith, ed., *State-Building in Russia: The Yeltsin Legacy and the Challenge of the Future* (Armonk: M. E. Sharpe, 1999), 155–76; Mikhail Dmitriev, "Party Economic Programs and Implications," in Michael McFaul, Nikolai Petrov, and Andrei Ryabov, with Elizabeth Reisch, eds., *Primer on Russia's 1999 Duma Elections* (Moscow: Carnegie Moscow Center, 1999), 37–58; Steven L. Solnick, "Gubernatorial Elections in Russia, 1996–1997," *Post-Soviet Affairs* 14, no. 1 (1999), 48–80. But see Valerii Solovei, "Kommunisticheskaya i natsionalisticheskoi transformatsii Rossii," in Lilia Shevtsova, ed., *Rossia: Politicheskaya* (Moscow: Carnegie Endowment for International Peace, 1998), 195–272.

[9] See Richard Ahl, "Society and Transition in Russia," *Communist and Post-Communist Studies* 32 (1999), 175–93; David Mason and Svetlana Sidorenko-Stephenson, "Changing Public Perceptions and the Crisis of Confidence in the State: The Yeltsin Legacy," in

When combined, these examples carry one message: the capacity of the military in these contexts to make or break regimes.

In much of the postcommunist world, by contrast, there is a long tradition of civilian control over the military – a tradition that goes far back in Russian history and that, with the rise of state socialism, was maintained by Soviet leaders at home and eventually projected outward to the members of the Soviet bloc. Civil-military relations, in short, was one area – and not the only one – where the authoritarian past proved to be a benefit, not a burden insofar as democratization after state socialism was concerned.[10] If the military is not so much of a problem, however, the state is – as analyses of Russia in particular, but also Albania, Georgia, Bosnia, Moldova, Serbia and Montenegro, and the Central Asian states have made clear.[11]

Before we can explore this relationship between the state and democratization, however, some definitions are in order. Let us begin with democracy. Following the procedural and parsimonious proclitivities of the discipline, we can define democracy in the following way: as a type

---

Gordon B. Smith, ed., *State-Building in Russia: The Yeltsin Legacy and the Challenge of the Future* (Armonk: M. E. Sharpe, 1999), 155–76; Mikhail Dmitriev, "Party Economic Programs and Implications," in Michael McFaul, Nikolai Petrov, and Andrei Ryabov, with Elizabeth Reisch, eds., *Primer on Russia's 1999 Duma Elections* (Moscow: Carnegie Moscow Center, 1999), 37–58; Steven L. Solnick, "Gubernatorial Elections in Russia, 1996–1997," *Post-Soviet Affairs* 14, no. 1 (1999), 48–30. But see Valerii Solovei, "Kommunisticheskaya i natsionalisticheskoi transformatsii Rossii," in Lilia Shevtsova, ed., *Rossia: Politicheskaya* (Moscow: Carnegie Endowment for International Peace, 1998), 195–272.

[10] On the variable scholarly readings of the impact of the socialist past, see Bela Greskovits, "Rival Views of Postcommunist Market Society: The Path Dependence of Transitology," in Michel Dobry, ed., *Democratic and Capitalist Transitions in Eastern Europe: Lessons for the Social Sciences* (Dordrecht: Kluwer Academic Publishers, 2000), 19–48. For studies that recognize the power of the socialist heritage, see Pauline Jones Luong, *Institutional Change and Political Continuity in Post-Soviet Central Asia: Power, Perceptions and Pacts* (Cambridge: Cambridge University Press, 2002) and Grzegorz Ekiert and Stephen E. Hanson, eds., *Capitalism and Democracy in Central and Eastern Europe: Assessing the Legacy of Communist Rule* (Cambridge: Cambridge University Press, 2002).

[11] See, for example, Stephen Holmes, "What Russia Teaches Us Now," *The American Prospect* 32 (July/August 1997), 30–9; Charles King, *The Moldovans: Romania, Russia, and the Politics of Culture* (Stanford: Hoover Institution, 2000); Ghia Nodia, "Putting the State Back Together in Post-Soviet Georgia" and Vadim Volkov, "Who Is Strong When the State Is Weak? Violent Entrepreneurship in Russia's Emerging Markets," both in Mark Beissinger and Crawford Young, eds., *Beyond State Crisis? Postcolonial Africa and Post-Soviet Eurasia in Comparative Perspective* (Washington, D.C.: Woodrow Wilson Center/Johns Hopkins University Press, 2002), 81–104 and 413–45, respectively. On stateness problems in Latin America, see Guillermo O'Donnell, "On the State, Democratization and Some Conceptual Problems," *World Development* 28 (1993).

of regime – or one approach to the organization of political power – that combines civil liberties, political rights, and institutionalized competition for political office. Even more succinct is the definition offered by Adam Przeworski: democracy as uncertain political outcomes.[12]

The state refers to a political entity combining two monopolies: a spatial monopoly and a monopoly over the legitimate exercise of coercion. What distinguishes a state from other political constructs, therefore, is the existence of spatially bounded political authority – or what was defined at Westphalia in the seventeenth century as the geographically bounded maintenance of political order.[13] States vary, of course, in the degree of contestation over boundaries and over the exercise of political authority within those boundaries. In weak states, contestation is high; in strong states, a monopoly is in place. Put more concretely: weak states feature such characteristics as permeable boundaries (given secessionist pressures and/or repeated international interventions), conflicts involving the definition of the nation, the privatization of coercion, low levels of popular compliance, and state failure to collect revenues and meet financial obligations.

THE WEAKNESS OF THE RUSSIAN STATE

The Russian Federation exhibits all of these deficiencies. As a number of studies have demonstrated, laws in Russia are irregularly used to conduct political or economic transactions, in large measure because other mechanisms are both more familiar and still functional.[14] Moreover, the

---

[12] See Adam Przeworski, *Democracy and the Market* (Cambridge: Cambridge University Press, 1991). Also see Robert Dahl, *Polyarchy* (New Haven: Yale University Press, 1971) and Philippe C. Schmitter and Terry Lynn Karl, "What Democracy Is...and Is Not," *Journal of Democracy* 2 (1991), 75–88.

[13] See Charles Tilly, *Coercion, Capital and European States, AD 990–1992* (Cambridge: Basil Blackwell, 1998); Charles Tilly, ed., *The Formation of Nation-States in Europe* (Princeton: Princeton University Press, 1975); Jeffrey Herbst, *States and Power in Africa* (Princeton: Princeton University Press, 2001); Michael Mann, *The Sources of Social Power: A History of Power from the Beginning to AD 760*, Vol. I (Cambridge: Cambridge University Press, 1986); Anna Grzymala-Busse and Pauline Jones Luong, "Reconceptualizing the State: Lessons from Postcommunism," *Politics and Society* 30 (December 2002): 529–54.

[14] See Kathryn Hendley, "Rewriting the Rules of the Game in Russia: The Neglected Issue of the Demand for Law," *East European Constitutional Review* 8, no. 4 (Fall 1999), 89–95; Cheryl W. Gray and Kathryn Hendley, "Developing Commercial Law in Transition Economies: Examples from Hungary and Russia" and Thomas Owen, "Autocracy and the Rule of Law in Russian Economic History," both in Jeffrey Sachs and Katharina Pistor,

Russian state lacks spatial harmonization of its laws, such that local laws are in repeated conflict with the laws of the center.[15] Perhaps the most dramatic testimony to the problem of law in Russia, however, is the statistic that in the Russian Federation in 1996, twenty-six tax collectors were murdered.[16]

The absence of a rule of law culture and the spatial fragmentation of the legal system together mean that in practice the Russian state encloses – or, more accurately, attempts to enclose – a number of micro-states within its boundaries. These micro-states are sufficiently well-defined that the political boundaries demarcating these units also function as economic boundaries. The result is a spatially segmented polity, economy, and state, with many units highly protectionist in both an economic and political sense. The weakness of the state, in short, goes hand-in-hand with the weakness of the Russian economy – a hardly surprising situation, given the central role of the state in creating the market integration necessary for capitalist economies to function effectively.[17] Finally, publics question the authority of the state; they tend to define their political allegiances in terms of local political units; and local officials take as their mandate the administration of local laws and the defense of the locality from encroachments by the center.[18]

If the internal boundaries of the Russian Federation are "too strong," then the external boundaries of this state are "too weak." Public agreement on the boundaries of the state is lacking, reflecting in large measure the weakness of Russian national identity. Why Russian identity is so weak reflects a number of factors, including the absence during the Soviet period of institutions that forge such an identity; the divisions within the Soviet and then Russian elite stratum over whether and how to define

---

eds., *The Rule of Law and Economic Reform in Russia* (Boulder: Westview, 1997), 139–68 and 23–40, respectively; and George Yaney, "Law, Society, and the Domestic Regime in Russia in Historical Perspective," *American Political Science Review* 59 (June 1965), 379–90.

[15] Kathryn Stoner-Weiss, "Central Weakness and Provincial Autonomy: Observations on the Devolution Process in Russia," *Post-Soviet Affairs* 15 (1999); Kathryn Stoner-Weiss, *Resisting the State: Reform and Retrenchment in Post-Soviet Russia* (Cambridge: Cambridge University Press, forthcoming).

[16] Holmes, "What Russia." This echoes an earlier period of political turmoil in Russia – that is, the years between the 1905 and 1917 revolution – when public officials were also the target of considerable violence. See Sheila Fitzpatrick, *The Russian Revolution* (Oxford: Oxford University Press, 1991).

[17] David Woodruff, *Money Unmade: Barter and the Fate of Russian Capitalism* (Ithaca: Cornell University Press, 1999).

[18] See, in particular, Stoner-Weiss, *Resisting the State*.

this identity; and, finally, the considerable constraints on the construction of a coherent identity when the particular proto-nation in question is located in the core, not the periphery, within an empire, not within a state.[19] With national identity poorly defined and liberalism orphaned as a consequence of the costs of the Russian transition, Russian nationalism has often become the preserve of an extreme right that blames a conspiracy of foreigners and domestic minorities for Russian travails.[20] Moreover, with both the state and the economy compartmentalized, the external boundaries of the state have been subject to considerable conflict. This is evidenced most dramatically by the ongoing wars in Chechnya.[21] To summarize, then: Russia exhibits a pattern precisely opposite to that of strong states – soft, not hard external boundaries, and hard, not soft internal boundaries.

Finally, there is the economic crisis that has engulfed Russia. The seriousness of this crisis can be seen, for example, in the following estimate: if Russia were to grow at 5 percent a year from 2000–15 (which is an optimistic forecast), it would only manage then to return to its economic size in 1989, when the transition began.[22] There are many factors, of course, that have contributed to this dismal record, but one of the most important – as identified in cross-national studies of economic performance in the postcommunist world – seems to be the weakness of the Russian state.[23]

---

[19] See, especially, Yitzhak Brudney, *Reinventing Russia: Russian Nationalism and the Soviet State, 1953–1991* (Cambridge: Harvard University Press, 1998); Veljko Vujacic, "Historical Capacities, Nationalist Mobilization, and Political Outcomes in Russia and Serbia: A Weberian View," *Theory and Society* 25 (December 1996).

[20] See, especially, Stephen Shenfield, "Foreign Assistance as Genocide: The Crisis in Russia, the IMF, and Interethnic Relations," in Milton Esman and Ronald Herring, eds., *Carrots, Sticks and Ethnic Conflict: Rethinking Development Assistance* (Ann Arbor: University of Michigan Press, 2001).

[21] Anatol Lieven, *Chechnya: Tombstone of Russian Power* (New Haven: Yale University Press, 1998) and Matthew Evangelista, *The Chechen Wars: Will Russia Go the Way of the Soviet Union?* (Washington, D.C.: Brookings Institution, 2002). On the issue of bargaining between the regions and the center, see Solnick, "Gubernatorial Elections"; Daniel Treisman, "Russia's Ethnic Revival: The Separatist Activism of Regional Leaders in a Postcommunist Order," *World Politics* 49 (January 1997), 212–49; Valerie Bunce, "Conflict, Compromise and Cooperation: Explaining Center-Regional Bargaining in Ethnofederations," paper presented at the annual meeting of the International Studies Association, Portland, Oregon, February 27, 2003.

[22] As estimated by Vladimir Popov. See "The Political Economy of Growth in Russia." Program on New Approaches to Russian Security, No. 17, Davis Center, Harvard University, 2000.

[23] Ibid. For an analysis that addresses the difficulties federalism poses for structural adjustment policies, see Karen Remmer and Erik Wibbels, "The Subnational Politics of

This is a state that, as already noted, has failed to integrate the economy; that has yet to develop a geographically consistent commercial code; that has great difficulties collecting taxes, paying its bills, delivering energy, or providing public order; that devotes much less money to ordinary governing functions than other states; that has overseen both a demonetization of the economy; and, more generally, that struggles to enforce contracts and monopolize coercion.[24] Although the Russian economy is no more corrupt than a host of other economies that are judged, nonetheless, to be effective, at least for now (for example, China), corruption in Russia becomes a serious problem because it is both reflects and adds to the deficiencies already noted.[25]

If there is a consensus that the Russian state is weak, there is also a consensus that this poses a serious problem for Russian democracy.[26] As Stephen Holmes has argued: "Today's Russia makes excrutiatingly plain that liberal values are threatened just as thoroughly by state incapacity as by despotic power."[27] This line of argument has also been treated as a more general proposition: "no usable state, no democracy."[28] Far less clear, however, is *how* state capacity affects democracy – an issue that has been largely ignored for a number of reasons. For example, most definitions of democracy assume the existence of a capable state (which was a reasonable assumption for both the West and Latin America, given their felicitous sequencing of state-building, then democratization); the crafting of democracy in both Latin America and southern Europe has tended to specialize in regime transition, while holding the state constant[29]; and those interested in transitions from authoritarianism to democracy, like their counterparts pressing for neoliberal economic reforms, have been

---

Economic Adjustment: Provincial Politics and Fiscal Performance in Argentina," *Comparative Political Studies* 33, no. 4 (2000), 419–45.

[24] See, especially, Vadim Volkov, "Between Economy and State: Private Security and Rule Enforcement in Russia," *Politics and Society* 28, no. 4 (December 2000), 437–82.

[25] See, for example, Dmitry Glinski and Peter Reddaway, 'The Ravages of 'Market Bolshevism.'" *Journal of Democracy* 10, no. 2 (1999), 19–34.

[26] See, for example, Alfred Stepan, "Russian Federalism in Comparative Perspective," *Post-Soviet Affairs* 16 (April–June 2000), 133–76 and Stephen Hanson, "Defining Democratic Consolidation: Reflections on the Institutionalization of Postcommunist Regimes," in Richard Anderson, M. Steven Fish, Stephen Hanson, and Philip Roeder, eds., *Postcommunism and the Theory of Democracy* (Princeton: Princeton University Press, 2001).

[27] "What Russia Teaches Us Now," *The American Prospect* 32 (July/August 1997), 33.

[28] As observed in "Russia on the Brink: Democracy or Disaster?" *Newsletter of the Helen Kellogg Institute for International Studies* (Notre Dame) 31 Fall 1998), 17.

[29] See, especially, Robert Fishman, "Rethinking State and Regime: Southern Europe's Transition to Democracy," *World Politics* 42 (1990), 442–60.

prone to emphasize the value of what can be called state "subtraction."[30] Just as diverting were two other assumptions – that authoritarian states, especially of the state socialist variety, were big and therefore capable, and that pervasive violence indicates political control (when it may suggest the very opposite).[31] Finally, both the literature on democratization and on state-building seemed to suggest that the two could not be combined, because they "exhibit contradictory logics."[32] As Dankwart Rustow argued more than thirty years ago, democracy cannot enter into the zone of realistic political choice unless the national and state questions have been resolved.[33]

THE RELATIONSHIP BETWEEN THE STATES AND REGIMES

The postcommunist experience – with its twenty-two new states, only seven of which can be deemed consolidated democracies – asks us to reconsider these arguments. We can begin to assess the relationship between the state and democracy by recognizing a more general point: the close interdependence between states and regimes. To be effective, regimes of whatever type must function as an ideological monopoly across space. If regimes are contested within the borders of a state, they are by definition less sustainable. Regimes, therefore, depend on the state – to provide ideological consistency within state borders, to define the nation that then constitutes the basis for citizenship and compliance, and to give the regime the spatial reach it requires to govern effectively. Weak states, in short, are necessarily associated with weak regimes, whether the regime in question is democratic or authoritarian. Just as the deregulation of the regime's ideological monopoly can deregulate the state's spatial monopoly, a decline in the state's capacity to project authority consistently across space is usually accompanied by a proliferation of regimes.

It is, therefore, far from accidental that revolutions tend to combine spatial with ideological fragmentation; that is, the trilogy of secessionist

---

[30] For a counterargument that economic reforms are in part state-building exercises, see Hector Schamis, *Re-Forming the State: The Politics of Privatization in Latin America and Europe* (Ann Arbor: University of Michigan Press, 2003, forthcoming). Also see Erika Weinthal, *State-Making and Environmental Cooperation* (Cambridge, MA: MIT Press, 2002).
[31] As noted by Herbst, *States and Power*, 91
[32] The phrase is taken from Hector Schamis, *Re-Forming the State*, 206–7.
[33] "Transitions to Democracy: Toward a Dynamic Model," *Comparative Politics* 2 (1970), 337–63.

movements, the collapse of the state's coercive capacity, and the multiplication of regimes. Note, for example, the Bolshevik Revolution, with its signifying indicators of dual power and leakage of the Polish and Baltic parts of the Russian empire (which some political leaders of Ukraine attempted to emulate, but without success). It is also not accidental that the weakening of authoritarian regimes is often accompanied, especially in multinational contexts where minorities are geographically concentrated, by growing demands for regional autonomy and sometimes independent statehood.[34] Here, the Spanish and Mexican cases are instructive; so, most obviously, are the Soviet Union, Yugoslavia, and Czechoslovakia during the last decade of authoritarian rule.

The theoretical boundaries that social scientists have erected to distinguish between the domains of the state and the regime – boundaries that are often in practice discarded with state and regime used interchangeably – are in an empirical sense highly porous and interactive, especially at the extremes of a continuum defined by weak and strong poles.[35] Thus, deficits in one domain usually carry with them deficits in the other. Put differently: the ideological and the spatial sides of politics – or the domain of the regime and of the state, respectively – tend to be infectious, with liabilities transferable across the two political arenas. Assets also travel. Strong regimes can build strong states. By strong regimes, I refer to regimes that are based on a widespread public consensus about – and elite compliance with – the rules of the political game. When regimes are strong, they can lend power to states. This is one reason why at least some of the new states in the postcommunist region – for example, the Czech Republic, Slovenia, and the Baltic countries – have been so successful with respect to both state-building and democratization. A popular consensus about statehood and regime form was joined with two assets carried over from the state socialist period: well-defined boundaries and a nationalism rooted republican institutions and aligned with a liberal political agenda.

It was precisely the absence of many of these assets that made the Russian Federation's transition to independence and democracy so

---

[34] Daniel Conversi, "Domino Effects or Internal Developments: The Influence of International Events and Political Ideologies on Basque and Catalan Nationalism," *Western European Politics* 16 (July 1993), 245–70.

[35] On the failure to distinguish between the regime and the state, see Fernando Henrique Cardoso, "On the Characterization of Authoritarian Regimes in Latin America," in David Collier, ed., *The New Authoritarianism in Latin America* (Princeton: Princeton University Press, 1979), 33–57.

difficult. In that context, weak national identities and limited public consensus regarding both statehood and democracy locked the new regime and new state into a vicious circle. What also contributed to the problematic interaction between state-building and democratization were five other features of the Russian context that also happen to describe the situation in much of postcolonial Africa: poor correspondence between national and state boundaries as a consequence of imperial mischief; the difficulties of administering large expanses of territory with sparse populations; fragmented domestic markets; sudden independence; and institutional legacies from the imperial past that worked against a common identity, state capacity, and a popular and elite consensus regarding the ideological complexion of regimes-in-the-making.[36]

THE STATE AND DEMOCRATIZATION

With these more general observations in mind, we can now turn to the specifics of the relationship between the state and democratization. As argued above, democracy combines rights, liberties, and competition. There is no mention of the state. However, a capable state is nonetheless implied. Can there be civil liberties and political rights in the absence of rule of law? To meet the democratic standard, civil liberties and political rights must be expansive, guaranteed, and consistently applied across individuals, circumstances, and space. It is precisely the state that provides these necessary conditions.[37] At the same time, can political competition function effectively in a weak state? Again, the answer is no – in three ways. First, competition itself must take place through elections that are free, fair, and regular. In the absence of standard operating procedures that the state provides, these guarantees would ring hollow. Second, the rules governing competition for political office must be democratic, irrespective of where and when they take place. Put differently, the internal borders of the state – that is, the administrative subunits that make up the whole – can diversify the electoral context, but not in ways that violate democratic standards. Again, the key issue is spatial hegemony, legal consistency, and

---

[36] Herbst, *States and Power*. These are long-standing issues in Russian history, evident long before and even during "high Stalinism." See Anatole Leroy-Beaulieu, *The Empire of the Tsars and the Russians* (New York: Putnam and Sons, 1989) and James Harris, *The Great Urals: Regionalism and the Evolution of the Soviet System* (Ithaca: Cornell University Press, 1999).

[37] See Barry Weingast, "The Political Foundations of Democracy and the Rule of Law," *American Political Science Review* 91 (June 1997), 245–63.

compliance. Finally, if those exercising power are not elected officials and if elected officials cannot access the resources necessary to meet public expectations and implement the decisions they make, then the relationship between competitive elections and political accountability – a relationship assumed by most definitions of democracy and required for democratic governance – cannot materialize.

What I am suggesting, therefore, is that the attributes commonly used to denote democracy are best understood as necessary, but not sufficient defining conditions. They recognize the forms of democracy, but ignore its foundations. Thus, in a weak state context, the attributes of democracy do not have the same meaning, nor do they have the desired – or, for that matter, the assumed and the required – effects.

Indeed, the same holds true for capitalism – as David Woodruff has argued.[38] Without well-defined borders, consolidated and consistently exercised political authority within those borders, and the rule of law and administrative procedures that render the state a "cage of reason," the state is too weak to secure either the capitalist or the democratic project.[39] Ideological fragmentation, therefore, goes hand-in-hand with spatial fragmentation. To return to the specific case of the Russian Federation: democracy is not in fact the only game in Russian towns.

BRIDGING VERSUS BREAKAGE

Specialists in Latin American and southern European politics have devoted considerable attention to identifying optimal approaches to democratization – an issue prompted not only by their normative commitments to democracy, but also by their assumptions that new democracies are inherently fragile enterprises, that they can be crafted (and quickly) by political elites, and that their forms and future reflect, as a consequence, the quality of elite crafting.[40] Although disagreements abound concerning the payoffs attached to various decisions, such as the relative

---

[38] David Woodruff, "Rules for Followers: Institutional Theory and the New Politics of Economic Backwardness in Russia," *Politics and Society* 28, no. 4 (December 2000), 437–82.
[39] Bernard Silberman, *Cages of Reason: The Rise of the Rational State in France, Japan, the United States and Great Britain* (Chicago: University of Chicago Press, 1993).
[40] See, especially, Guiseppe Di Palma, *To Craft Democracy* (Berkeley: University of California Press, 1980); O'Donnell, Schmitter, and Whitehead, eds., *Transitions from Authoritarian Rule*; Terry Lynn Karl, "Dilemmas of Democratization in Latin America," *Comparative Politics* 23 (1990), 1–22.

costs and benefits of opting for parliamentary versus presidential systems of government, there is, nonetheless, a consensus that the best approach to transition is one that forges *compromises* between two sets of elites: authoritarian leaders and leaders of the democratic opposition. Without such compromises, the two camps are polarized and the future of democracy, already uncertain, becomes even more so. Thus, the key to successful democratization in the early stages of the transition seems to be those strategies that find ways to bridge the old and the new orders.

To understand the logic here, we must recognize that democratization requires movement on three fronts: ending authoritarian rule, creating democratic institutions, and yet attaching authoritarians to the new political order. The trick, therefore, is finding ways to shift from authoritarian to democratic politics, but without unleashing a political backlash from those groups facing a deregulation of their political monopoly. For specialists on southern Europe and Latin America, these seemingly contradictory demands counseled a cautious approach to transition; that is, one that slows down the pace of or obscures the downward political mobility of the former privileged elites, while providing them with incentives to play by the new, not the old political rules.[41]

These considerations have led analysts to prefer three specific strategies. First, they advocated pacting – or agreements struck between authoritarians and democrats that specify to mutual liking (or at least tolerance) when and how politics is to be deregulated. The second preference is for free, fair, and competitive founding elections that give support not just to opposition parties, but also to parties that contain representatives of the authoritarian order. Finally, democratization, it is argued, is well-served by interim leaders who have popular support and who combine a forward-looking commitment to democracy with backward-looking connections to the authoritarian past. What I have just described is precisely the Spanish model of democratization – a transition to democracy that, despite widespread fears of failure, was successful, largely because of what many have seen as the quality of elite crafting.[42]

---

[41] This is the theme, for example, of O'Donnell, Schmitter and Whitehead, eds., *Transitions from Authoritarian Rule*. Moderate strategies, however, do not mean moderate politics; indeed, such strategies arise in response to high levels of political conflict. See Nancy Bermeo, "Myths of Moderation," *Comparative Politics* 29 (1997), 305–22.

[42] This has been argued most straightforwardly by Richard Gunther. See "Spain: The Very Model of a Modern Elite Settlement," in John Higley and Richard Gunther, eds., *Elites and Democratic Consolidation in Latin America and Southern Europe* (Baltimore: Johns Hopkins University Press, 1992), 36–80.

If moderation is preferred in the political realm, moreover, it also emerges as the strategy of choice for the economic arena. The key issues here are the following. First, given changes in international economic norms and the mounting economic costs of import substitution industrialization, many new democracies must contend not only with building a democratic order, but also introducing neoliberal economic reforms. Second, in the short-term, such reforms tend to concentrate losers while dispersing winners. Finally, what these reforms seem to require is precisely what is in short supply in new democracies; that is, patient publics and powerful political leaders, insulated from the wrath of voters and vested interests and committed to staying the difficult economic reform course. Put simply, then, there are serious tensions between democratization and economic reform.[43]

There are, however, three ways in which such tensions can be alleviated. One is through pacting, as Karen Remmer has observed:

Not only have they (pacts) created the political space necessary to adopt drastic policy measures, pacts have also inhibited popular participation in policy formation processes, thereby offering guarantees of economic policy continuity and limited social redistribution to propertied elites who have historically mounted the major challenges to democracy in the region.[44]

A second approach is designing economic reforms in ways that bring old economic interests on board. Here, the argument is that political coalitions must be built that bridge the old and the liberalized economy and that transform in effect old rent seekers into new ones. Such a strategy invests, in turn, in state capacity – a vital component of both sustainable democracy and sustainable and beneficial economic reforms.[45] The final approach advocates where possible a sequencing of reforms. For example, Spanish leaders consolidated democracy first and only later

---

[43] See, for example, Stephan Haggard and Robert Kaufman, *The Political Economy of Democratic Transitions* (Princeton: Princeton University Press, 1995) and Leslie Armijo, Thomas Biersteker, and Abraham Lowenthal, "The Problems of Simultaneous Transitions," in Larry Diamond and Mark Plattner, eds., *Economic Reform and Democracy* (Baltimore: Johns Hopkins University Press, 1997). For the African case, see Henry Bienen and Jeffrey Herbst, "The Relationship between Political and Economic Reform in Africa," *Comparative Politics* 29 (October 1996), 23–42.
[44] Karen Remmer, "The Political Impact of Economic Crises in Latin America in the 1980s," *American Political Science Review* 85 (September 1991), 734.
[45] See Schamis, *Re-Forming the State* and Bela Greskovits and Hector Schamis, "Democratic Capitalism and the State in Eastern Europe and Latin America," paper presented at the Annual Meeting of the American Political Science Association, Atlanta, September 2–5, 1999.

introduced needed economic reforms.[46] This strategy has two related advantages: it secures democracy and, in so doing, invests in the regime's future capacity – through enhanced political legitimacy – to introduce and implement neoliberal reforms. It is an approach that reconciles the contradictory nature of economic reform; that is, the concentration of power necessary to introduce such reforms and the legitimacy required to assure their full and sustained implementation.

Whether we focus on the politics or the economics of transition, the recommendation seems to be the same. The best strategy is one that reconciles the contradictions of transition by bridging the old and the new orders. All of these arguments would seem to be even more compelling when applied to the postcommunist region. Here, we can note, for example, the greater economic and political costs attached to a transition to capitalism, given the Communist Party's conjoined economic and political monopoly, the unusually unfavorable economic point of departure for these transitions, and in many cases the role of mobilized publics in bringing down the old order.

However, what we discover in the postcommunist region is that the opposite strategy – that is, breakage, not bridging – emerges as the most successful approach to political and economic transition.[47] Thus, the most well-defined and full-scale democracies in the postcommunist area – that is, Poland, Hungary, the Czech Republic, Slovenia, and the Baltic states – differ in a number of respects but share one commonality: an early and thoroughgoing rejection of both the politics and economics of the state socialist past.

To elaborate: whereas the transitions in Hungary, Poland, and Slovenia were pacted, the transitions in the Czech Republic and the Baltic states were not. Thus, there seems to be no particular reason to privilege pacting over, say, mass mobilization as the optimal way to begin the transition to

---

[46] See, for example, Haggard and Kaufman, *The Political Economy*; Jose Maria Maravall, "Politics and Policy: Economic Reforms in Southern Europe," in Pereira, Jose Maria Maravall and Adam Przeworski, eds., *Economic Reforms in New Democracies: A Social Democratic Approach* (Cambridge: Cambridge University Press, 1993), 77–131. New democracies, however, may be unusually capable of implementing economic reforms because of increased political legitimacy. See Karen Remmer, "The Politics of Economic Stabilization: IMF Standby Programs in Latin America, 1954–1984," *Comparative Politics* 19 (October 1986).

[47] See Bunce, "The Political Economy"; Michael McFaul, "The Fourth Wave of Democracy and Dictatorship: Noncooperative Transitions in the Postcommunist World," *World Politics* 54 (January 2002), 214–44; Timothy Frye, "The Perils of Polarization in the Postcommunist World," *World Politics* 54 (April 2002) 308–37.

democracy. Second, what is common to all the successful cases of democratization in the postcommunist world – and what distinguishes them from all those regimes that fall short of the democratic standard – is the outcome of the founding election. Where the opposition forces won handily – and, thus, where the ex-communists suffered a decisive electoral defeat – is precisely where the consolidation of democracy has gone the furthest. Finally, this pattern continues with respect to economic reform. In the postcommunist world, there is a very high correlation between democratization and economic reform. Thus, the most democratic regimes are also the regimes that have made the greatest progress in shifting from a socialist to a capitalist economy. By contrast, the regimes that have remained authoritarian have failed to introduce economic reforms, and the regimes that fall in between the political stools of democracy and dictatorship evidence one of two patterns: moderate progress on economic reforms or introduction of significant reforms that were then either halted or sabotaged.[48]

What makes these observations all the more compelling are the following considerations. First, there are no cases in the region of democratization without economic reforms. Second, economic reforms tend to be introduced early or not at all. Finally, to join the observations about economic reform with some of the earlier arguments, we can conclude that the pronounced pattern in the cases of successful democratization in the postcommunist setting has been a substantial victory of the opposition forces in the founding election followed by rapid introduction of large-scale economic reforms and democratic consolidation. Put succinctly: political and economic breakage do not only go together, but they also seem to be mutually supportive – a pattern at variance with the experiences of Latin America and southern Europe.

RETURNING TO RUSSIA

With these generalizations in mind, let us return to the Russian case. Russia occupies the middle position; that is, a regime where the founding election produced divided support between the communists and the

---

[48] See Bunce, "The Political Economy"; Frye, "The Perils"; M. Steven Fish, "The Determinants of Economic Reform in the Post-Communist World," *East European Politics and Societies* 12 (Winter 1998), 31–78. But also see Jeffrey Kopstein and David Reilly, "Geographical Diffusion and the Transformation of the Postcommunist World," *World Politics* 53 (October 2000), 1–37.

opposition forces (facilitated by a mixed presidential-parliamentary system); where democracy has been compromised; and where radical economic reforms were introduced early, even before democratic institutions were fully fashioned, only to be sabotaged by various interests and ultimately by decision makers themselves. The design of the Russian economic reforms, moreover, was based on the perceived necessity of coopting the support of those interests privileged in the old order.[49] This, in turn, created a "politics of partial reform," wherein powerful interests – the short-term winners in the reform process – were able to access a steady stream of rents precisely because the economy was perched between state socialism and capitalism.[50] To complete the economic transition would deny them their rents, just as completing the political transition would do the same for democratization.

A strategy of bridging, therefore, has been very costly for Russia, whether we focus on democratization or economic reform. The weakness of accountable government is matched in the Russian setting by abysmal economic performance. The question then becomes: why do strategies of bridging and breakage have such different consequences in Latin America and southern Europe versus the postcommunist region? Suffice to note here that what seemed to influence variations by region in the costs and benefits of these two strategies were two interrelated factors: the desire and the capacity of the opposition forces to move quickly on political and economic fronts. In the most successful southern cases, desire was moderate and capacity was low, given such considerations as the absence in many instances of widespread public mobilization against authoritarian rule, the constraining historical memories associated with democratic breakdown, the continuing power of the military, and the highly uncertain nature of these transitions (largely because they began before democracy had shown itself to be a global enterprise).

By contrast, the most successful eastern cases combined high desire and high capacity. This reflected such considerations as the regionwide character of the collapse of state socialism and the many precedents of successful transition elsewhere, the absence in many cases of democratic breakdowns in the past, the long-institutionalized distancing of the military from politics, and the clear message, given mass protests and the outcome of the

---

[49] See Andrei Shlaifer and Daniel Treisman, *Without a Map: Political Tactics and Economic Reform in Russia* (Cambridge: MIT Press, 2000).
[50] Joel Hellman, "Winners Take All: The Politics of Partial Reform in Postcommunist Transitions," *World Politics* 50 (1998) 203–34.

first election, that citizens were quite supportive of democracy. Equally important was the widespread belief that failure to break with state socialism and take advantage of the political honeymoon would necessarily compromise both the democratic and the capitalist project. Just as important was a final consideration. In some cases, nationalism was defined as an anti-communist and anti-Soviet project, and, precisely for those reasons, a pro-western and pro-liberal project. With the end of state socialism, the Soviet bloc, and sometimes even the state, nationalism then functioned to lengthen the political horizons of the public, forge a consensus among ruling elites, confer considerable power on newly elected leaders, and, finally, place democratization and economic reform at the top of the political agenda.[51]

The contrast between the east and the south, therefore, can be put straightforwardly: the contexts of the two sets of transitions were different, these differences produced different calculations about both the capacity to change and the necessity of doing so, and the resulting actions produced in turn a different array of costs and benefits. Thus, the south had one path to success and the east quite another, and this reflected not regional differences per se but rather differences in both authoritarian legacies and transitional timing. There is no inherent advantage, therefore, to approaching the transition as a matter of either bridging or breakage. Indeed, as I will elaborate below, there is also no reason to assume that all of these politicians were confronted with the same choices.

THE QUALITY VERSUS THE SUSTAINABILITY OF DEMOCRACY

As already observed, the literature on recent democratization tends to converge on two key assumptions. The first is that elites are disproportionately responsible for both the founding and the survival of democracy. The other is that the quality of democracy reflects in large measure the quality of elite choices – with the quality of democracy understood as the degree to which democratic practices meet the standards of rule of law, expansive civil liberties and political rights, institutionalized competition for political office, and full accountability of elected officials. To these

---

[51] On nationalism lengthening political horizons as well as forging a political consensus that empowered newly elected leaders, see Rawi Abdelal, *Economic Nationalism after Empire: A Comparative Perspective on Nation, Economy and Security in Post-Soviet Eurasia* (Ithaca: Cornell University Press, 2001). Also see Rasma Karklins, *Ethnopolitics and Transition to Democracy: The USSR and Latvia* (Baltimore: Johns Hopkins University Press, 1993).

assumptions can be added a third: that the quality of democracy predicts in turn its durability.

The Russian case provides us with a welcome opportunity to rethink these assumptions and, with that, to confront an issue central to comparative inquiry. Whereas a great deal has been written about the strategies of case selection, much less attention has been paid to a related question. How do the causal assumptions we make shape the conclusions we draw from comparisons among cases?

Let us begin this methodological exercise by focusing on the Russian presidency. As is widely recognized, Boris Yeltsin played a central role in the rise of democracy in Russia, yet many of his actions, beginning in 1993, would seem to have compromised the democratic project and, for that matter, economic reform and state capacity.[52] Moreover, given his background and his commitment to recentralization of the Russian state, Yeltsin's successor, Vladimir Putin, could be viewed as a force against democratic politics. Thus, it is fair to say, especially in view of what has been argued earlier concerning the poor performance of the Russian regime, state, and economy, that Russia could very easily defect from the democratic column in the future. This prediction is especially compelling given the parallels between contemporary Russia and Weimar Germany – for example, disastrous economic performance, downward mobility in the international system, and the combination in both cases of presidential-parliamentary government, with important discretionary powers reserved for the presidency.[53]

There are, however, several problems with this line of argument. One is that there are some good reasons to be optimistic about Russian democracy. First, since independence, Russia has held five elections at the national level – and hundreds more at the local and regional levels. These

---

[52] Three helpful analyses of the Yeltsin era are: Lilia Shevtsova, *Yel'tsin's Russia: Myths and Realities* (Washington, D.C.: Brookings Institution, 1999); Michael McFaul, *Russia's Troubled Transition from Communism to Democracy* (Ithaca: Cornell University Press, 2001); and George Breslauer, *Gorbachev and Yeltsin as Leaders* (Cambridge: Cambridge University Press, 2002).

[53] Stephen E. Hanson and Jeffrey S. Kopstein, "The Weimar/Russia Comparison," *Post-Soviet Affairs* 13 (July–September 1997), 252–83. These two cases, however, vary with respect to political polarization and development of civil and political society. See James Gibson, "Social Networks, Civil Society, and the Prospects for Consolidating Russia's Democratic Transition," *American Journal of Political Science* 45 (January 2001), 51–69; Sheri Berman, "Civil Society and the Collapse of the Weimar Republic," *World Politics* 49 (April 1997), 401–29; and Marc Howard, *The Weakness of Civil Society in Postcommunist Europe* (Cambridge: Cambridge University Press, 2003).

elections have been by and large free and fair, they have invited (especially at the central level) considerable competition, and power has changed hands repeatedly. For example, in the gubernatorial elections of 1996–7, fully one-half of the incumbent candidates were defeated – an important consideration, as one indicator of democratic consolidation is peaceful turnover in political power.[54] Second, the rules of the political game have been relatively stable since the referendum on the 1993 Constitution. Third, the number of parties on the ballot for the Duma has declined over time. In 1995, there were forty-three and in 1999, twenty-six. Not surprisingly, this, plus a 5 percent threshhold for representation, has also translated into a sharp decline in wasted votes – shifting from 50 percent in 1995 to 18.6 percent in 1999.[55] Fourth, there is evidence that regional governors are interested in greater cooperation with the center and that the Duma and the president can cooperate in policy making. Fifth, although there are some extremists in the Duma, Russian public opinion tends to cluster at the center of the political continuum and evidences consistent support for democratic procedures. Finally and most important, there is the obvious point that, gloomy predictions to the contrary, Russian democracy has continued. This, in turn, introduces two questions – most obviously, why Russian democracy has lasted, and, less obviously, whether that is in spite of, or because of, its democratic deficits.

We can begin to answer these questions by addressing the question of comparative standards. Yeltsin has been criticized for his role in weakening the state (through, say, bilateral treaties with various regional governors), tolerating the accumulation of considerable power by various economic interests, compromising economic reform in ways that serve those interests, and, therefore, giving Russia a capitalism that does not work, a state that has difficulty extracting resources and commanding compliance, and a democracy that lacks accountability. What is often implied in these critiques is that Yeltsin should have made other choices that supported, rather than undermined, the state, democracy, and capitalism. But this introduces a key question. Were those other choices effectively available? The answer to that question is rarely provided. Instead, another

---

[54] See Steven L. Solnick, "Putin and the Provinces." Program on New approaches to Russian Security, Policy Memo Series, no. 115, Davis Center, Harvard University, May 2000 and Solnick, "Gubernatorial Elections."

[55] See Robert Moser, *Unexpected Outcomes: Electoral Systems, Political Parties, and Representation in Russia* (Pittsburgh: University of Pittsburgh Press, 2000); Michael McFaul, "Russia's 1999 Parliamentary Elections: Party Consolidation and Fragmentation," *Demokratizatsiya* 8 (Winter 2000); and Smyth, "Power as Patronage."

case – say, Poland or the Czech Republic – is brought in to demonstrate the costs of the Russian approach to political and economic transition.

There are good reasons to pair Russia with either Poland or the Czech Republic, especially when the comparison produces a more subtle understanding of such complex terms as shock therapy and voucher privatization.[56] However, the problem is with a second step that is sometimes taken, once smaller or larger "n" comparisons are carried out – a step that verges on the automatic, given the emphasis in the literature dealing with democratization and with economic reforms, on the existence of optimal approaches that apply to a wide range of contexts, and on the power of individual decision makers to choose among strategies that range from ideal to disastrous. That step is to argue, on the basis of variations in strategies and in economic and political outcomes, that the Russian leadership did it wrong and that they should have adopted the approaches taken by their more successful counterparts. Both arguments ignore the power of context in shaping the effectively available menu of policy choices. They presume, in short, that outcomes are a function of elites making good or bad choices.

Ignoring context can be highly misleading. For example, the Polish political leadership had the rare luxury of being positioned to make a choice that was at once radical and easy. I use both adjectives advisedly. By accident and by its specific functioning, communism in Poland created a popular consensus supporting liberal politics and economics. Indeed, even in 1980 this consensus was apparent, as one out of every three members of the Polish United Workers' Party (or the Communist Party) joined Solidarity. When the communist system finally made its formal departure, therefore, the new Polish leadership was both liberal and liberated. It was not just that Soviet power had retreated and, with that, the Polish United Workers Party. It was also that the new Polish leadership enjoyed a large mandate, thanks to the outcome of the June 1989 elections and the formation of a Solidarity-led government in August of the same year. At the same time, Polish rent seekers, long suspecting that the game was soon to be up, had begun to reposition themselves, even as early as the mid-1980s, to reap benefits from the more liberalized order to come. They were, in short, partners, not antagonists.

---

[56] See, for example, the instructive comparisons offered by Peter Murrell, "What Is Shock Therapy? What Did It Do in Poland and Russia?" *Post-Soviet Affairs* 9 (1993), 111–40 and Hilary Appel, "Voucher Privatization in Russia: Structural Consequences and Mass Response in the Second Period of Reform," *Europe-Asia Studies* 49 (1997), 1443–59.

In Russia, by contrast, there was much less consensus among publics or among elites about the regime-in-the-making, and the movement toward the new order was compromised as a result, and because of that, necessarily solicitous of rent seeking in both political and economic terms. The rent seekers, moreover, were perched between the old and the emerging order. Rather than jumping on the bankwagon, as in Poland, they were waiting for a bandwagon to form. In the process, they reaped considerable benefits from partial economic reform and partial democracy. The Russian variation on this process, it must be emphasized, did not originate with Yeltsin or even with Gorbachev. It was also characteristic of the Brezhnev era, when, as with the more recent leaders, central control over politics and economics was reduced in order to prolong the regime and keep rent seekers within the game rather than pushing them outside. Simply put, Brezhnev gave up power in order to keep it – and the weakness of the regime, the weakness of the state, and the abysmal performance of the economy all testified to how costly those compromises were.

In the absence of consensus, then, the "choice" in Russia, more recently as during the Brezhnev era, was neither stark nor simple. It was, instead, "ordinary" politics – to reverse Leszek Balcerowicz's apt characterization of the "extraordinary politics" present during the early stages of the Polish transition; that is, the unusual capacity of Polish leaders in 1989–90 to chart a radical, yet highly popular political and economic course.[57] As Andrei Shlaifer and Daniel Tresiman have argued with respect to economic reform, choice in Russia was severely circumscribed: "The task of a reformer in a weak state is to persuade stakeholders to give up more socially inefficient ways of receiving rents in exchange for less socially costly payoffs." The same holds true if we shift our attention to the political realm. The task of a democratizer in a weak state is to persuade stakeholders – say, regional governors and powerful economic lobbies – to give up more politically inefficient ways of receiving rents in exchange for less politically costly payoffs.

What I am suggesting, therefore, is the following. The emphasis on elite choice, so central to the study of recent democratization and so reflective of the remarkable confluence among some rational choice models; the preferences for proximate and not distal influences on politics; and the derivation of options from comparisons across cases rather than the realistic alternatives built into each setting have created two problems.

---

[57] See *Socialism, Capitalism, Transformation* (Budapest: Central European University Press, 1995).

One is a failure to recognize most decisions as choices among competing opportunity costs. The other is a pronounced tendency, especially when "unusual politics" provides a comparative standard, to overestimate what leaders can do. The first oversimplifies choice while ignoring the thicket of constraints. The second transforms decision makers into heroes or villains.

If elite choice needs to be reconsidered, so too does the relationship between the quality and the survival of democracy. As Michael McFaul has observed: "The stability of a regime and the quality of a regime are analytically separate categories that should not be subsumed under one word – consolidation."[58] The Russian case provides two insights here. First, it may be that the causal arrow runs in the opposite direction; that is, that the sustainability of democracy could be construed as an investment in its quality. Second, it could be argued – albeit with some trepidation – that the low quality of Russian democracy may explain why it has survived. Thus, it is precisely the democratic deficits in Russia that prolong the democratic experiment. This interpretation can be most readily supported by considering the only alternative to Yeltsin's policies that might have furthered democracy, a strong state, and a well-functioning capitalist economy. What if Yeltsin had proceeded by, say, building a party, strengthening democratic institutions, empowering the state, and staying the course on economic reform? Assuming for a moment that these actions were possible, they would have alienated the rent seekers. What could then have happened was a coalition among authoritarians and the decentralizers, both of which at present are divided, not united.[59] This in turn would produce a walkout – on the economy, the state, and democracy. A radical approach, in short, could have both terminated the experiment with democracy and capitalism and destroyed the state – for example, by transforming secessionist demands, now used primarily for bargaining purposes, into secessionist actions.

All this can be put relatively simply. Yeltsin's options were threefold: to resist a liberal revolution, to embrace this revolution fully, or to proceed but in compromised fashion. It can be argued that the first and the third are less likely than the second to produce a democratic outcome. Thus, democracy was short-changed, but durable; capitalism was distorted, but implanted; and the state, although weak and vulnerable to challenges,

[58] *Russia's Troubled Transition*, Ch. 9, 1–2.
[59] On the instability of these coalitions, see Philip Roeder, "The Rejection of Authoritarianism in the Soviet Successor States" and Hanson, "Defining Democratic Consolidation," both in Richard Anderson, M. Steven Fish, Stephen Hanson, and Philip Roeder, *Postcommunism and the Theory of Democracy* (Princeton: Princeton University Press, 2001).

nonetheless survived. If nothing else, if a weak state tempts regions to defect, so an even weaker state can make the act of defection (but not the games of threat) irrelevant. The survival of the Russian state, democracy, and capitalism, therefore, may not be in spite of their low quality but rather precisely because of that. Because the rent seekers are powerful and secure advantages only under the conditions of deficits in the state, democracy, and capitalism, they have a vested interest not only in preventing further democratization, further progress toward capitalism, and a more capable state, but also, just as importantly, in supporting all three as currently configured. Here, we can add yet another variation on the relationship between the quality and the sustainability of democracy. It could be that the sustainability of Russian democracy is an investment in its low quality.

CONCLUSIONS

The purpose of this chapter has been to use the Russian experience, supplemented by other cases in the postcommunist region, to rethink the definition of democracy, optimal approaches to democratization, and the relationship between the quality and the sustainability of democracy. Four arguments were presented. First, democracy depends on a capable state. The definition of democracy, therefore, should highlight this precondition. More generally, the study of democracy, as with the study of any regime, should recognize the interdependence between the regime and the state. Second, historical legacies, together with more immediate influences, seem to determine what constitutes the most successful approaches to democratic transition. Precisely because these legacies were so different in the east versus the south, the most successful approach in the former was breakage and in the latter, bridging. Third, comparative analyses are valuable for identifying causal relationships, but more problematic when used to generate recommendations about how transitions should proceed. Such recommendations ignore the power of context while exaggerating both the power of elites and the range of policy options available to them. Finally, whereas high quality democracies tend to be durable democracies, the opposite is not necessarily the case. Thus, in some contexts, low quality democracy may account for its sustainability. To return to an earlier point: although bridging may have compromised both the democratic and the capitalist project in Russia, it may also account in that particular context for the surprising durability of the Russian political and economic experiment.

7

Russians as Joiners: Realist and Liberal Conceptions of Postcommunist Europe[1]

James M. Goldgeier and Michael McFaul

Immediately after the collapse of communism in Europe, many students of international relations predicted a return to balance-of-power politics among the great European powers. Others foresaw new balancing between the United States and Europe as the international system moved from a bipolar order to a multipolar world. A decade later, the distinguished observer Joseph Joffe argued that Western Europe and Russia might join together to offset American power: "Ten years after victory in the cold war, the United States is still No. 1 by any conceivable measure. But the lesser actors – Russia, Europe, China – are beginning to make true what history and political theory have predicted all along: Great powers will generate 'ganging up.' Nos. 2, 3, and 4 will seek to balance against Mr. Big."[2] And a recent book by a leading Europe scholar, Charles Kupchan, predicts that a united Europe will emerge as America's main long-term strategic challenger.[3]

Joffe, Kupchan, and other realists like John Mearsheimer and Kenneth Waltz eventually may be right. Perhaps the German, French, and Russian coalition during the 2003 Iraq war is just the beginning. In the future, *realpolitik* and balance of power may return as the organizing principles of international politics on the European continent. Someday, the "lesser" powers may seek to balance against the United States. To date, however, what is more striking is how wrong these realist predictions since 1989

---

[1] This chapter builds on an earlier essay that appeared in *Perspectives on European Politics and Society* (Spring 2001).
[2] Josef Joffe, "A Warning from Putin and Schroeder," *New York Times*, June 20, 2000.
[3] Charles A. Kupchan, *The End of the American Era: U.S. Foreign Policy and the Geopolitics of the Twenty-first Century* (New York: Knopf, 2002).

have proven to be. To be sure, Russian, Chinese, and even some French and German elites have devoted much rhetorical attention to the inevitability of the reemergence of a multipolar world in which American hegemony is balanced by new powers and new alliances, and this was particularly true of President Chirac in 2003.[4] To date, however, the rhetoric about balance-of-power politics has greatly exceeded actual balance-of-power behavior on the European continent. The evidence of balancing suggested by Joffe and others is just as thin today as it was over a decade ago when realists first penned their gloom and doom scenarios for Europe after the end of bipolarity.

To understand why, we need an alternative view regarding the structure of international relations. Rather than accepting realist assumptions about the state as a unitary actor seeking to survive in an anarchic world through balancing strategies, we organize the international system into two worlds – the liberal core and the realist periphery.[5] In the liberal core, shared values and expectations as well as material incentives lead to the absence of war and the management of international conflict through negotiation; in the Hobbesian periphery, peace is tenuous, both between states and within states, and is maintained only through traditional power balancing. The United States, as the leading liberal state, is the key actor in both worlds. Although Robert Kagan has argued that the United States plays in the world of Hobbes while Europe enjoys its Kantian peace, in fact the United States operates in both arenas, which is the key to understanding how Europe and the world have evolved since 1989.[6]

The core and the periphery, however, are not permanently divided. In Europe, the interaction is dynamic. At times, the intentions of the core toward countries in the periphery like Russia have been ambiguous. On balance, however, the core powers have moved to expand their zone of peace and prosperity eastward rather than seeking to insulate themselves from this unstable part of Europe. As the largest country in the European periphery, Russia should feel threatened by this eastern expansion and act to thwart it. Such behavior would be consistent with realist approaches to international relations. Yet, despite increasingly hostile anti-western rhetoric, Russia has generally pursued a policy of integration with the

---

[4] For an overview of rhetoric even before 2003, see Peter Rodman, "The World's Resentment: Anti-Americanism as a Global Phenomenon," *The National Interest*, No. 60 (Summer 2000), pp. 33–41.
[5] James M. Goldgeier and Michael McFaul, "A Tale of Two Worlds: Core and Periphery in the Post-Cold War Era," *International Organization* 46 (Spring 1992), pp. 467–92.
[6] See Robert Kagan, *Of Paradise and Power* (New York: Knopf, 2003).

West since the late Soviet period and across three very different Soviet/ Russian presidencies. Russia's integrationist tendencies have resulted from a combination of (1) core strategies aimed at drawing Russia into the West and (2) domestic politics in Russia – specifically, the continued victory of integrationist coalitions in Russia's domestic political struggles. In the West, state leaders have privileged integrationist policies when dealing with Russia, even when initially pursuing realist policy hedges against the possibility of a resurgent, belligerent Russia. In Russia, state leaders also have championed integrationist policies, even though occasionally tempted to react to western hedge policies or rhetoric by seeking to balance western power. Since the end of the Cold War, the pull of the liberal core has overcome the push of realist balancing.

To demonstrate the virtues of the core-periphery approach in general and its explanatory value for understanding international politics in Europe in particular, this essay proceeds as follows. The next section examines key features of the core-periphery approach, with specific reference to security relations in Europe. Section three then looks at the security strategy pursued by the core toward countries in the European periphery – Central and Eastern Europe, and the states that emerged from the collapse of the Soviet Union. This section demonstrates that those norms developed to regulate state behavior in the core can influence the behavior of states on the core's borders, including even Russia. And core countries have aimed explicitly to integrate Russia into the western core rather than to balance Russian power. In section four, we then turn to an examination of Russia's behavior toward the West. Russia has pursued integration rather than confrontation, even to the point of ceding its sovereignty in an unprecedented attempt to integrate into the western-led order rather than to isolate itself or to balance against the West.

THE CORE-PERIPHERY APPROACH

Realism argues that the recurrence of balance-of-power politics is the defining feature of international relations. Because the lack of a central authority in international politics forces states to provide for their own security, realists posit that states will balance against the hegemonic aspirations of any one state and that military alliances will disappear after they have served their balancing purpose. Many realists also argue bipolar systems are more stable and prone to great power peace; multipolar systems – because of the uncertain distribution of power and the threat of shifting alliances – are more unstable and prone to great power war.

Not surprisingly, therefore, most realists feared the uncertainties brought about by the end of the Cold War. These scholars and analysts argued that the collapse of the Soviet Union and the end of bipolarity would lead to a return to multipolarity and the kind of balancing behavior that would reproduce pre-1945 unstable and conflictual patterns of state relations in Europe. Without the Soviet threat to unite them, the United States and Europe would be unlikely to sustain cooperation given the challenges each could potentially pose to the other. Germany would turn economic strength into military power, as it did in the first half of the twentieth century. Even now, prominent realists point to Europe's efforts to develop a common foreign and security policy as evidence that balancing is a norm.[7]

To date, the predictions that realists offered more than ten years ago have not come to pass. To frame post-Cold War international politics, especially in Europe, in terms of balancing among major powers fails to explain the central dynamics of great power politics in the 1990s. Multipolar balancing has not reconfigured international politics on the European continent. Although Europe and the United States engage and will continue to engage in economic competition, there is no sign of military balancing, let alone on the scale that occurred in the 1930s and 1940s. And Russia, for so long hostile to western interests, has for the past decade sought not to balance against the West but to join it.

A more compelling realist case comes from William Wohlforth, who has argued that unipolarity will be stable and durable. Wohlforth emphasizes that the United States is so dominant in every power category while additionally blessed by geography that no country will even try to balance against it in the foreseeable future. The problem of misperception that has so often influenced balancing behavior in the past is not an issue given that no one can fail to see the gap, and Wohlforth quite rightly declares, "Most of the counterbalancing that has occurred since 1991 has been rhetorical."[8]

---

[7] Kenneth M. Waltz, "The Emerging Structure of International Politics," *International Security*, Vol. 18, No. 2 (1993), pp. 44–79; Kenneth M. Waltz, "Evaluating Theories," *American Political Science Review* 91 (1997); John J. Mearsheimer, "Back to the Future: Instability in Europe after the Cold War," *International Security*, Vol. 15, No. 1, (1990), pp. 5–56; Christopher Layne, "The Unipolar Illusion: Why New Great Powers Will Rise," *International Security*, Vol. 17, No. 4, (1993), pp. 5–51; Peter W. Rodman, *Drifting Apart? Trends in U.S.-European Relations* (Washington: Nixon Center, 1999).

[8] William C. Wohlforth, "The Stability of a Unipolar World," *International Security*, Vol. 24 (1999), p. 35.

This argument about America as the dominant power is fine as far as it goes, and is an important complement to our own position given the role that America has played in creating and maintaining the liberal core. But it fails to capture the diversity of state behavior in the international system as a whole. Whereas balancing is absent among the great powers and in the liberal world, it is still prevalent and necessary in many other regions, including in Europe's periphery (witness the Caucasus). Even if divided on issues like Iraq, the international relations between France, Germany, and Great Britain today, however, bear little resemblance to their interactions in previous centuries. Importantly and in contrast to previous international systems, the ebbs and flows of balance-of-power politics in most of the periphery do not affect directly interstate politics in the core. Therefore, rather than focus on unipolarity or the kind of polarity in the system as a whole, we identify a different structural feature of the international system: the existence of two worlds, the core and the periphery. Liberal theories that emphasize the role of democracy, markets, and international institutions in creating what Karl Deutsch called a "security community" or Hedley Bull called an "international society" are better at explaining international politics in the core.[9] The realist analysis of balance-of-power politics better explains dynamics in the periphery.

Scholars have explored both normative and structural reasons why liberal states do not go to war with one another. These include the costs to populations that can hold leaders accountable as well as norms of self-restraint regarding threats to use force against populations in other constitutionally based political systems.[10] Other analysts point to the reduced levels of uncertainty that occur in strategic interaction involving democratic states. Democratic leaders in one country assume that their counterparts in another democracy must contend with the same set of constraints that they confront. In established democracies, those democratic norms that produce compromise within states also will spawn compromise between liberal democratic states.[11]

---

[9] Karl W. Deutsch, et al., *Political Community and the North Atlantic Area* (Princeton: Princeton University Press, 1957); Hedley Bull, *The Anarchical Society: A Study of Order in World Politics* (London: Macmillan, 1977).

[10] On the historical emergence of democratic states, see Kurt Taylor Gaubatz, "Kant, Democracy, and History," *Journal of Democracy*, Vol. 7, No. 4 (October 1996) pp. 136–50. There is a huge literature on the sources of the democratic peace. Leading authors include Michael Doyle, Bruce Russett, and John Owen. A particularly good collection of articles by these authors and others is Michael Brown, Sean Lynn-Jones, and Steven Miller, eds., *Debating the Democratic Peace* (Cambridge: MIT Press, 1996).

[11] Russett, "Why Democratic Peace?" in Brown et al., *Debating the Democratic Peace*, p. 97.

Over time, repeated, nonviolent interactions between the core democracies have produced self-enforcing institutions from which no state has an incentive to defect.[12] These democratic states form a Kantian "pacific union" or an international society in which interstate interaction is much more predictable and peaceful than interstate relations either between nondemocratic states or between democratic states and nondemocratic states. The international institutions that form out of this peaceful interaction in turn help to keep the peace. Other interactions that may serve to reduce uncertainty and thereby enhance peace include alliances, trade, and the presence of transnational actors. Nowhere has this been more true than in Europe.

Although consolidated and strengthened by a shared historical experience of the Cold War, the liberal democratic core does not have fixed or clearly delineated boundaries. In general terms, however, the distinction between core and periphery arises from a combination of geography, history, and the character of internal institutions within member states. The core encompasses Western (and now increasingly Central) Europe, North America, and parts of East Asia and its leading powers are the United States, Germany, and Japan. Historically, this region grew closer together when the United States created a post-World War II liberal capitalist order to counter the Soviet threat. Internally, these states have a set of political and economic institutions that can be defined as democratic and market-based, respectively. Externally, these states keep the peace not by balancing against each other, but rather by creating and developing security institutions of mutual benefit. The periphery includes Africa, Central and South Asia, the Middle East, and *parts* of Latin America, Eastern and Southeastern Europe, and East Asia. Historically, these peripheral regions were not linked together during the Cold War era, but instead served frequently as the arena of U.S.-Soviet rivalry. Internally, the states in these regions include both authoritarian and democratic regimes and display varying degrees of capitalist development. Externally, many of the states in these regions must rely on the balance of power as the only means of security.

In an earlier article, we outlined the central theoretical assumptions and analytical advantages of a core-periphery approach, focusing in particular on how interstate relations within the core differ from interstate relations

---

[12] Randall Calvert, "Rational Actors, Equilibrium, and Social Institutions," in Jack Knight and Itai Sened, eds., *Explaining Social Institutions* (Ann Arbor: Michigan University Press, 1995), pp. 57–94.

within the periphery.[13] We argued that a next stage of research should focus on relations between these two worlds – the subject of this chapter. Much of the analysis of the "democratic peace" has tended to ignore this interaction except to note that although liberal states do not go to war with one another, they have no such inhibitions with nonliberal states. But can we say anything more systematic about these relationships?[14]

Core-Periphery Interactions

If there is no military balancing in the core, core states will not engage in military balancing in the periphery, and thus globally the core and periphery will generally grow divorced from one another.[15] The United States and the Soviet Union balanced each other everywhere in the world as part of their worldwide struggle. With the Cold War straitjacket removed, wars in the developing world typically will not be deterred or promoted by core state intervention. Rather, core state military engagement in the periphery will be motivated primarily by vital interests such as access to oil and strategic mineral supplies and to a lesser extent by special interests of domestic constituents. The West defined Bosnia and Kosovo as vital interests only because they are close to the core geographically; the humanitarian rationale resonated because it was *Europe*. Compare this behavior not only to the lack of reaction to genocide in Rwanda but to the relative absence of concern for the civil wars in Sierra Leone, Liberia, Sudan, and Ethiopia, or even interstate clashes in central Africa, that is, the same type of events that attracted great power intervention during the Cold War. Even in Afghanistan, where the United States acted after September 11, 2001 (but not during the decade before) to eliminate the Taliban regime and its support for Al Qaeda, there is once again a growing lack of interest in the internal affairs of that country.

This argument about a growing divorce between core and periphery must be qualified by a second hypothesis. If liberal core states have obtained increased security through the development of an international

---

[13] Goldgeier and McFaul, "A Tale of Two Worlds."
[14] Barry Buzan, "New Patterns of Global Security in the Twenty-First Century," *International Affairs*, Vol. 67, No. 3 (1991), pp. 431–51, is an important earlier work examining relations between core and periphery. Michael W. Doyle, *Ways of War and Peace* (New York: W. W. Norton, 1997), pp. 268ff, also discusses several hypotheses relevant to core-periphery relations.
[15] On this point, see also Buzan, "New Patterns of Global Security in the Twenty-First Century," p. 435.

society in the core, then we should expect the liberal core to promote democracy and markets in those peripheral states located *geographically closest* to the core. The effort of core enlargement will be greatest in those states contiguous to the core that are most likely to consolidate liberal institutions. Core state leaders believe that democratic and capitalist institutions create stability, predictability, and economic wealth. The core will seek to expand its zone of liberal peace and prosperity to places that most resemble the core and will promote political and economic reform to help potential members meet core norms. States remaining opposed to those norms will be ignored if they are far away and extremely weak (Liberia), or isolated and deterred if they are closer and/or pose a potential threat to the liberal peace (Milosevic's Serbia or Saddam's Iraq). The ultimate goal is a larger liberal zone bringing the expected security and economic benefits from democracy and markets. To achieve this objective of enlargement, core states not only have pursued government-to-government engagement policies but also have deployed their powerful international institutions: for example, the International Monetary Fund, the World Bank, the World Trade Organization, NATO, transnational nongovernmental organizations, and even international associations of western political parties.

Power, interest, geography, and liberal norms are closely linked in this potential expansion of the liberal zone. Michael Doyle has noted that historically liberal states have suffered from, in Hume's words, "supine complaisance." This manifests itself as both "a failure to support allies [and] a failure to oppose enemies." In the past, liberals generally have not made much effort to support liberalism in places where it was just getting started, for example, Weimar Germany in the 1920s. The exception, writes Doyle, is "when one Liberal state stood preeminent among the rest, prepared and able to take measures, as did Britain before World War I and the United States following World War II, to sustain economically and politically the foundations of Liberal society beyond its borders."[16] The United States played this role in the first post-Cold War decade, and any further extension of the core or actions to prevent reversals in those places where the core has already expanded will depend on American leadership, as we have seen in recent years in Afghanistan and Iraq.

---

[16] Doyle, *Ways of War and Peace*, pp. 275–6. See also Timothy Garton Ash, "Europe's Endangered Liberal Order," *Foreign Affairs*, Vol. 77, No. 2 (March–April 1998) pp. 51–65.

The historical tendency toward complaisance enhances the role of geography in affecting where the core attempts to expand. Neighboring areas are more likely to be targets of opportunity because, quite simply, it is easier to include them, and this proximity is particularly important as core states define their security interests; instability in areas close to the core is of greater concern. Even in the economic sphere, contiguity can increase the core's interest, as in the case of trade via road and rail transport, although geography is less relevant in banking, information, and service sectors.

How a state in the periphery responds to the core depends on two factors – the opportunities the core provides for joining the liberal world and the makeup of domestic coalitions in the peripheral states. As already stated, core states are more likely to reach out to peripheral states contiguous with core states and less likely to embrace those far away. In addition, core states are more likely to reach out to liberal states or liberalizing states in the periphery rather than illiberal regimes. Finally, in Europe, core states have seen the integration of Russia as important not because of its proximity but because its success on the liberal path would have profound effects for core security given its size and its nuclear arsenal.

States outside of the core can pursue three basic strategies regarding relations with core states: they can seek to isolate themselves from the core; they can seek to overturn the liberal order in the core; or they can attempt to integrate into the core. Why peripheral states make the choices they do depends in part on the core strategy toward them: that is, to what extent the core seeks to integrate or isolate their state. But a state's response also depends on the balance of power of domestic interest groups. Those groups that stand to gain from democratization and markets will push for greater integration into the core. Those threatened by liberalization in the political and economic spheres will try either to isolate or balance against the core. Jack Snyder has told this story well for Soviet foreign policy, as zero-sum oriented party ideologues and the military-industrial complex competed over policy with the urban middle class and cultural and technical intelligentsia who sought better relations with the West.[17] We seek to extend this type of analysis to post-Soviet Russia, where the handful of very profitable corporations, their political allies, and Russian voters as a whole have provided sustained momentum for continued integration

---

[17] Jack Snyder, "The Gorbachev Revolution: A Waning of Soviet Expansionism?" *International Security*, Vol. 12, No. 3 (1987/88), pp. 93–131.

with the West and have prevailed in foreign policy debates over those who have opposed integration.

EXPANDING WESTERN SECURITY INSTITUTIONS

The North Atlantic Treaty Organization (NATO), the West's premier security institution, has served as a primary tool in the core's effort to extend its reach into the parts of Europe formerly dominated by Moscow. With the London declaration of 1990, NATO began shifting its emphasis from the Cold War alliance built to contain the Soviet threat to a political-diplomatic entity designed to facilitate the creation of an undivided Europe. It retained its collective defense function, and the Article V guarantee that an attack on one would be considered an attack on all was still its central feature, but it also began to emphasize its role as a bridge-building institution as the Warsaw Pact crumbled. In Rome the following year, the North Atlantic Cooperation Council (NACC) was created. The NACC was open to all of the former Warsaw Pact and former Soviet states, and it established a regular forum for interaction between the Transatlantic core and the nations to the East.[18]

As the United States military grew increasingly concerned about the potential for "other Bosnias" in Europe's periphery, it began to think about ways to develop peacekeeping capabilities for regional action that would lessen the need for the use of American troops. Promoted strongly by General John Shalikashvili, first in his role as Supreme Allied Commander in Europe and later as Chairman of the Joint Chiefs of Staff, the Partnership for Peace (PFP) emerged as a central policy initiative and was endorsed by NATO's Heads of State at their summit in January 1994.[19]

By the end of 1994, however, the United States was moving well beyond PFP to promoting the idea of NATO's enlargement into Central Europe. It is true that making an argument that the United States came to support enlargement in 1994 as part of a strategy of integration in Central Europe and not primarily to balance against a future threat from Russia is difficult since the first steps in carrying out this policy – namely the accession of

---

[18] On these issues, see Robert L. Hutchings, *American Diplomacy and the End of the Cold War: An Insider's Account of U.S. Policy in Europe* (Washington: Woodrow Wilson Center Press, 1997); Philip H. Gordon, ed., *NATO's Transformation: The Changing Shape of the Atlantic Alliance* (Lanham, MD.: Rowman and Littlefield Publishers, Inc., 1997).

[19] See James M. Goldgeier, *Not Whether But When: The U.S. Decision to Enlarge NATO* (Washington: Brookings Institution, 1999), chapter two.

Poland, Hungary, and the Czech Republic to NATO membership – would be consistent with either approach. But several pieces of evidence help support our argument. First, extensive process tracing of the decision within the Clinton administration through interviews with dozens of government officials shows that the handful of people who supported the policy inside the executive branch did so as part of their policy of assisting liberal transitions in Central and Eastern Europe.[20] Second, if balancing against a future Russian threat was of primary importance, Slovakia should have been included in the first group for geostrategic reasons. While Slovakia was on the initial list as part of the "Visegrad four," its failure to proceed with political reform led NATO to exclude it until after it had reformed and could be invited at the 2002 NATO summit in Prague. Finally, NATO made a concerted effort to reassure Russia about this process by trying to foster new institutional arrangements that gave Russia the ability to participate to some degree in NATO deliberations. Not surprisingly, realist proponents of NATO expansion (whose goal was to ensure that Russia could not again dominate its western neighbors) vehemently denounced this particular policy move by NATO leaders.

Interviews with U.S. government officials suggest that there were a number of reasons, including domestic political considerations, why the United States led the push to extend NATO east. But the key *foreign policy* rationale was to help peripheral countries in Europe make the leap into the core. U.S. national security adviser Anthony Lake had first put forth the Clinton administration's general policy of "enlargement" in September 1993. Taking the view that states in the core (a term he himself used) of democracies and market economies had a different type of relations than those elsewhere in the international realm, Lake argued for a foreign policy that would seek not merely to strengthen relations within the core but that would also reach out to others, like those in Central and Eastern Europe, in order to enlarge it. "The successor to a doctrine of containment," he argued, "must be a strategy of enlargement – enlargement of the world's free community of market democracies."[21]

The key early proponents of NATO enlargement within the administration argued that without the prospect of membership in a key western

---

[20] Ibid.
[21] Anthony Lake, "From Containment to Enlargement," *Vital Speeches of the Day*, Vol. 60 (October 15, 1993), pp. 13–19. Clinton emphasized this approach less than a week later at the UN General Assembly. See Clinton, *Public Papers of the Presidents of the United States*, p. 40.

institution, Central and Eastern European countries would lose the momentum for reform. Their thinking was that NATO and the European Union (EU) were the premier institutions in Europe, and the EU, absorbed in the internal problems associated with the Maastricht Treaty, would postpone its own expansion, as it did until fifteen years after the fall of the Berlin Wall. These officials wanted to encourage states such as Poland and Hungary to continue on the path of reform – to adopt civilian control of the military, to build a free polity and economy, and to settle border disputes – by providing the carrot of NATO membership if these countries succeeded.[22]

Most of the administration in 1993–4 was opposed to enlargement, and there was no great groundswell of support within Europe (NATO Secretary-General Manfred Wörner and German Defense Minister Volker Rühe were among the few early European proponents). But the opposition came largely from those pursuing a different liberal impulse – namely integration of Russia into the core – who feared enlargement would overturn these efforts. Within the Clinton administration, proponents of enlargement believed that it was possible both to bring the Central Europeans into the West and maintain a good relationship with Russia, whereas opponents believed that if NATO expanded, Russia would be lost. Neither group used balance-of-power arguments to support their policy positions; one focused on extension of the liberal core to stabilize Central Europe; the other focused on extension of the liberal core to prevent backsliding by Russia.

This argument does not ignore considerations of power. The U.S. government under both Presidents George H. W. Bush and Bill Clinton wanted to keep NATO as the key security institution in Europe in large part because of American leadership in the organization; NATO is the primary vehicle by which the United States dominates security policy in Europe. Still, despite the power considerations behind the U.S. emphasis on NATO's role, one needs to look at the way this power has been used and at the nature of the process of enlargement.[23] Both realist advocates and opponents of NATO enlargement clearly believed that the institution's

---

[22] For an early exposition of these ideas, see Stephen J. Flanagan, "NATO and Central and Eastern Europe: From Liaison to Security Partnership," *The Washington Quarterly* (1992), pp. 141–51. See also Strobe Talbott, "Why NATO Should Grow," *The New York Review of Books*, August 10, 1995; Richard Holbrooke, "America, a European Power," *Foreign Affairs*, Vol. 74, No. 2 (1995), pp. 38–51.

[23] For the classic realist argument about hegemonic power, see Robert Gilpin, *War and Change in World Politics* (Cambridge: Cambridge University Press, 1981).

central objective was to keep Russian power in check.[24] There is no question that many supporters of the first round of post-Cold War NATO enlargement in the U.S. Senate and within the governments of Central Europe believed initially the key objective was taking the fruits of the Cold War victory and preventing Russia's return to its traditional sphere of influence. But although some in both the East and West spoke openly about a "hedge" strategy against a resurgent Russia, the primary focus of the leading western governments has been on the integrative rather than the containment function. And the integrative function was clearly primary in the second round of enlargement, when seven more countries were invited to join the Alliance.

If the goal was to balance Russian power, why did the Clinton administration establish a NATO-Russia Founding Act to assuage Russian concerns about the extension of its former adversary into the East and would give Russia a voice in NATO affairs, and why did George W. Bush agree to the creation of a NATO-Russia Council to accompany round two? Although Russia has complained at various times that enlargement violates previously reached understandings, that it humiliates a weakened Russia, and that it threatens Russian security, the West clearly has sought to extend this major institution in a way that minimizes conflict with Russia, a country on which the West also has spent vast resources for the purpose of integration.[25]

The European core (led by the United States) has pursued as policy bringing into the fold those closest geographically (Central and Eastern Europe), supporting on a smaller scale those a bit further away (e.g, Georgia and Azerbaijan), containing those with an anti-western agenda (Serbia before Milosevic's ouster and Belarus), and integrating Russia. No doubt, the efforts have been uneven. The European Union has been more sensitive to enlargement costs than NATO and went more slowly on enlargement, but its major enlargement of 2004 will solidify the post-Cold War integrationist project. Although disagreements have emerged between the Europeans and the United States, there has been no dispute that

---

[24] For realist proponent arguments, see Henry Kissinger, "Helsinki Fiasco," *Washington Post*, March 30, 1997; Zbigniew Brzezinski, "The Premature Partnership," *Foreign Affairs*, Vol. 73, No. 2 (1994). For the realist opponent view, see Michael Mandelbaum, *The Dawn of Peace in Europe* (New York: Twentieth Century Fund Books, 1996).

[25] Note, for example, the criticism by those such as Kissinger that the Founding Act would be devastating for NATO's future by giving Russia too great a voice. See Henry A. Kissinger, "The Dilution of NATO," *Washington Post*, June 8, 1997, C9.

would warrant notions of new balancing between the leading European powers and America.

The one country from the East with the most potential to upset core efforts over the long term is Russia, which although much weaker than in the mid-1980s still has great disruptive capability. And Russians could have seen (and rhetorically in many ways did see) many western policies – for example, NATO enlargement, the wars in Kosovo and Iraq, support for a Caspian pipeline to Turkey, U.S. military bases in Central Asia – as part of a new American policy of containment. But what is fascinating is the way in which Russia has responded to core entreaties. It is only half of the story to look at western security policy. To date, what is most compelling in Europe is the absence of return to balancing between Russia and the West.

RUSSIA AND THE WEST

Many Americans and Russians have warned that Russia is likely someday to become once again an enemy of the West. Russia, so the argument goes, feels threatened by NATO expansion, potential U.S. missile defense, and American hegemony more generally, and as a traditional great power will therefore seek to balance against this threat. Others argue that Russia's historical and cultural proclivities as an imperial power will compel this state to return to the balance-of-power game once Russia has recovered from its current weakness.[26]

After the election victory of Vladimir Zhirinovsky in December 1993, many analysts predicted a "correction" in Russian foreign policy.[27] Two years later, the Communist Party electoral victory in the 1995 parliamentary elections confirmed for many Russia's drift away from international liberalism.[28] Soon after the 1995 election, Yeltsin replaced his liberal, pro-western Foreign Minister, Andrei Kozyrev, with Yevgeny Primakov, an experienced Soviet foreign policy specialist known for his "realist" and anti-western views.[29] Upon assuming this office, Primakov argued

---

[26] Brzezinski, "The Premature Partnership"; Ariel Cohen, *Russian Imperialism* (Westport, CT: Praeger, 1996).
[27] Jack Snyder, "Russian Backwardness and the Future of Europe," *Daedalus*, Vol. 123 (1994), p. 181.
[28] Peter Reddaway, "Red Alert," *The New Republic*, January 29, 1996.
[29] On the ascendancy of the "pragmatic nationalists" and the waning of "liberal westernizers," see Margot Light, Stephen White, John Lowenhardt, "A Wider Europe: The View from Moscow and Kyiv," *International Affairs*, Vol. 76, No. 1 (January 2000), pp. 77–88. The labels come from Neil Malcolm, Alex Pravda, Roy Allison, and Margot

for a return of multipolarity in the international system, a strategy he continued to advocate as Russia's prime minister in 1998–9. President Vladimir Putin, a career KGB officer, uttered similar phrases early in his, tenure.

Despite domestic pressures, personnel changes, and rhetorical statements, Boris Yeltsin and his governments never abandoned their overriding objectives of emulating domestic institutions of the core states and integrating into the core. In foreign affairs, Russian leaders denounced NATO enlargement in words, but continued to cooperate with the alliance in deeds, particularly in peacekeeping forces in Bosnia and Kosovo (even after temporarily canceling cooperation in Brussels due to the 1999 war). President Putin has demonstrated an indifference to democracy, violating human rights and the rule of law when they have come in conflict with other goals.[30] At the same time, Putin has demonstrated a real commitment to promoting market reforms and devoted tremendous time and energy to courting European leaders. Fundamentally, he believes that Russia is a *European* nation. And even after receiving very little from the United States for his post-September 11 show of solidarity with the West, he has made good relations with George W. Bush a top priority.[31]

Periodically, Russian leaders have threatened to recreate the Soviet Union to act as a bulwark against western expansion. Yet even the simplest step toward reunification – the incorporation of Belarus – has been delayed for years by economic concerns.[32] Occasionally, Russian leaders have hinted at creating a Russian-Chinese alliance and even a Russia-China-India alliance to balance against western power, but none of these countries have ever taken even the first steps toward realizing such an alliance. And while joining France and Germany against the U.S.-led war in Iraq, Putin has been much more careful in his stance than President Chirac or Chancellor Schroeder.[33]

Light, *Internal Factors in Russian Foreign Policy* (Oxford: Oxford University Press, 1996).

[30] Michael McFaul, "Putin in Power," *Current History* 99 (October 2000), pp. 307–14.

[31] During his first term, Putin has seemed to believe that he could separate the objectives of European integration and economic growth from his plans for "reform" of the polity, but in the long run, continued backsliding in Russian democracy will be an obstacle to integration.

[32] On the rhetoric of Russian "muscular" foreign-policy community versus the reality of Russian capabilities, see Sherman Garnett, "Russia's Illusory Ambitions," *Foreign Affairs*, Vol. 72, No. 2 (1997), pp. 61–76.

[33] See Sherman Garnett, ed., *Rapprochement or Rivalry: Russia-China Relations in a Changing Asia* (Washington: Carnegie Endowment for International Peace, 2000).

Central to Russia's choice regarding its foreign policy trajectory has been the continued victory of pro-western coalitions within Russia and the policies and institutional changes that they have pursued. Throughout the 1990s, Russian liberals – defined here most minimally as those committed to markets, free trade, individual rights, and democracy – were challenged repeatedly, be it at the ballot box or in internal elite struggles. Led by Boris Yeltsin, however, Russia's liberal forces advocating capitalism and democracy at home and integration with the West abroad dominated Russian politics. Those in Russia who may have stood to gain from more anti-western foreign policies – be they radical communists, extreme nationalists, segments of the armed forces, or parts of the military-industrial complex – have persistently lost in political struggles for state control. Over time, many of these losers have readjusted their goals and now accept the basic principles of democracy, capitalism, and western integration. Since the election of Vladimir Putin as Russia's president in March 2000 (and reelection in March 2004) the future of Russian democratic institutions has become more uncertain. To date, however, the collapse of Soviet communism has allowed for the protracted and partial emergence of liberal economic and political institutions, an outcome that in turn has fostered Russian integration with rather than balancing against the West.

Russia's Liberal Revolution

After the collapse of the Soviet Union in 1991, Yeltsin and his government delayed reforms in their first two years of rule, a calculation that helped to precipitate a constitutional crisis and eventually military standoff between the president and the Russian Congress in the fall of 1993. Since then, however, the adoption of a new constitution (ratified in a popular referendum in 1993) and elections for the parliament (1993, 1995, 1999 and 2003), the president (1996, 2000 and 2004), and regional heads of administration (1995, 1996, 1997, 2001) signal that Russian leaders have an interest in at least mimicking the political practices of the core states, if not fully adopting them over the long run. All major political actors in Russia today recognize that they are better off acquiescing to the democratic process than pursuing political power (or retaining political power) through nondemocratic means.[34]

---

[34] This observation concerns the interest-based commitment to democracy of all major actors, not a norms-based commitment to democracy.

Russia is not a liberal democracy. The Russian political system lacks many of the supporting institutions that make democracy robust.[35] Russia's party system, civil society, and the rule of law are weak and underdeveloped. Executives, both at the national and regional level, have too much power, and Putin has increased the powers of the presidency. Crime and corruption are still rampant. Over the last several years, Russia's media has lost a great deal of its independence and has become increasingly dependent on oligarchic business empires and Putin's favors. The Russian state still lacks the capacity to provide basic public goods, and the Russian economy continues to sputter. All of these attributes impede the deepening of democratic institutions. Nonetheless, although the Russian political system is not a fully liberal democracy, it is an electoral democracy.

Russia also has made progress toward developing market institutions. The market, not Gosplan, now determines most prices in Russia, while individual owners, not the state, now control most enterprises and shops. Russia's pace of marketization and subsequent return of economic growth has been much slower than expected. Partial reform has produced substantial and sustained rents for economic actors with access to the state.[36] Nonetheless, no serious political force in Russia today, including even the Communist Party of the Russian Federation, advocates the restoration of the command economy.[37] Likewise, a majority of Russians are nostalgic for the stability of Brezhnev's economic system, but most nonetheless believe that some form of a market economy is necessary for Russia.

Western Engagement: Incentives and Resources for Russian Domestic Change

Accompanying the creation of partial democratic and market institutions at home, Yeltsin actively pursued closer relations with the West during his entire tenure. Given the kind of economy and polity Russian leaders hoped to build, engagement with the West made sense since Russia's first postcommunist leaders looked to western democracies and their capitalist economies as models to be emulated. Yeltsin and his supporters,

---

[35] Michael McFaul, "One Step Forward, Two Steps Back," *Journal of Democracy* 11 (July 2000), pp. 19–33.
[36] Joel Hellman, "Winners Take All," *World Politics*, Vol. 50, No. 2 (1998), pp. 203–34.
[37] On the migration of the CPRF toward more market-oriented policies, see Mikhail Dmitriev, "Party Economic Programs and Implications," in Michael McFaul, Nikolai Petrov, and Andrei Ryabov, eds., with Elizabeth Reisch, *Primer on Russia's 1999 Duma Elections* (Washington: Carnegie Endowment for International Peace, 1999), pp. 31–60.

therefore, welcomed the collapse of the bipolar system and the potential enlargement of the core. According to initial calculations by the Russian government and western experts, the faster Russia entered this new international system, the more likely democratic and market reforms would succeed.[38]

Given this initial orientation, Yeltsin and his first post-Soviet Foreign Minister, Andrei Kozyrev, placed friendly relations with the West and the United States in particular as Russia's highest foreign policy priority. In return for embracing without qualification the western model, Yeltsin's government hoped to receive western financial assistance and private capital investment. Acting Prime Minister Yegor Gaidar's strategy for macroeconomic stabilization, in fact, hinged on infusions of financial credit from the International Monetary Fund (IMF) and, to a lesser extent, the World Bank.

At times, Russian leaders pursued this aim of core integration at the expense of their own domestic sovereignty – a violation of one of the core assumptions of realism. Most starkly, Russian leaders ceded some of their autonomy regarding economic decision making. After independence, the IMF quickly established contact with the new Russian government and soon thereafter, Russia became one of the largest recipients of IMF funds.[39] These transfers did not come without constraints. Although Russia enjoyed more flexibility regarding IMF conditionality than most borrowers, the Russian government had to conform to the anti-inflationary measures recommended by IMF stabilization plans. The IMF also provided advice on a whole range of policy reforms, including bankruptcy laws, tax reform, and central bank reorganization. In the estimation of the IMF's former Managing Director, Michel Camdessus, "*In part because of IMF support*, Russia now has a professional central bank."[40] In other words, an institution dominated by the core powers has actively intervened to reform one of Russia's key economic institutions.

The task of transforming the Soviet command system into a Russian market economy is one of the most ambitious economic transformations

---

[38] Jeffrey Sachs, "Helping Russia: Goodwill Is Not Enough," *The Economist* (December 21–January 3, 1992), p. 104; and Yegor Gaidar, *Days of Victory and Defeat* (Seattle: University of Washington Press, 1999).

[39] Michael Gordon, "Russia and IMF Agree on Loan for $10.2 Billion," *New York Times*, February 23, 1996, p. 1.

[40] Michel Camdessus, "Russia and the IMF: Meeting the Challenges of an Emerging Market in a Transition Economy," address to the U.S.-Russian Business Council (Washington, DC, April 1, 1998), p. 2.

ever attempted. To facilitate this revolutionary undertaking, Russia's new government not only solicited advice from international financial institutions, but also invited western economists and lawyers to work in their government agencies. At the State Property Committee (GKI), western advisers worked closely with their Russian counterparts to draft laws and regulations on privatization. Although the presence of these (mostly American) advisers at GKI elicited a strong visceral reaction from Russian nationalists and communists, this external intervention in the internal affairs of Russia lasted several years. Later, through programs sponsored by the U.S. Agency for International Development, American consultants both worked directly for or developed contractual arrangements with virtually every Russian government agency involved in the economic reform process, including the Central Bank, the Ministry of Finance, the Ministry of the Economy, and the Federal Securities Commission.[41]

To a lesser extent, Russian leaders also have paid a price regarding their autonomy over political decision making in return for acceptance into the core community of states. Like other postcommunist countries, Russian leaders recognized that they must construct democratic political institutions in order to be accepted *into* the core community of states. To this end, they allowed a flood of western advisers on political reform to operate in Russia. For example, western advisers have been involved in drafting the Russian constitution, crafting the Duma and presidential electoral laws, writing the civil code (the "economic constitution" of Russia), assisting the formation of political parties, monitoring Russian elections, and instituting jury trials. Literally dozens of Russian government agencies have received direct financial assistance or equipment from western countries. In the case of the United States, almost all of these transfers came from the Agency for International Development, a U.S. government organization.[42] Most European and Canadian programs are also funded by governments, either by individual countries or the European Union.[43] Likewise, hundreds of Russian political leaders and state bureaucrats

---

[41] See James M. Goldgeier and Michael McFaul, *Power and Purpose: U.S. Policy toward Russia after the Cold War* (Washington: Brookings Institution Press, 2003).

[42] For a list and discussion of the programs, see Goldgeier and McFaul, *Power and Purpose*, chs. 5, 14.

[43] For an overview of the actors involved, see Michael Pinto-Duchinsky, "The Rise of 'Political Aid,'" in Larry Diamond, Marc Plattner, Yun-han Chu, and Hung-mao Tien, eds., *Consolidating the Third Wave Democracies: Regional Challenges* (Baltimore: Johns Hopkins University Press, 1997), pp. 295–324.

have been (re)trained in European and American educational programs, schools, and universities. State-owned television networks have even allowed Americans to produce and air programs about democracy and the rule of law that were funded by the U.S. government. Finally, through the Cooperative Threat Reduction (Nunn-Lugar) program, the United States government pays U.S. firms to destroy Russian strategic weapons, including ICBMs, bombers, and submarines.

If Russian leaders aspire to balance against the West, why have they allowed these core-power interventions into their economic, political, and security affairs? Even President Putin has not discontinued some of the most intrusive programs, such as the Cooperative Threat Reduction program. The sustained acceptance of these various interventions is especially surprising given their limited results. Even as western analysts deride these programs as destructive to Russian national interests, the Russian government has remained engaged with these western-sponsored programs.[44]

Russian Foreign Policy after Communism

In parallel to this acquiescence to massive western intervention domestically, Russian leaders also have pursued an integrationist foreign policy regarding the core's international institutions. Russian rhetoric about international relations has at times sounded like nineteenth-century *realpolitik*. Russian actions in the real world, however, look more like twentieth-first-century integrationism.[45] In June 1992, Russia made its first foray into core integration by joining the International Monetary Fund and the World Bank. Since then, Russia pursued entrance into a myriad of western institutions, including the Paris Club and the G-7 (recast the "group of eight" to accommodate Russia's presence) as well as dozens of international treaties regarding everything from dumping to accounting practices. Negotiations on Russia's entry into the World Trade Organization (WTO) have been delayed, but Russia's intentions are clear: Russia is a joiner of western institutions, not a bulwark against them.[46]

---

[44] For one such denunciation, see Janine Wedel, *Collision and Collusion: The Strange Case of Western Aid to Eastern Europe 1989–1998* (New York: St. Martin's Press, 1998).

[45] On this disconnect between Russian rhetoric and behavior, see Roland Dannreuther, "Escaping the Enlargement Trap in NATO-Russian Relations," *Survival*, Vol. 41, No. 4 (Winter 1999–2000), pp. 145–64.

[46] On the basic strategy of integration, see Russian Foreign Minister Igor Ivanov, "Russia, Europe at the Turn of the Century," *International Affairs* (Moscow), Vol. 46, No. 2 (2000), pp. 1–11.

As already mentioned, Russian foreign policymakers even continue to pursue the institutionalization of relations with NATO, a western security institution designed originally to repel Russian aggression in Europe and whose enlargement and war in Kosovo deeply angered the Russia elite. In his visit to Great Britain in the spring of 2000, then acting president Putin even floated the idea of Russian membership into NATO by asking rhetorically, "Why not?"

As Russia's new market institutions have consolidated, they have helped to create economic actors with interests in greater Russian integration into the core. Oil and gas companies, mineral exporters, and bankers have emerged as the main societal forces pushing for greater western integration.[47] Foreign policy issues of concern to companies like Lukhoil, Most-Media, or even Ilyushin Design Bureau are not shaped by *realpolitik* calculations about Russia's place in the world, but rather by concrete interests regarding specific foreign policy decisions. Russian exporters desire access to western markets, importers need western goods, and Russian bankers seek partnerships with western capital.

This coalition for western engagement within Russia has a rather limited scope of interests. Above all else, these individuals have sought to maintain access to western capital and markets. When "security" issues such as opposition to NATO enlargement threaten these interests, liberals within the Russian government and their allies in Russia's economic society have cooperated to sustain engagement. Regarding other foreign policy issues that are not seen to have a direct relationship to these economic interests, this liberal coalition either has neglected the problem altogether or allowed other foreign policy entrepreneurs to assume center stage. For instance, this coalition has shown little interest in arms control issues, allowing other interest groups to dominate debate on issues like START II in the 1990s. Similarly, this engagement coalition has ceded arms trade promotion to the Ministry of Atomic Energy and individual enterprises of the military industrial complex.

Countervailing forces both domestically and internationally have challenged this general policy of engagement and integration with the West. Internally, Russia's rocky transition to the market and democracy has stimulated intermittently illiberal nationalist and communist political groups

---

[47] See the several articles devoted to these issues in a special edition of Moscow's *International Affairs*, Vol. 46, No. 2 (2000) called "Russia's Oil and Gas Strategy in the 21st Century."

that have deplored this western integrationist trajectory in foreign policy. Externally, NATO enlargement and the Kosovo war have served to unify a disparate anti-western coalition within Russia. Yet, when push comes to shove, Russian liberals and economic interest groups that benefit from western integration have not allowed nationalists or communists at home to derail Russian relations with the West.[48] After more than a decade of limited success with liberal reforms and western engagement, President Putin's government has had even more liberals in senior positions than any previous Yeltsin government.

Similarly, Putin's foreign policy actions have been pro-western, and especially pro-European. Putin does not overdo the rhetoric of multipolarity or wax on about a third way for Russia. Instead, he claims to want to make Russia a normal western power. His international heroes come not from the East or the South, but from the West.[49] During the Iraq war in spring 2003, he appeared to want to put greater emphasis on Europe and less on Russia's relations with the United States. Some have interpreted such initiatives since the start of his presidency as new evidence of balance-of-power politics in Europe.[50] Yet, such analysts grossly underestimate the ties that bind the core together and underestimate the value that Putin and Russians place on integrating into this core. To be sure, Putin does not appear to have a romantic attachment to the West. He has stated repeatedly that Russia must have a foreign policy that serves Russian national interests. Yet, Putin also has stated that he sees integration into the West as a Russian national interest, as he confirmed most dramatically in the days following September 11. Russia's trajectory is still toward integration with the core, albeit at a slower pace than most in the West would like.

Some have posited an alternative hypothesis to explain Russia's lack of balancing against the West – weakness. If Russia could, then Russia would pursue more belligerent policies toward the West. A stronger Russia could repel rather than submit to western institutions. Since the Soviet collapse in 1991, Russia's capacity to project military power has vastly weakened. Russia's military industrial complex is a shadow of its former

---

[48] Sergey Rogov, *Russia and NATO's Enlargement: The Search for Compromise at the Helsinki Summit* (Alexandria, VA: Center for Naval Analysis. 1997).
[49] See *Ot pervogo litsa: razgovory s Vladimirom Putinym* (Moscow: Vagrius Books, 2000).
[50] Joffe, "A Warning from Putin and Schroeder"; and Amos Perlmutter, "Tilting the Balance of Power," *Washington Times*, June 29, 2000.

self. Russia's only real military asset is its nuclear arsenal, although even this symbol of superpower status is eroding. Russia's ability to project military power throughout the world has been lost.

Weakness, however, is not a good indicator of intention, as the end of the Cold War itself demonstrated. It was not the erosion of Russian military that ended the Cold War. Rather, it was the collapse of communism *within* the Soviet Union and then Russia that suspended the international rivalry between the United States and the Soviet Union and reshaped fundamentally the international system. Only a change of similar proportion in an anti-western, illiberal direction within Russia will reinvigorate U.S.-Russian rivalry.

CONCLUSION

In this chapter, we have made the case for understanding the post-Cold War order not in terms of balance-of-power politics but rather as a tale of two worlds, core and periphery. Building upon earlier work that focused on international relations within the core and within the periphery, we have offered a set of hypotheses about the interaction between core and periphery. We deliberately selected core expansion into the European periphery and Russian reaction to it as critical cases. Given the aspirations to great power status of countries in the region, realist expectations about balance-of-power politics should have been borne out.

They have not been. Our examination of the core policies toward the European periphery, including Russia, and Russia's reaction to these policies has suggested a different dynamic at play. To date, core expansion is seen as a shared interest of elites in the major "European" capitals, be they in Paris, London, Washington, Warsaw, or even Moscow. Western state leaders seek expansion of the core to extend the perimeter of democratic and capitalist states in Europe. Enlargement of the core means greater security for core states. At the same time, Russian government leaders seek to join the core to enjoy the benefits of membership and avoid the costs of isolation and balancing against the core. An alternative project – be it an ideological, economic, or military counterforce – has not yet crystallized in the periphery. In Russia, several domestic groups have attempted to articulate this anti-core project, but so far have failed. Given Russia's protracted transition from communism and its halting progress toward consolidating liberal economic and political institutions, the argument we make is a contingent one. If anti-western coalitions succeed in gaining power in Russia and destroying its fragile democratic and market institutions, Russia will be unlikely to continue the foreign policy of its first post-Soviet decade. To date, however, what is most surprising is how little balancing against the West or the United States in particular has occurred.

Although this article has not explored this phenomenon outside of Russia in the former Soviet bloc, one sees dramatic evidence of domestic decisions about political and economic structures being driven throughout the region by the desire to join the West. This is most obvious in the case of the new and incoming members of NATO. Poland developed civilian control over the military, and Hungary and Romania solved their potential ethnic/territorial disputes to ensure they could join the core. The governments of Romania and Bulgaria went against popular sentiment during the Kosovo war in order to curry NATO's favor. And it is also true elsewhere in the region. Whereas some predicted that Ukraine might seek control over the strategic nuclear weapons on its soil in order to balance Russia's military power, under pressure from the West it fulfilled the provisions of the Trilateral Accord that it signed with the United States and Russia to transfer the warheads back to Russia. In these cases, and numerous others, a key aspect of the internal debate was the material and nonmaterial benefits of being part of Europe and the West.

Exceptions in Europe – Lukashenko's Belarus, Milosevic's Serbia, and Meciar's Slovakia – support our argument. The autocratic, protectionist government of Lukashenko in Belarus has chosen to isolate or balance against the West and has asked for, but not received, support in this endeavor from Russia. The economic penalties for this course have been severe. When Slovakia's government failed to proceed with political reform, it lost the chance to gain NATO membership in the first wave of enlargement; its new government strove mightily to respond to popular pressure to regain its place in the queue and is now joining both NATO and the EU. And Milosevic's agenda ensured both high economic costs as well as NATO's efforts to contain his militarism. In all three cases, failure to adopt the core's liberal agenda, even if only temporary in some cases, posed significant costs to these countries.

This essay has explained both the core's attempts to integrate the states of the former Warsaw Pact and Russia's striking willingness to suffer encroachments of domestic sovereignty and external security in order to keep open the possibility of admission into the core. An important issue for the future will be the implication of the western strategy for the future of the western institutions themselves as new members from the East expand the scope and size of NATO and the EU. The core-periphery relationship is an evolving dynamic, and future research should look further not only at how the West has affected the East in Europe but also at how integrating the East may in turn affect the West. Finally, comparisons with other regions would help refine the hypotheses about core-periphery relations that we have presented.

Index

Acceptance, international, 33, 35
Adigeia, 136
Afghanistan, 239
Africa, 93
  postcolonial, 218
Agency for International Development, 250
Akaev, Askar, 79, 89, 91
Al Qaeda, 238
Albania, 84, 107, 211
Aldrich, John H., 187
Aliev, Heydar, 90
American Political Science Review, 5
American Voter, The, 182, 184, 187
Ancien regime, 59, 60, 62, 63, 69, 73, 74, 75, 76, 77, 78, 79, 80, 81, 82, 83, 87, 90, 91, 92, 94
Anderson, Benedict, 57
Angola, 70
Arkhangelsk, 135
Armenia, 87, 92
Article 71, 135, 137
Article V, 241
Asia, 94
Austria, 93
Austro-Hungarian Empire 55
Authoritarian regimes, 110, 117, 120
Authoritarianism, 115
Azerbaijan, 84, 88, 90

Balcerowicz, Leszek, 229
Baltic countries, 217
Baltic states, 42, 222
Bashkortostan, 137

BEEPS. *See* Business Environment and Enterprise Performance Survey (BEEPS)
Belarus, 41, 79, 80, 86, 88, 90, 92, 100, 102, 108, 109, 113, 255
Belarussian Popular Front, 80
Belgorod, 135
Belovezhskaia-Pushcha Agreements, 41
Berlin, 92
Berlin Wall, 243
  crumbling of, 58
Bipolar international system, 7
Bipolarity, 235
Blaney, Geoffrey, 70
Bolshevik Revolution, 3, 9, 217
Borders, disputed, 87, 88
Bosnia, 42, 211
  defined by the West, 238
Bosnia-Herzegovina, 87
Botswana, 115
Brezhnev, Leonid, 229, 248
Britain, 239
British North America Act, 36
Bulgaria, 84, 91, 92, 255
Bull, Hedley, 236
Bunce, Valerie, 18, 19, 22, 207
Bush, George H.W., 35, 243
Bush, George W., 245
Business Environment and Enterprise Performance Survey (BEEPS), 161

Camdessus, Michel, 249
Capitalism, 219
Capture economy, 161

Carnegie Endowment for International
    Peace, 205
Caspian pipeline, 245
Castaniera, Micael, 116
Caucasus, 90, 91
Ceausescu, Nicolae, 92
Central Africa, 238
Central Asia, 91, 211
Central Bank, 250
Central Electoral Commission, 163
Central Europe, 109
Centrally planned economy (CPE), 101
Ceteris paribus, 202
Challenges, ethnonational, 37, 48
Champion of isolationism, The, 122
Chechen conflict, 139
Chechnya, 46, 134, 214
Cheliabinsk, 163
Chile, 114, 115
China, 97, 100, 101, 104, 105, 107, 109,
    114, 115, 121, 156, 232
Chinese index of economic freedom, 100
Chirac, Jacques, 232, 233
Civil liberties
    absence of rule of law and, 218
Clinton administration, 242, 243
Clinton, Bill, 243
Cold War, 19, 94, 232, 234, 235, 237, 238,
    239, 241, 254
Colton, Timothy, 15, 16, 17, 46, 173
Command economy, 68
Common-state, withering away of, 41, 42
Communism
    Soviet, 9
Communist federations
    unraveling of, 37
Communist party, 228
    Czechoslovakia and, 41
    Soviet Union and, 41
    Yugoslavia and, 41
Communist Party of Belarus, 80
Communist Party of the Russian Federation
    (KPRF), 176, 195, 199, 202, 204
Communist Party of the Soviet Union
    (CPSU), 173, 185, 195, 196, 202, 204
Comparative democratization, 18
Comparative Study of Electoral Systems
    (CSES), 177
Congress of Vienna, 23
Consecutive terms, 169
Constitution, 15
    Article 135, 137
    regional governments of, 133

Constitutional Court, 136, 155, 168
Contracts
    regulation of, 133
Converse, Philip E., 180, 185
Cooperative Threat Reduction (Nunn-Lugar)
    program, 251
Core-periphery approach, 234, 238, 241
Council of Ministers, 177
Coup attempt, 78
CPE. See Centrally planned economy (CPE)
CPSU. See Communist Party of the Soviet
    Union (CPSU)
Crime rate, 96, 108
Croatia, 42, 58, 87, 91, 93
CSES ID module, 189
Cuba, 104
Cult of the Individual, 80
Currency crisis, 15
Czech Republic, 58, 86, 217, 222, 228
Czechoslovakia, 67, 77, 86, 217

De facto nation-states, 56
Death rates, 96
Debt financing, 126
December 1991 Referendum, 27
Decentralization, 155
Decolonization, 35, 93
Deepening democracy in a fragmented
    world, 116
Defections, 42, 43
Defense expenditures, 31
DeMelo et al., 99
Democracy
    definition of, 211
    fourth wave of, 58, 95
    levels of, 116
    quality vs. sustainability, 225, 231
    threats to, 210, 212
Democratic peace, 238
Democratic regimes, 117, 120
    strong vs. weak, 111
Democratization, 63, 65, 94, 95, 117, 118,
    175, 220
    economic reform and, 223
    recent, 207, 208
    Spanish model of, 220
    state and, 218, 219
Demokratizatsiia, 26
Deutsch, Karl, 236
Dictatorship
    fourth wave and, 58, 95
Divannyye partii, 176
Domestic fuel prices, 123

Index

Downsizing
  government and, 108
Doyle, Michael, 239
Duma, 176, 250
  number of parties and, 227
Dunlop, John, 27
Durkheim, Émile, 32
Duverger, Maurice, 174, 175, 205
Dvoinoe podchinenie, 143

East Germany, 77
Eastern Europe, 101
Eastern expansion, 19, 233
EBRD Transitions Report, 113
Economic decentralization, 130, 131, 134
Economic performance, 31, 33, 96, 129
Economic reform, 13
Economy
  Russia's, 248
Elections
  participation in, 175
Electorate
  age gradient and, 181
Estado Novo, 180
Estonia, 41, 58, 77, 100, 102, 108, 109, 113, 128
Estonia's Communist Supreme Soviet, 26
Estonian Popular Front, 78
Ethiopia, 238
Ethnofederalism, 12, 57
Ethnonational challenges, 37, 48
Ethnonational crisis
  probability of, 52
Europe, 232
European Bank for Reconstruction and Development, 99
European Core, The, 244
European Union (EU), 92, 243, 255
Evans, Geoffrey, 189
Evgenii Nazdratenko, 168
Evil empire, 29
Exchange rate, 126
Expenditures, on defense, 31
Export restrictions, 123

False negatives, 18
Far Eastern Republic, 54
Federal funds, 144, 148
Federal Securities Commission, 250
Federalism, 6, 155
Federation Council, 167, 177
Fidrmuc, 116
Fifth Republic France, 180

Financing, inflationary, 125
Finland, 105
500-Day Plan, 82
Foreign policy
  after communism, 251, 254
Foreign trade, value of, 34
Fourth wave, 58, 67, 69, 93, 94, 95
France, 56, 95
  party system in, 188
Franquist regime, 185
Freedom House, 13, 74, 115, 116
French Revolution, 9
Friedman, Daniel, 64
From Plan to Market, 99
Furnivall, J.S., 32

Gaidar, Yegor, 249
Gamsakhurdia, Zviad, 90
GDP, 96
Georgia, 42, 87, 88, 90, 91, 92, 211
Germany, 93, 235
Gilpin, Robert, 25, 29
Gingrich Revolution, 7
Glasnost', 26
Goldgeier, James, 19, 232
Gorbachev, Mikhail, 75, 76, 81, 82, 102, 157, 173, 229
Gosplan, 248
Gran Colombia, 55
Great Depression, 98
Greater Horde, 44
Green, Donald, 183
Gross domestic product, 33
Gubernatorial regimes, 169
Gurr, Ted Robert, 50

Havel, Vaclav, 75, 89
Hedge strategy, 244
Hegemonic autocrats, 79, 81
Hellman, Joel, 18
Heritage Foundation, 100
Heywood, Paul, 185
Hitler, Adolf, 90
Hodnett, Grey, 38, 44
Holmes, Stephen, 215
How Russia Votes, 184
Human Development Report, 116
Hume, 239
Hungarian Socialist Party, 77
Hungary, 58, 75, 77, 81, 86, 222
Huntington, Samuel, 62
Hyperinstitutionalization
  state and, 171

Illegal tariffs, 159
Illiberal democracies, 117, 129
Ilyushin Design Bureau, 252
Import substitution, 102, 122
Income
  indirect redistribution of, 127
  inequalities in, 96, 124
Independence, claims to, 35
Indigenization, policy of, 38
Industrial policy, 121
Inflationary financing, 125
Infrastructural power
  central state and, 141, 156
Institute of Sociology of the Russian
  Academy of Sciences, 206
Institutional collapse, 101
Institutional weapons, proliferation of,
  37, 38
Internal trade barriers
  removal of, 133
International acceptance, 33, 35
International Monetary Fund (IMF), 239,
  249, 251
International society, 236
Interwar facism, 187
Investment, 96
  foreign, 133
Iraq, 239
  war in, 245, 253
Irkutsk, 135, 137
Islamic uprisings, 84

Jacobins, 64
Japan, 93
Jaruzelski, Wojciech, 76
Joffe, Joseph, 232, 233
John Marttila Communications, 206
Jowitt, Kenneth, 10

Kabardino-Balkaria, 136, 137
Kagan, Robert, 233
Kalmikia, 137
Karachai-Cherkessia, 136
Kareliia, 135
Karimov, Islam, 80
Karl, Terry Lynn, 62, 64
Kazakhs, 44, 45
Kazakhstan, 79
Khanti-Mansii, 137
Khodjenti clan, 84
Kiev's International Sociological Institute, 28
Kocharian, Robert, 88
Kohn, Hans, 55

Kol'skii Nuclear Power Station, 163
Komi, 137
Korenizatsiia, 38
Kosolapov, Mikhail, 206
Kosovo, 252
  defined by the West, 238
  war in, 245, 253, 255
Kozyrev, Andrei, 245, 249
Kozyreva, Polina, 206
KPRF. *See* Communist Party of the Russian
  Federation (KPRF)
Krasnodor, 136
Kravchuk, Leonid, 28, 83
Kupchan, Charles, 232
Kyrgyzes, 44
Kyrgyzstan, 45, 79, 90, 91, 92

Laitin, David, 2
Lake, Anthony, 242
Landsbergis, Vytautas, 75
Latgalian nationalism, 54
Latin America, 94, 193, 207, 208, 210
  democratization in, 63
Latvia, 58, 77, 78
Latvian National Independence Movement,
  78
Latvian Popular Front, 78
Latvian Supreme Soviet, 78
Law on Cooperatives, 157
Law on State Enterprises, 157
LDPR. *See* Liberal-Democratic Party of
  Russia
Leaders, 88, 91
Legal separatism, 165
Leningrad, 166
Levine, Daniel, 66
Liberal-Democratic Party of Russia, 192
Liberalization, 14, 98, 99
Liberalization index, 119
Liberia, 238
Life expectancy, 96, 98
Lithuania, 58, 77, 78, 81
Lithuanian Supreme Soviet, 78
Living standards, 98
Logit analysis, 49
London Declaration of 1990, 241
Lukashenko, Aleksandr, 80, 90, 255
Lukhoil, 252
Luzhkov, Yurii, 136, 192

Maastricht Treaty, 243
Macedonia, 42, 56
Macro-economic reform, 132

Index

Macro-stabilization, 98, 127
Macroeconomic instability, 127
Macroeconomic policy, 121
Macroeconomic populism, 102
Macroeconomic stabilization, 99
Mainwaring, Scott P., 174
Makhkamov, Khakhor, 84
Managed democracy, 204
Mann, Michael, 16, 55
March 1991 Referendum, 27
Market economy, 69
Marketization dividend
Marxism, 3
Marxist-Leninist regime, 184
May 14, 1995 Referendum, 28
Mayall, James, 34
McAllister, Ian, 184
McFaul, Michael, 13, 19, 58, 205, 230, 232
Mearsheimer, John, 232
Media
  Russia and, 248
Medical Insurance Fund, 142
Military
  as threat to democracy, 210
Military coup d etat, 210
Military fitness, 29
Military juntas, 184
Miller, Arthur H., 189
Miller, William, 185
Milosevic, Slobodan, 92, 255
Ministry of Atomic Energy, 252
Ministry of Finance, 250
Ministry of Justice, 137, 155
Ministry of the Economy, 250
Mobilization, catalysts of, 89
Moldova, 42, 56, 70, 81, 82, 84, 86, 94, 211
Moldovan Popular Front (MPF), 81
Mongolia, 70, 81, 84, 107
Montenegro, 211
Morlino, Leonard, 183
Moscow, 135, 136
Most-Media, 252
Motyl, Alexander, 28
MPF. *See* Moldovan Popular Front (MPF)
Multiparty politics
  acceptance of, 175
Multipolarity, 235
Murder rates, 96
Murmansk, 163
Muslims, 44

Nabiyev, Rakhman, 84
NACC. *See* North Atlantic Cooperation Council (NACC)

Nagorno-Karabakh Republic, 88
Nation-state
  relationship of nationalism to, 55
  triumph of, 21, 25
National Council for Eurasian and East European Research, 206
National identity, 24
National Salvation Front (NSF), 92
National Science Foundation, 206
National self-determination, 47
Nationalism, 25, 28
  defined, 225
  relationship to nation-states, 55
NATO, 92, 239, 241, 243, 255
  enlargement of, 19, 245, 253
NATO's Heads of State, 241
NATO-Russia Council, 244
NATO-Russia Founding Act, 244
Nazarbaev, 80
New Deal, 183
9+1 Accord, 82
Niyazov, Saparmurad, 80
Nizhnni Novgorod, 135
Nomenklatura, 42, 56
Non-compliance patterns, 139
North Atlantic Cooperation Council (NACC), 241
North Atlantic Treaty Organization. *See* NATO
North Korea, 104, 122
North Ossetiia, 135
Novosibirsk, 135
NSF. *See* National Salvation Front (NSF)

O'Donnell, Guillermo, 60, 62, 63, 65
Oblasts, 38
Okrugs, 38
Olson, Mancur, 115
Omsk, 135
Ordeshook, Peter, 5
Orenburg, 147
Over-militarization, 101
Overindustrialization, 101

Pacific union, 237
Pacted transition, 81
Pacts, function of, 68
Palmquist, Bradley, 183
Parliamentary democracy, 82
Partisanship, 17, 181, 188
  age and, 195
  community size and, 196
  democratic political regime, 199
  education and, 196

Partisanship (*cont.*)
  erosion of, 188
  ideal number of parties and, 198
  interest in politics and, 197
  left-right scale, 199
  parties and ordinary people and, 198
  past CPSU membership and, 196
  sex and, 196
  social characteristics and, 195
  sources of, 194, 203
  talking politics and, 198
  viewing TV news and, 197
  winner in reforms and, 196
Partnership for Peace (PFP), 241
Party identification, 182, 188
  estimates of, 200
  question wording as indices of, 189
Party of Power, 205
Party system, 175, 181
PCE, 184
Peace dividend, 103
Pension Fund, 142
Perestroika, 31, 173
Petrosian, Ter, 88
PFP. *See* Partnership for Peace (PFP)
Pharr, Susan J., 183
Pierce, Roy, 180, 185
Poland, 58, 75, 76, 77, 81, 86, 95, 105, 222, 228
Policies, 120, 128
Polish United Workers' Party, 228
Political decentralization, 130, 131, 134
Political engagement, 197
Political liberalization, 132, 157
Political opinions, 198
Political party, 17
  ideal number of, 180
  psychological identification with, 182
Pomor'e Republic, 46
Popov, Vladimir, 13, 96, 116
Popular Front, 26, 80
Populism
  macroeconomics of, 124
Portugal, 193
  right-wing regime in, 184
Post-communism studies, 19
Post-stalinist period, 38
Postsocialism, 210
Pre-transition distortions, 104
Presidential electoral laws, 250
Presidential system, 82
Presidium of the Council of Ministers, 37
Presidium of the Supreme Soviet, 37

Price controls, 122, 125
Primakov, Yevgenii, 192, 245
Primor'e Republic, 46
Primorskii Krai, 168
Privatization, 158
  early stages of, 159
  vouchers and, 160
Pro-Kremlin Unity bloc, 192
Property rights, protection of, 133
Proto-nation states, decision making rights of, 36
Przeworski, Adam, 58, 62, 65, 116, 212
PSOE, 184
Public officials, survey of, 154
Putin, Vladimir, 29, 130, 140, 166, 168, 170, 175, 177, 192, 195, 204, 226, 246, 247, 248, 251, 253
Putnam, Robert D., 9, 183

Rawlsian veil, 65
Realpolitik, 232, 251, 252
Recession, 104
  magnitude of, 101, 102
  supply-side, 105
Referendum May 14, 1995, 28
Referendum of December 1991, 27
Referendum, March 1991, 27
Reform, economic, 13
Regime change, cooperative approaches to, 60, 67
Regional resistance
  roots of, 156, 171
Remmer, Karen, 221
Republic of Komi, 163
Republic of Sakha (Yakutia), 163
Reunification, 246
Revolution, 8
  Russia's liberal, 247, 248
Rodrik, Dani, 116
Roeder, Philip, 12, 65, 66
Romania, 86, 91, 92, 255
Romanian Communist Party, 92
Rome, 241
Rose, Richard, 176, 184
Rostov, 136
Ruble, 127
  devaluation of, 122
Rühe, Volker, 243
Rule of law (CIS), 129
Russia, 41, 70, 81, 82, 84, 86, 92
  core security and, 240
  economic crisis of, 214
  levels of literacy and urbanization, 209

Index

media and, 248
parallels between Weimar Germany and, 226
presidency in, 226
problem of law in, 213
the West and, 245
weakness of economy, 213
Russian Federation, 174, 185
  boundaries of the state, 213
  constitution of, 134
  national diversity of, 209
Russian Ministry of Justice, 136
Russian nationalism, 214
Russian state
  weakness of, 212, 216
Rustow, Dankwart, 60, 67, 216
Rwanda, 238

Sakha, 137
Sakhalin, 163
Samara, 135
Schickler, Eric, 183
Schmitter, Philippe, 60, 62, 63, 65
Schroeder, Chancellor, 246
Second wave, 93
Sectoral inequalities, 124
Security community, 236
Segment states
  citizenship rights of, 36
  leaders of, 36
Segmental incorporation, failure of, 35, 37
Segmental institutions, 22, 48
Segmentation
  reasons for, 37
Sejm, 76
Self-determination, 34
Selznick, Philip, 38
Sen, Amartya, 115
September 11, 238, 246, 253
Serbia, 19, 42, 91, 92, 211
Shadow economy, 108
Shalikashvili, John, 241
Shevardnadze, Eduard, 82, 87, 90, 91
Shlaifer, Andrei, 229
Shock therapy, 228
Shushkevich, Stanislav, 80
Siberian Republic, 46
Sierra Leone, 238
Skalnik Leff, Carol, 22
Slavic states, 90
Slovakia, 86, 242, 255
Slovenia, 42, 58, 86, 217, 222

Snyder, Jack, 240
Social characteristics
  partisanship and, 195
Social Science Research Council, 207
Social Security Fund, 142
Sofa parties, 176
Soldiers' Mothers, 162
Solidarity, 76, 86, 228
South Korea, 114, 115
Southern Europe, 94, 207, 208, 210
  democratization in, 63
Soviet communism, 9
Soviet Union, 67, 217
  collapse of, 235
Sovietology, 3, 6
Spain, 95, 184, 193
Spruyt, Hendrik, 25
SPS. *See* Union of Rightist Forces
Stanford University, 205
START II, 252
State Duma, 167, 168, 204, 205
State hyperinstitutionalism, 171
State Property Committee (GKI), 250
State-creation, 22
State-society relationships, 15
States and regimes
  relationship between, 216, 218
Stavropol, 136
Stockholm International Peace Research Institute, 50
Stoner-Weiss, Kathryn, 15, 16, 130
Subsidies, 127
  maintaining under budget constraints, 126
Substitution policies, 127
Subtraction, 216
Sudan, 238
Suicidal nationalism, 35
Suicide rates, 96
Sultangalievism, 42
Suny, Ronald, 22
Super districts, 166
Supreme Court, 37
Supreme Soviet, 80
Sverdlovsk, 169

Taiwan, 114, 115
Tajikistan, 56, 70, 81, 83, 84, 91
Taliban regime, 238
Tatarstan, 45, 137, 163, 169
Tax avoidance, 108
Tax collection
  increased, 133

Third wave democratization, 59, 67, 69, 70, 72, 81, 93, 94
Tiumen, 135, 163
Transition economies, 107, 111, 123
Transition, actor-centric theory of, 93
Transitional partisanship, 188
  props of, 204
Transitional regimes, 13, 58
Transitions from Authoritarian Rule, 60
Transitologists, 4, 62
Transylvanian Hungarians, 54
Treisman, Daniel, 164, 229
Trilateral Accord, 255
Tripartite typology, 74
Tudjman, Franjo, 87
Turkestan, 44, 45
Turkic Muslims, 44
Turkic republics, 42
Turkmenistan, 41, 79, 86, 100
2002 NATO summit, 242
2003 Iraq War, 232
Tyva, 137

U.S. Agency for International Development, 250
U.S. Civil War, 183
Ubangi-Shari, 55
Ukraine, 41, 81, 83, 84, 217, 255
Ukrainian Communist Party, 83
Under-institutionalization, 15
Union of Rightist Forces, 192
Unipolarity, 235
United Russia Party, 205
United States, 232, 233, 239
Unity bloc. *See* United Russia Party
University of Iowa, 189
Urals Republic, 46
Uzbekistan, 79, 80, 86, 100, 102, 107, 108, 109, 113, 128
Uzbeks, 45

Vietnam, 97, 100, 101, 104, 105, 107, 113
Visegrad four, 242
Volgograd, 135
Voronezh, 135, 136
Voucher privatization, 228

Walesa, Lech, 75, 89
Waltz, Kenneth, 6, 232
War, fear of, 31
War-making capacity, 29
Warsaw Pact, 241, 255
WDR. *See* World Development Report (WDR)
Weak states
  characteristics of, 212
Weber, Max, 88, 89
Weimar Germany
  parallels between Russia and, 226
West, The, 91, 92
  GDP in, 98
  policy of integration with, 233
  Russia's relations with, 19, 245, 254
Western security institutions
  expanding, 241, 245
White, Stephen, 184, 185, 188
Whitefield, Stephen, 189
Whitehead, Laurence, 60
Why Parties?, 187
Wohlforth, William, 235
Woodruff, David, 219
World Bank, 159, 161, 239, 249, 251
World Development Report (WDR), 99
World fuel prices, 122
World Trade Organization (WTO), 239, 251
World War I, 239
World War II, 96, 239
Wörner, Manfred, 243

Xiaoping, Deng, 156

Yabloko party, 192
Yakovlev, Alexander, 82
Yavlinskii, Grigorii, 192
Yeltsin Constitution of 1993, 174
Yeltsin, Boris, 82, 90, 91, 102, 135, 156, 158, 165, 175, 177, 195, 205, 226, 229, 230, 245, 247, 248, 253
  criticism of, 227
Yugoslavia, 42, 67, 86, 217

Zhirinovsky, Vladimir, 90, 192, 245
Zimmerman, William, 206
Zubarevich, Natalia, 166
Zviad Gamsakhurdia, 87

For EU product safety concerns, contact us at Calle de José Abascal, 56–1°, 28003 Madrid, Spain or eugpsr@cambridge.org.

www.ingramcontent.com/pod-product-compliance
Ingram Content Group UK Ltd.
Pitfield, Milton Keynes, MK11 3LW, UK
UKHW011319060825
461487UK00005B/186